P9-DTQ-576

INCREDIBLE VICTORY

Books by Walter Lord

INCREDIBLE VICTORY

THE PAST THAT WOULD NOT DIE

PEARY TO THE POLE

A TIME TO STAND

THE GOOD YEARS

DAY OF INFAMY

A NIGHT TO REMEMBER

THE FREMANTLE DIARY

INCREDIBLE
Victory

By WALTER LORD

BURFORD BOOKS

ISBN 1-56865-867-2

4966

To William Rushton Calfee

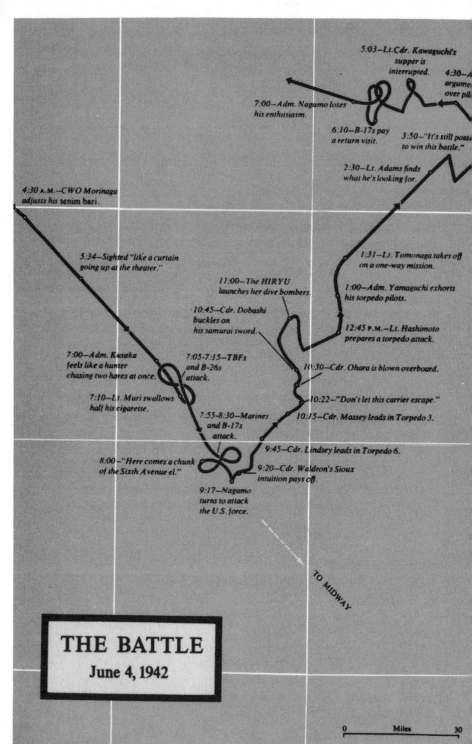

5:03—Lt.Cdr. Kawaguchi's supper is interrupted.

4:30—A argumen over pil

7:00—Adm. Nagumo loses his enthusiasm.

6:10—B-17s pay a return visit.

3:50—"It's still poss to win this battle."

2:30—Lt. Adams finds what he's looking for.

4:30 A.M.—CWO Morinaga adjusts his senim bari.

1:31—Lt. Tomonaga takes off on a one-way mission.

5:34—Sighted "like a curtain going up at the theater."

11:00—The HIRYU launches her dive bombers.

10:45—Cdr. Dobashi buckles on his samurai sword.

1:00—Adm. Yamaguchi exhorts his torpedo pilots.

12:45 P.M.—Lt. Hashimoto prepares a torpedo attack.

7:00—Adm. Kusaka feels like a hunter chasing two hares at once.

7:05-7:15—TBFs and B-26s attack.

10:30—Cdr. Ohara is blown overboard.

7:10—Lt. Muri swallows half his cigarette.

10:22—"Don't let this carrier escape."

7:55-8:30—Marines and B-17s attack.

10:15—Cdr. Massey leads in Torpedo 3.

9:45—Cdr. Lindsey leads in Torpedo 6.

8:00—"Here comes a chunk of the Sixth Avenue el."

9:20—Cdr. Waldron's Sioux intuition pays off.

9:17—Nagumo turns to attack the U.S. force.

TO MIDWAY

THE BATTLE
June 4, 1942

0   Miles   30

180°

179°

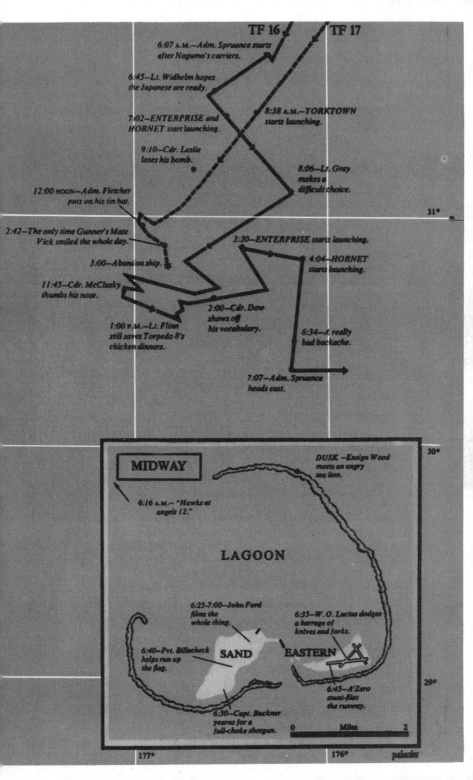

Contents

Illustrations follow page 116.

Foreword

By any ordinary standard, they were hopelessly outclassed.

They had no battleships, the enemy eleven. They had eight cruisers, the enemy twenty-three. They had three carriers (one of them crippled); the enemy had eight. Their shore defenses included guns from the turn of the century.

They knew little of war. None of the Navy pilots on one of their carriers had ever been in combat. Nor had any of the Army fliers. Of the Marines, 17 of 21 new pilots were just out of flight school—some with less than four hours' flying time since then. Their enemy was brilliant, experienced and all-conquering.

They were tired, dead tired. The patrol plane crews, for instance, had been flying 15 hours a day, servicing their own planes, getting perhaps three hours' sleep at night.

They had equipment problems. Some of their dive bombers couldn't dive—the fabric came off the wings. Their torpedoes were slow and unreliable; the torpedo planes even worse. Yet they were up against the finest fighting plane in the world.

They took crushing losses—15 out of 15 in one torpedo squadron . . . 21 out of 27 in a group of fighters . . . many, many more.

They had no right to win. Yet they did, and in doing so

they changed the course of a war. More than that, they added a new name—Midway—to that small list that inspires men by shining example. Like Marathon, the Armada, the Marne, a few others, Midway showed that every once in a while "what must be" need not be at all. Even against the greatest of odds, there is something in the human spirit—a magic blend of skill, faith and valor—that can lift men from certain defeat to incredible victory.

CHAPTER 1

A Single Stroke

PETTY OFFICER HEIJIRO OMI didn't have a word to say in excuse. As the Admiral's chief steward, he was responsible for the food at this party—and that included the *tai*, a carefully selected sea bream cooked whole. It had been a happy inspiration, for *tai* broiled in salt meant good luck in Japan. But this time the chef had broiled it in bean paste—*miso*, to be exact—and as every superstitious Japanese knew, that extra touch meant crowning good luck with bad.

Obviously it was just a slip. The chef hadn't been thinking, and Omi had been off attending to some other detail of the party. Still, even the smallest mistake was humiliating when one had the privilege of personally serving Admiral Isoroku Yamamoto, the universally worshiped Commander in Chief of the Combined Fleet of the Imperial Japanese Navy. Now Omi stood forlorn and silent as Commander Noboru Fukusaki, the Admiral's flag secretary, dressed him down. The Admiral himself hovered in the background; a humorless half-smile flickered across his face.

Well, no time to brood about it. The guests were already swarming aboard the flagship *Yamato*, riding gracefully at her red buoy in the anchorage of Hashirajima. Some 200 officers soon packed the quarterdeck—dark, scowling Admiral

Nagumo of Pearl Harbor fame . . . a dozen young destroyer skippers . . . the enormously popular Captain Yanagimoto of the carrier *Soryu* . . . promising staff officers like Commander Sasabe, whose Naval Academy Class of '23 seemed to be getting so many good jobs.

Admiral Yamamoto had invited them all this spring evening of May 25, 1942, to help celebrate a very auspicious occasion. A huge Japanese armada was about to set forth across the Pacific, and its goal was in keeping with its size: capture the American base at Midway, lure the U.S. fleet to destruction, and hopefully win the war for Japan at a single stroke.

Cheers and *banzais* echoed across the water, past the scores of ships that packed the quiet anchorage. If any one noticed the *tai* served with *miso,* it was long since forgotten. Toasts to the nation; toasts to the fleet; toasts to past triumphs and future hopes. The warm *sake* stirred visions of limitless glory, and even the flowered cups seemed auspicious—they had been presented to Admiral Yamamoto by the Emperor himself.

Victory was in the air . . . not just at Hashirajima but throughout Japan. For six months she had enjoyed an unbroken string of triumphs beyond the wildest imagination— Pearl Harbor . . . the *Repulse* and the *Prince of Wales* . . . Hong Kong . . . Manila . . . Singapore . . . Bataan. By April Vice Admiral Chuichi Nagumo's big carriers were ravaging the Indian Ocean, smashing Colombo, sinking two British cruisers, plus the carrier *Hermes* off Trincomalee. Then Coral Sea and still more glory. Later, men would call it a strategic defeat—it permanently blunted the Japanese thrust toward Australia—but who could see that now? A generously inflated communiqué ticked off a satisfying toll of smashed U.S. carriers, battleships and cruisers.

Heady stuff, making it easy to believe still more. The village radios crackled with bulletins of a demoralized America. Newspapers described U.S. cities "ghostlike" under a new blackout law. Reports told how "unwilling American women are dragged from their homes into munitions factories." (Years later any American would recognize that this referred to the robust "Rosie the Riveter.")

Best of all, the press described how the American people were beginning to waver. One article told how Cordell Hull was desperately trying to rally a war-weary people, but "it is like trying to drive an unwilling horse into a bull fight arena." Another report said that a San Francisco radio announcer stammered when he tried to defend democracy. "DISSATISFACTION WITHIN CAMP OF ALLIES CONTINUES TO MOUNT," happily announced the Japan *Times and Advertiser*, quoting Father Charles E. Coughlin, "the brave and well-known Catholic missionary in America."

One Japanese who did not buy all this was Admiral Yamamoto. Born in 1884 during the great awakening of the "Meiji Restoration," blooded at Tsushima under the heroic Admiral Togo, and now the leading apostle of naval air power, Yamamoto stood perfectly for all the greatness of new Japan. But he also knew his America. He had studied at Harvard, served as naval attaché in Washington, traveled around the country. Don't take taxis, take the bus, he used to tell new Japanese arrivals.

He knew America's resilience and optimism too. His enemies would later make much of a "boast" that he'd sign peace in the White House. Actually, he said that Japan could never win short of signing peace in the White House.

Above all, he understood American production. He may not have known that in 1940 the United States turned out 4,500,000 automobiles, while Japan made only 48,000; but he wouldn't have been surprised. He knew all too well that Japan was overmatched, and that it was only a matter of time before American production would begin to tell. "If I am told to fight regardless of the consequences," he confided to Premier Konoye in 1941, "I shall run wild for the first six months or a year, but I have utterly no confidence for the second and third years of the fighting."

To Yamamoto there was only one solution: a quick, decisive victory before America got rolling. If he could crush the weakened U.S. fleet—especially those carriers missed at Pearl Harbor—he'd control the whole Pacific. Then just possibly Washington might settle for a peace favorable to Japan, rather than face the agony of the long road back.

Admittedly it was a long shot, but what was so wrong with that? He had always been a gambler. In his American days two of his favorite diversions were bridge and poker. "Do you like to gamble?" he once asked an apprentice secretary at the Embassy in Washington. When the young man hesitantly said he hadn't yet tried, Yamamoto shut him off: "People who don't gamble aren't worth talking to."

So the stakes were right. Trouble was, Admiral Chester W. Nimitz, commanding the U.S. Pacific Fleet at Pearl Harbor, refused to play along. Well aware that his crippled force was still in no shape to risk an all-out test, Nimitz contented himself for the moment with hit-and-run carrier thrusts and morale-building raids. Yamamoto decided that the only way to draw him out was to take something the Americans couldn't afford to lose. Then when their fleet emerged to meet the challenge, he'd pounce on it with everything he had.

Midway seemed the perfect bait. It was only a small U.S. outpost in the central Pacific, but its capture offered several advantages—it would strengthen the homeland's defenses; it would be a useful patrol plane base—but above all, it would lure the U.S. fleet out. Standing only 1,136 miles from Pearl Harbor, Midway was a place the Americans would just have to defend. They would come; and he would get them.

The idea first began brewing as early as February 1942. Japan was nearing the end of what it called the "first phase" of its conquests, and the problem was what to do next. One school wanted to go west—seize Ceylon, eventually link up with Rommel in the Near East. Another group—the bright desk boys at Naval General Staff—wanted to head south; they'd isolate Australia by taking New Caledonia, Samoa and Fiji.

Midway was the product of Combined Fleet Headquarters, and this fact alone meant a certain amount of jealous sniping from the Naval General Staff. But apart from the traditional rivalry between deck and desk sailors, the plan seemed open to several objections. Midway was far away—the attack would have no shore-based air support. By the same token, it was well within the range of U.S. planes based in Hawaii. To many it seemed too small and remote to be a good patrol base. Holding it would use shipping badly needed elsewhere. Above all, there wasn't enough time to gather all the supplies and equipment needed for such a long jump—the proposed June deadline was a killer.

Yet Midway had one great advantage that outweighed everything else: Yamamoto was for it. No one would openly stand up against him; so on April 5 the Naval General Staff finally gave the plan a somewhat reluctant blessing. As a conciliatory gesture, Yamamoto tied in the Fiji-Samoan operation as the next step afterward. Then, since the Naval General Staff was worried about possible bombings from the Aleutians, he also added an Aleutian attack to the Midway plan. He had plenty of ships, and it might help confuse the Americans.

But intraservice rivalries die hard, and by mid-April it was clear the Naval General Staff was still dragging its feet. Now they wanted to postpone the attack for a month.

All the squabbling ended on April 18. It was just another spring day when Prime Minister Hideki Tojo took off that morning on a routine inspection trip. Then, as his party headed toward the small port of Mito, suddenly a "most curious" brown plane was seen flying toward them. A moment of puzzling . . . then the frantic realization that it was an American bomber. Tojo's plane veered wildly out of the way as the bomber flashed by, intent on its business.

All Japan was just as surprised, as Lieutenant Colonel Jimmy Doolittle's 16 B-25s swept in on their famous raid. The Japanese had sighted the U.S. task force, indeed expected a visit the following day when the carriers were close enough to launch their regular planes. But nobody dreamed the Americans could launch long-range bombers from a carrier's flight deck. The damage was small, but the shock and wounded pride were enormous.

No one took it harder than Admiral Yamamoto. The Emperor's safety was an obsession with him. After the raid he holed up in his cabin on the *Yamato* and brooded alone for a day. Chief Steward Omi had never seen him so pale or downhearted.

No more doubts about Midway now. The operation took on new importance as a way to strengthen Japan's defensive perimeter, while Yamamoto was more determined than ever to bring on the battle that would finish off the U.S. fleet. The Naval General Staff stopped their sniping, urged the Admiral to get going.

On the *Yamato* Senior Operations Officer Captain Kameto Kuroshima went into one of his trance-like periods of contemplation. It was his function to hammer together the operation, and all agreed he was born for the job. He ate, slept, lived only for operations. While working on an idea, he'd disappear into his cabin for days. Sometimes he'd burn incense and ponder in the dark; other times he'd sit at his desk, buried in paper, as the cigarette butts piled up. (He put them in a glass half filled with water because the crew wouldn't trust him with an ashtray.) Lost in thought, he'd forget everything else—people said he even slept in his shoes. The orderlies rather irreverently called him *Boke-Sambo*—"foggy staff officer"—but Yamamoto knew better. The Admiral put up with any amount of outlandish behavior because the brilliant Kuroshima was, the whole staff agreed, "the God of Operations."

The plan that emerged was worthy of the man. It called for an intricate naval ballet, involving no less than 16 different groups of ships performing with perfect coordination. All was built around "N-Day"—the day scheduled for the landings on Midway. On N-3 Day Admiral Hosogaya would open the show with his attack on the Aleutians. Then on N-2 Day Admiral Nagumo's superb Striking Force of six carriers would hit Midway from the northwest, softening the place up for easy capture. On N-Day itself the Invasion Force would arrive from the west, supported by Vice Admiral Nobutake Kondo's Second Fleet. Meanwhile the Main Force—Admiral Yamamoto's great array of battleships—would lie between the two . . . lurking about 300 miles in the rear, waiting to jump the U.S. fleet when it rushed out to rescue Midway. To the north, some of Hosogaya's supporting ships would lie near enough to join Yamamoto when he moved in for the kill.

To be on the safe side, Kuroshima also arranged for reconnaissance. Two cordons of submarines would be placed between Hawaii and Midway. They would spot and report the U.S. fleet as it came out, and maybe get a little target practice.

Of course, these were just the bare bones of the plan. Now the scene shifted from the scented gloom of Kuroshima's cabin to the bright linoleum of the operations room, where the staff would contribute its expertise. Commander Yoshiro Wada, the chief signal officer, struggled to work out a feasible communications system . . . Commander Yasuji Watanabe labored over tactical problems . . . Commander Akira Sasaki projected planes and pilot requirements . . . Others took on headaches like fueling, navigation and support for the troop landings.

Admiral Yamamoto often joined them. In the last analysis it was his plan, and he wasn't the kind of leader who used his staff for advice; they were there to carry out *his* decisions. For large meetings they pulled together the desks in the operations room to form a sort of conference table; for smaller sessions they sat around in a square of brown leather sofas. On a table in the center there was always a box of Sakura cigarettes, some cheese, and that great symbol of their victories—a bottle of Johnny Walker Red Label whisky "liberated" from Singapore.

Yamamoto himself didn't drink or smoke, but he was no

prig. He could joke with his staff and was always considerate of the enlisted men. Rather formal on the job (no one ever saw him take off his coat), he was disarmingly human off duty. His sweet tooth, his zest for *shogi*, his weakness for Hechima cologne, all made him so much more a creature of flesh and blood than the national monument he had now become.

Toward the end of April he received his two top commanders, Admirals Nagumo and Kondo, in his red-carpeted office just aft of the operations room. They were back from the Indian Ocean, knew nothing of Midway; now they had come to get the word. Nagumo was indifferent—his carriers could do anything—but Kondo began rattling off some of the old objections. Yamamoto cut him short—all that was settled long ago.

May 1, and the days of planning were over. That morning the various task force commanders swarmed aboard the *Yamato* for four days of briefing and table-top maneuvers. As they tried out the plan on the game board, Red Team (the U.S. fleet) unexpectedly caught Blue Team (Nagumo's carriers) while their planes were off bombing Midway. Under the rules nine hits were scored, the *Akagi* and *Kaga* sunk. Rear Admiral Matome Ugaki, Yamamoto's shrewd chief of staff, hastily reversed the umpire; six hits were erased and the *Akagi* refloated.

Success thus assured, the mimeograph machines began rolling. May 5, Imperial General Headquarters Navy Order No. 18 directed the Combined Fleet to "carry out the occupation of Midway Islands and key points in the western Aleutians in cooperation with the Army." Other orders followed, and finally that ultimate badge that changed any military plan from dream to reality, an official code name. From now on the project would be the "MI Operation," with the Aleutians to be referred to as "AO" and Midway itself as "AF."

One final touch. Thinking back on those table-top maneuvers, Captain Kuroshima did feel it might be useful to know just a little bit more about what the U.S. fleet was doing. So around May 8 he added an extra precaution: seaplanes refueled from submarines would reconnoiter Pearl Harbor the week before the attack, to give up-to-the-minute information on enemy movements.

Ships began creeping out. Early May several submarines quietly headed south, each carrying a midget sub piggyback. Hopefully they could stage diversionary attacks on Sydney and Madagascar, throwing the enemy even more off guard. Other submarines glided east—they would refuel the sea-planes to reconnoiter Pearl Harbor. Others went to set up the cordons that would alert the fleet when the Americans came out. Still another moved east alone—the clever Lieu-tenant Commander Yahachi Tanabe was taking the *I-168* to the enemy's very doorstep. It would reconnoiter Midway itself and report what was going on.

Commander Yasumi Toyama could use a little good intel-ligence. He was responsible for working out the actual land-ings, yet he knew depressingly little about Midway. As he later confessed, "It was just a spot on the ocean." He had no photos; the plane meant to take them had been shot down as it approached. His maps were sketchy and ancient. Idly, he decided to land on the south side where the reef was close to the shore. He never realized that there was a large gap in the reef to the north.

He had no better idea what they'd find when they got there. A Navy estimate suggested 750 U.S. Marines; the Army thought 1,700. Most sources agreed Midway might have 50-60 planes, maybe ten antiaircraft guns, about the same number of shore-defense guns. Not much else.

In any case, the Japanese were bringing enough. It would be a joint Army-Navy affair, amounting to some 4,600 men altogether. Colonel Ichiki's 28th Infantry could take care of themselves anywhere; so could his engineers and rapid-fire gun company. Captain Ota's 2nd Combined Special Naval

Landing Force was equally tough, as were the Navy construction men and even the weather team. They all had plenty of fire power too—the Navy alone was bringing 94 guns.

The only real problem was landing craft, and that was more an embarrassment. Commander Shiro Yonai, chief of staff for the Navy contingent, knew they'd need flat-bottomed boats to get over the reefs, yet there wasn't a single one in the whole Japanese Navy. Finally he buried his pride and borrowed some from the Army Infantry School.

May 15, and the Navy occupation force began moving out, bound for the staging area at Saipan. May 18, Colonel Ichiki visited the *Yamato* for a personal briefing from Admiral Yamamoto. Then he and his troops were on their way too.

That same day Chief Warrant Officer Takayoshi Morinaga, torpedo pilot on the carrier *Kaga*, swooped down in a mock attack on some cruisers maneuvering in the Inland Sea. The fliers were getting in some final practice, and Morinaga was a good example why they were the best at their trade in the world. Starting with the China incident in 1937, he had now been flying combat for five years.

On the *Akagi*, flagship of the carrier fleet, Admiral Nagumo's staff bustled about pulling together supplies, planes and pilots. The attack was now firmly set for June 4, and Nagumo's roly-poly chief of staff, Rear Admiral Ryunosuke Kusaka, thought this was much too soon. The pilots should have 40-50 days ashore to rest and help train the new men coming up. But like everyone else who counseled delay, he got a quick brush-off from Combined Fleet Headquarters.

Nor was even Kusaka overly concerned. They might have too little time to prepare, but he spent much of it trying to put through posthumous promotions for the naval aviators killed at Pearl Harbor. Truth was, he felt it really didn't matter anyhow: "We can beat the Yankees hands down with a single blow."

They would soon have their chance. May 20, Admiral Yamamoto fixed the final tactical grouping of his forces, and now the heart of the fleet—70 great warships—gathered at Hashirajima anchorage for the last time. Dwarfing them all was the 64,000-ton *Yamato*, back from a quick trip to Kure for supplies. Biggest battleship in the world, her 18.1-inch guns could hurl a broadside more than 25 miles. But big as she was, the center of attention was Admiral Nagumo's Striking Force of massive carriers—the *Akagi*, 30,000-ton ugly dowager of the carrier fleet . . . the *Kaga*, most powerful of them all . . . the more modern *Hiryu* and *Soryu*, listed as 10,000 tons for purposes of the old London Naval Treaty, but actually a good 18,000 tons each.

At that, there should have been two more of them. The superb new carriers *Shokaku* and *Zuikaku* were meant to be on hand, but detached for the Coral Sea affair, they had run into a little trouble. On May 17 *Shokaku* limped back into Kure, her flight deck shattered and her bow burnt out by American bombs. *Zuikaku* followed two days later, undamaged but her air group badly mauled. Between them, the two ships had only six torpedo planes and nine dive bombers left.

So there was no question of bringing them along. Four carriers should be enough anyhow. The Americans had little left. That "*Saratoga*-type" carrier was certainly sunk at the Coral Sea, and the *Yorktown* probably so. Even if she survived, it would make no difference. If *Shokaku* couldn't make Midway, how could *Yorktown*?

Far from giving pause, Coral Sea actually strengthened everyone's confidence. After all, that fight had been carried on by the 5th Air Squadron, generally scorned as the worst in the fleet. If this group of nobodies could hold their own against the best the Americans could offer, it should be child's play for the 1st and 2nd Air Squadrons now heading out—they were the cream of Japanese naval aviation. "Son of concubine gained a victory," ran the mildly coarse joke that swept the wardrooms, "so sons of legal wives should find no rival in the world."

Convinced of this, one headquarters told the post office at Yokosuka Naval Base simply to forward its mail to Midway. Combined Fleet sent down a new name for the islands: "Glorious Month of June." Officers who had brought ashore their personal belongings at the time of Pearl Harbor now lugged them all on board again—cameras, trinkets, framed pictures of the family, sets of *go* and *shogi*. Chief Warrant Officer Morinaga thought how different it was from the start of the war. Then he lay awake all night. Now he slept perfectly. Midway would be simple . . . "as easy as twisting a baby's arm."

No wonder spirits were high at the gala send-off party on May 25. No wonder they clinked the Emperor's cups and shouted their toasts. In contrast, the 26th was a day of quiet briefing, a last chance to button down the million details that went into winning a great victory. Far to the south, the transports were now assembled at Saipan. The troops busily practiced landings, splashing ashore through the surf. The mine sweepers, subchasers and patrol boats began streaming out of the harbor that afternoon, getting a head start so they could refuel at Wake. From the northern port of Ominato, the first units of the Aleutian force were pulling out too. Led by the light carriers *Ryujo* and *Junyo*, they soon disappeared east, lost in a swirling fog.

Six A.M. Wednesday, May 27, at the Hashirajima anchorage. A signal flag suddenly fluttered from the mast of Nagumo's flagship *Akagi:* "Sortie as scheduled." Anchor chains clattered, and the Striking Force began moving: first the light cruiser *Nagara*, leading the 11 destroyers of the protective screen . . . then the cruisers *Tone* and *Chikuma* . . . then the battleships *Haruna* and *Kirishima* with their odd pagoda masts . . . and finally the *Akagi*, the *Kaga*, the *Hiryu*, the *Soryu*.

As they crept single file past the ships still at anchor—Yamamoto's and Kondo's great collection of battleships and cruisers—sailors lined the rails, cheering and waving their caps. The sun blazed down, and it seemed a good omen after the cloudy, muggy days they'd been having. But the best omen of all, as everyone knew, was the day itself. For this 27th of May, 1942, was Navy Day—the 37th anniversary of Admiral Togo's great victory over the Russians at Tsushima.

Slowly they moved down the Inland Sea, through the Bungo Strait, and into the great blue swells of the open Pacific. Gradually the homeland faded into the haze; shipboard routine picked up; some men began doing calisthenics on the *Akagi's* flight deck. The engines pounded faster . . . they were on their way.

Back at Hashirajima anchorage that evening Admiral Yamamoto retired as usual to his cabin on the *Yamato*. This was when he liked to write letters, and it was always quite a ritual. The orderly would lay out brush and ink on a table; then, neatly spreading his paper on the carpet, Yamamoto would kneel down and start to write in a beautiful Chinese script. His letters were of all kinds—many to children—but some were on a special stationery used for no other purpose. These were the ones for Chiyoko Kawai, the geisha girl he kept in Tokyo.

Tonight his letter to her was serious; he was clearly still aware of his all-or-nothing risk. He told her he would like to give up everything, escape the world and be alone with her. But now he was off again, commanding all the fleet in the Pacific. The days ahead would be critical—"I imagine that very delightful moments may be few."

May 28, the Attu and Kiska invasion forces slipped out of Ominato harbor. Down at Saipan the Midway Invasion Force was starting too. Promptly at 5 P.M. the light cruiser *Jintsu* led 12 grimy transports and the tanker *Akebono Maru* out of the harbor. Several patrol boats joined up, and the seaplane tenders *Chitose* and *Kamikawa Maru* brought up the rear. They were to peel off later, hoping to take the tiny island of Kure just west of Midway and set up a seaplane base to support the invasion.

That same afternoon Admiral Kurita's supporting group of

heavy cruisers steamed out of Guam and took a parallel course. They were superb ships—the *Kumano, Suzuya, Mikuma* and *Mogami*—and should play a big part in covering the landings.

At Hashirajima the Main Force still rode quietly at anchor. On the *Yamato* the band gathered as usual outside the staff dining room at 11:50 A.M. Five minutes later the officers entered, stiff in their starched whites, and took their places. Then promptly at noon Chief Steward Omi knocked on Admiral Yamamoto's door as the band broke into a march. The Admiral emerged—he was always ready—and strode down the corridor into the dining room while the staff bowed their heads in respect. It was a daily ceremony when the flagship was in port, and today was no exception—but it would be the last time for a long, long while.

May 29, at the first light of day, the remaining ships began moving out too. First came Admiral Kondo's powerful force, designed to add still more beef to the invasion: a couple of battleships, five tough cruisers, the light carrier *Zuiho*, a swarm of destroyers.

And finally, the Main Force itself. Promptly at 6:00 A.M. the engines began turning over, and Admiral Yamamoto's 34 ships—heart of the Combined Fleet—got under way. Led by the mighty *Yamato*, seven great battleships glided through the Bungo Strait and headed into the Pacific. Around them bustled the usual screen of destroyers, cruisers and planes from the escort carrier *Hosho*. They were the last to leave, but that was just the point—these were the ships that would lurk in the wings while Nagumo and Kondo drew the enemy out; then they'd move in and deliver the knockout.

"The chief gunnery officer delivered a stirring appeal," wrote Takeo Ikemoto, a young seaman in the Main Force. "We will keep it in our minds forever."

"A beautiful day, a most appropriate day for such a cheerful departure," an engineer on the *Fuso* scribbled in his diary. The whole crew, he went on to say, were in high spirits.

And why not? How could this huge armada lose? It all

added up to 11 battleships, 8 carriers, 23 cruisers, 65 destroyers, scores of auxiliaries—some 190 ships altogether. Advancing eastward across the Pacific, they stretched over 1,800 miles in a great arc from the Kuriles to Guam. On this one operation their engines were using more oil than the peacetime Japanese Navy used in a year. Supporting them in this new age of aerial warfare were 700 planes, sea- and land-based—261 on Nagumo's crack carriers alone. Manning them were 100,000 men, including a dazzling army of 20 admirals. Commanding them was Isoroku Yamamoto himself.

And what was against them? The Combined Fleet estimate put the U.S. strength at 2 or 3 carriers (also possibly 2 or 3 escort types), perhaps 2 battleships, 11-13 cruisers, maybe 30 destroyers. Not much; and latest reports indicated there would be even less than that. On May 15 a patrol plane spotted two U.S. carriers down by the Solomons.

That meant there might well be no carriers at all in the Midway area. Then the operation would be even easier than expected, although, of course, they would also lose the chance of including carriers in the bag.

All that remained was for the U.S. fleet to do as planned. It must be in Pearl Harbor, then come out and fall into the trap. But of course this would happen. Even the orders said so. As Imperial General Order No. 94 explained, "We will destroy the enemy fleet which will appear when our operation is under way."

But what if the Americans knew what was up? Not a chance. Admiral Nagumo laid it on the line as his carriers raced toward the launching point. In his own intelligence estimate of the situation, paragraph (d) flatly declared, "The enemy is not aware of our plans."

JUST about this time, 7,000 miles to the east, in a chart room at the Navy Department in Washington a small group of officers were putting the finishing touches on a large chart of the Pacific Ocean. It was labeled in firm block letters, "STUDY OF AF AND AOB CAMPAIGNS, MAY 29, 1942."

The route of the Aleutian force was clear now, and it was carefully traced in magenta pencil, with the added note, "Assumed departure 0800, May 26." The movements of the Invasion Force were clear too—a red line headed out from Saipan, neatly marked, "Depart 28 May." Admiral Nagumo's Striking Force was causing a little more trouble. The May 27 departure date was clear enough, but the green line that slanted down from the northwest toward Hawaii was marked, "This course can be rejected." A new line ran more directly east, heading straight for Midway.

At the headquarters of the Commander in Chief, United States Pacific Fleet, in Pearl Harbor (CINCPAC), other officers worked on a similar chart. Experts at both places were in close touch with each other, exchanging data, comparing notes, sometimes differing in their interpretations. At Pearl, for instance, Admiral Nagumo's route ran farther to the north, then slanted southeast toward Midway, compass bearing perhaps 135°.

But here too there were uncertainties. Nobody seemed sure, for instance, just what was scheduled to happen at 6:00 P.M. on June 2 at a particular point some 650 miles west of Midway. It was obviously some sort of rendezvous, but the exact nature was hard to tell.

It seemed there were a few details that even a brilliant intelligence team couldn't work out.

CHAPTER 2

The Code and the Target

VISITORS were never welcome. To see anyone in the Navy's Combat Intelligence Unit at Pearl Harbor, it was first necessary to buzz a locked door at the top of some cellar steps. Eventually a man would appear and, if credentials were in order, the door would open. At the bottom of the steps was another locked door, and the same procedure would be repeated. When this second door opened, the visitor was finally in.

At first glance, the place seemed a shambles—about two dozen people working on top of each other, wading through a sea of paper. Any trace of a filing system had long since vanished. Stacks of folders simply piled up on the desks and chairs, then flooded out over the floor. Presiding over it all was a tall, thin, humorously caustic man in a red smoking jacket and carpet slippers—Commander Joseph J. Rochefort, Jr.

Joe Rochefort had been breaking codes for a long time now. In the early 1920s he helped another gifted young officer, Laurence F. Safford, set up the Navy's first center. In the doldrums of the '30s he amused himself by breaking the State Department's "gray" code. ("They were mad as hell.") In the fall of 1940 he helped crack the top Japanese naval code JN-25—by now he knew the language well.

May 1941, and he was at Pearl Harbor, setting up his Combat Intelligence Unit. Known in the trade as station "Hypo," it listened to Japanese traffic along with another station at Cavite ("Cash") and the home base in Washington ("Negat"). Technically Washington was headquarters, but the three stations really operated as a unit. Code-breaking was still a small world; the men in the business had worked together for years, sharing their findings, their theories, their hunches.

None of it did any good December 7, 1941. Japanese naval traffic had petered out, and Tokyo had also changed the key to JN-25, throwing everyone off for a few days. But the circuits soon started up again; the new key was solved by December 10, and once more there was plenty of good listening. Rochefort had spent the fall concentrating on the Japanese flag officers' system; now his unit joined the other stations in attacking JN-25.

Not that anyone understood much directly. The actual process of code-breaking rarely yielded more than 10%–15% of a message. The rest was all analysis: perhaps the name of a ship suggested another usually with it . . . or a past operation might help next time when the place names cropped up again . . . or a familiar operator's touch might give the source away; call letters could change, but a particular operator's "fist"—never.

It took a curious combination of talents to fathom all this—ideally a man should be sailor, linguist and puzzle fiend in about equal proportion—so it was not surprising that the Combat Intelligence Unit was known as an outfit of individualists. Nominally under the 14th Naval District, actually they were left on their own to exercise their special brand of genius. They lived for their work, and as the Japanese offensive rolled on, they got plenty of it. Gradually they absorbed a remarkable amount of unique knowledge.

One day toward the middle of April a totally unexpected

message arrived from Washington. It was, in fact, the first and only communication Rochefort ever received directly from Admiral Ernest J. King, Commander in Chief of the U.S. Fleet. COMINCH wanted Rochefort to give, based on the current flow of intercepts, his long-range estimate of Japanese naval intentions.

It was unusual, to say the least, for King to dip so far down the line in asking a question; yet it was understandable too at this particular moment. The Japanese had just raided Ceylon. Did this mean a major shift in the war toward India, or would they soon be back in the Pacific? A great deal depended on the answer.

Rochefort came up with a four-point estimate, reflecting the combined opinion of his staff: (1) Japanese operations in the Indian Ocean were over; the fleet was on its way home; (2) they weren't going to attack Australia; (3) they were planning an operation south of Rabaul, with forces already assigned; (4) there were signs of something else brewing in the Pacific, but he couldn't say when or where.

By late April the missing pieces were beginning to fall into place. The operation south of Rabaul was definitely aimed at Port Moresby—U.S. units headed for the Coral Sea. The other operation remained something of a mystery, but the Central Pacific seemed a strong possibility, and it was hard to look at the map without noticing Midway. Serving at various times as a coaling station, commercial cable relay point, and Pan American Clipper rest stop, Midway was currently a very useful but highly exposed Navy patrol plane base. It consisted of just two tiny islets, Sand and Eastern, lying side by side in a beautiful blue lagoon. There was nothing else worth anything for a thousand miles around. Midway was out in the Pacific alone—all alone.

Admiral Nimitz made a brief visit there May 2, spending a day with the officers in charge, Navy Commander Cyril T. Simard and Marine Lieutenant Colonel Harold Shannon.

Nimitz mentioned no specific threat but did ask what they'd need to defend Midway against an attack. The two men poured out their requirements.

"If I get you all these things you say you need, then can you defend Midway against a major amphibious assault?"

"Yes, sir."

Another week passed, and at Pearl Harbor Rochefort began to get a better picture. As always, it was a matter of piecing together the scraps gathered by all three stations—Pearl, Washington and a new unit in Australia replacing the one lost with the Philippines. Even so, there was nothing conclusive. It was all spotty . . . but nonetheless revealing. For instance, it was clear that Admiral Kondo's Battleship Division 3 was talking a lot to Nagumo's First Carrier Force . . . that certain transports were getting orders to Saipan, and BatDiv 3 was talking to them too . . . that Cruiser Division 7 was also heading for Saipan. Was there any connection between these things?

The traffic never gave any clear-cut answer. Often the pertinent messages were days apart. Yet Joe Rochefort had a knack of remembering them all, and as he pieced the picture together, it pointed to a massive operation involving most of the Imperial Combined Fleet.

But again, where? The Japanese never mentioned any particular spot, but gradually one name began cropping up more and more often—sometimes as a destination, sometimes as a place calling for certain equipment. In a sort of code-within-the-code this place was always called "AF."

Rochefort's little group racked their brains. Finally someone remembered that AF had also appeared in messages last March, at the time a couple of Japanese seaplanes made an abortive attack on Pearl Harbor. Papers flew as the whole office dug through the piles of intercepts, trying to track this vague clue down. Finally, there it was. The Japanese had indeed mentioned AF. Those seaplanes had refueled from a submarine at French Frigate Shoals, a tiny atoll lying toward

Midway, and one of the messages spoke of passing near AF.

For Rochefort, that settled it. AF must lie in the Midway area . . . and the only place worth taking around there was Midway itself. From now on, his estimates began stressing Midway as the probable target.

Not everyone saw it that clearly. The intercepts also referred to "AL," "AO," "AOB"—all definitely in the Aleutian area— and some high officers, especially in Washington, thought that the real target was Alaska or the West Coast. Admiral King himself leaned for a time toward Hawaii as a possibility, and the Army Air Force was always worried about a raid on San Francisco.

It was hard to change their minds. As usual, Rochefort's unit rarely managed to "read" more than 15% of an intercept, and to the average professional officer 15% seemed mighty little to go on. It was different in the old days when offices were smaller and the men knew each other better. Now there was tremendous turnover; whole new layers of command moved in, often staffed by men who knew little about radio intelligence. It was too much to expect them to understand the intricacies of cryptoanalysis. Nor did it help that the crypto-analysts were so secretive. They had to be, of course, but that didn't make it any easier to sell their wares to the bright new faces at COMINCH.

So the Navy Department had its skeptics . . . and so did the Army Air Force . . . and so, for that matter, did the high command in Hawaii.

But Rochefort also had his allies, and one of them was Nimitz's intelligence officer, Lieutenant Commander Edwin T. Layton. He too knew the Japanese and their language well. He spent two years at the Embassy in Tokyo just before the war, then was Admiral Kimmel's intelligence chief at the time of the Pearl Harbor disaster. Like the rest of Kimmel's staff, Layton wondered what would become of himself when Nimitz took over; and like the others, he felt that tremendous surge of morale when Nimitz asked them all to stay with him.

Intelligence, Nimitz told Layton, was something he knew nothing about. He had only this one suggestion: He hoped Layton would approach his job as though he were Admiral Nagano, or Yamamoto, or whoever was calling the tune in Tokyo. With the information at hand, he should put himself in Japanese shoes and come up with his best estimate of their plans and intentions.

With such sailing orders, it was easy to fall under the spell of Joe Rochefort's shop. Layton was completely sold, did his best to sell Nimitz too. The Admiral himself was half convinced, but no more.

Around May 8 Layton finally begged Nimitz to visit the Combat Intelligence Unit. Then he could see for himself. Layton was sure that once the Admiral watched the place in operation—saw how carefully the information was pieced together—then he too would become a true believer.

Nimitz couldn't come. Swamped with work on the Coral Sea battle, he was just too busy. But he did send Captain L. D. McCormick, his war plans officer. McCormick said he was busy too, but finally agreed to set aside two hours.

Down the stairs they went, and into the basement room, which for once the staff had made a halfhearted effort to clean up. On a makeshift table of planks and sawhorses Rochefort had spread all his intercepts. He patiently showed how one led to another, and how they all fitted together to form a composite picture.

McCormick was fascinated. In the end, he spent not two but three and a half hours poking around, flipping the material, asking a thousand tough, show-me questions. There were no velvet gloves on either side. . . .

"How do you *know* the *Kamikawa Maru* isn't just heading for her home port?"

"Well, if she is, that would be doing a tonsillectomy through the rectum."

In the end, McCormick came away completely convinced, and to sell McCormick was to sell Nimitz. From that day on, the Admiral was the staunchest ally Rochefort and Layton could hope to have.

Washington remained skeptical. For one thing, they still hadn't pinned down exactly what the Japanese meant by "AF." Rochefort was always sure it was Midway but he needed proof. Around May 10 he went to Layton with an idea. Could Midway be instructed to radio a fake message in plain English, saying their fresh-water machinery had broken down? Nimitz cheerfully went along with the ruse . . . Midway followed through . . . and two days later a Japanese intercept was picked up, reporting that AF was low on fresh water.

May 14, Nimitz filled in Major General Delos Emmons, the local Army commander, and declared a state of "Fleet Opposed Invasion." On the 15th, he began assembling his meager collection of ships. He had only three carriers and all were thousands of miles away in the South Pacific. Rear Admiral Frank Jack Fletcher's Task Force 17 was at Tongatabu, licking its wounds from the Coral Sea battle. The carrier *Yorktown* had not been sunk, as the Japanese claimed, but she was far from healthy. One bomb had ripped out her innards, and two near-misses had opened some seams. Vice Admiral William F. Halsey's Task Force 16 was marking time off the Solomons; he had arrived with the carriers *Enterprise* and *Hornet* just too late for Coral Sea. Nimitz radioed them all to hurry back.

At Tongatabu Fletcher quickly made a few patchwork repairs—then he was on his way. East of the Solomons, Halsey got the message May 16, local time, and immediately began collecting his scattered ships. He was rounding up the last of them on the 18th when a new message arrived from Nimitz. This one was only two words: "EXPEDITE RETURN."

As they swung northeast for Pearl, the *Enterprise*'s navigation officer, Commander Richard Ruble, had a satisfying thought. He recalled how, on the 15th, they had discovered an enemy patrol plane snooping about on the western horizon. Visibility was perfect, and it had plenty of time to get off a good contact report to Japanese headquarters firmly placing Task Force 16 deep in the South Pacific.

Back at Pearl Harbor the Combat Intelligence Unit labored on. Rochefort himself concentrated on the translations—so much depended on the nuances of the Japanese language even after a message was broken. He was now putting in 20-21 hours a day, curling up in some corner for occasional naps, going home "only when someone told me I ought to take a bath." The rest of the staff worked just as hard—Jasper Holmes, slaving over his ship positions; Tommy Dyer gulping keep-awake pills by the fistful; the brilliant Ham Wright buried in paper.

At CINCPAC, staff officers carefully noted the information on their charts. By now the composition of Nagumo's Striking Force was down pat—CarDivs 1 and 2, CruDiv 8, all the familiar names—but the route was more uncertain. Some clues suggested they'd come straight across; other clues said no, they'd go considerably to the north, then slant down. There was a theory they might even strike from the east. From all this, time was clearly another question mark.

There was less mystery about the Occupation Force coming up from the southwest. The route was clear; the only question was when it would arrive. Well, somebody figured, if the transport *Goshu Maru* left the Marshalls May 17, it could link up at Saipan on the 22nd, and the whole convoy would be at Midway on the 30th. On the other hand, there was much radio traffic about exercises, and maybe these would push the whole operation back a little. . . .

Carried away by the mounting excitement, it was hard for the insiders at CINCPAC to realize that some people were still dubious about the whole business. On May 16 or 17 Nimitz received a letter from General Emmons saying he appreciated the intelligence, but felt he ought to point something out. These estimates were based on enemy intentions rather than capabilities. It was safer to plan in terms of capabilities, and the Japanese were certainly capable of attacking Hawaii.

Nimitz called Commander Layton in—the Admiral's blue eyes twinkling with amusement as Layton exploded with exasperation. Yet Emmons's misgivings were understandable. Like most others, he knew little about Rochefort's work. Beyond that, there was the matter of Nimitz's order directing a state of "Fleet Opposed Invasion." This put all his Seventh Air Force bombers under CINCPAC control. But if the Navy was wrong and the Japanese did come to Hawaii, it would be Emmons, not Nimitz, who would feel the full blast from the War Department at being caught with no planes on hand.

Nimitz was not about to reverse course, but he did make a move typical of this most careful and conciliatory of men. He assigned one of his staff, Captain J. M. Steele, to the specific job of keeping an eye on the Combat Intelligence Unit's material. Steele became a sort of "devil's advocate," deliberately challenging every estimate, deliberately making Rochefort and Layton back up every point.

Steele really threw himself into the job. Layton rued the day it ever happened, but from Nimitz's point of view the assignment served two very useful purposes. First, it did something specific about General Emmons's letter without any real change in course; second, it provided a genuine check just in case they all were wrong, and the Japanese really did have an extra trick or two.

No more time for debating. The latest intercepts indicated that the attack might come as early as May 28. Nimitz warned Midway, and preparations at Pearl moved into high gear. Decisions were made in hours that normally might take days. What to do about the Aleutian side show? Nimitz decided to counter it with a small force that would keep the Japanese occupied and guard his own flank. How to use the submarines? Put them in an arc west of Midway to try and intercept the Japanese fleet coming in. What about the battleships on the

West Coast? Keep them there; they only got in the way. How about the *Yorktown*'s damage? Take a chance on repairing her at Pearl Harbor; an urgent message listed the things they'd need: arresting gear . . . 50 pneumercator gauges . . . and so on. In any other navy it might have seemed strange that this priority list also included a new freezer for the soda fountain.

The Army was now in high gear too. On May 18 the entire Seventh Air Force went on special alert for an attack on Midway or (the old fear persisted) an air raid on Hawaii. B-17s began pouring in from the West Coast. At the same time, big new PBYs were arriving for the Navy—these, in turn, hurried on to Midway.

They were all part of a sudden rush to beef up the place— a far cry from the old days when Midway seemed at the bottom of every supply depot's priority list. For months the Marines just couldn't get any barbed wire; now they got "hundreds of miles of it." Sandbags, antiaircraft guns, impregnated clothing, PT boats, reinforcements, all poured out in a steady stream. When the big railroad ferry *Kittyhawk* left for Midway on May 23, her decks bulged with fighters and dive bombers, even five light tanks.

But how to use this growing strength? And how best to coordinate it with the three precious carriers racing up from the South Pacific? On the 23rd Nimitz asked Admiral Pat Bellinger, his patrol plane chief, and Captain A. C. Davis, his staff aviation officer, to confer with the Army immediately on how to make best use of all the planes available—both Army and Navy, ashore and afloat. They should think in terms of possibly five Japanese carriers, and they must hurry. "TIME IS EVERYTHING."

The submarines were already moving out. The big *Nautilus* was lying in dry dock when her skipper Lieutenant Commander Bill Brockman was asked how soon he could get going. Brockman said about 48 hours. Everyone worked around the clock, and at 9:00 A.M. on May 24 she slipped down the channel, bound for her station in the arc west of Midway. Eleven other subs were out there too; seven more patrolled to the east in case Nagumo tried an unexpected dash for Hawaii.

May 25, there was new excitement at Pearl Harbor. This day the Combat Intelligence Unit came through with its hottest item yet—a long Japanese intercept that really laid it on the line. This message ticked off the various units, the ships, the captains, the course, the launching time—everything.

Rochefort was hard at work on the translation when word came that Nimitz wanted to see him personally at a certain time. Completely absorbed and wanting to finish it, he turned up at the Admiral's office half an hour late. This was too much for even the placid Nimitz, and his manner was chilly, to say the least. But he soon warmed up as Rochefort gave him, point by point, the exact battle order and operating plan of the Japanese Striking Force.

Nimitz rushed a new message to Midway, giving all the details. There were only two bright spots: Nagumo's Force no longer included the carrier *Zuikaku;* and the date of the attack would be later than they originally thought—it should fall some time around June 3–5.

Washington still had its skeptics. Now the big fear was a Japanese ruse; the enemy might be just feeding Nimitz these messages to cover up a major raid on Hawaii or the West Coast. After all, they used fake radio signals to fool CINCPAC just before the attack on Pearl Harbor. Maybe this was the same sort of thing. Nimitz should plan his defenses with this threat in mind.

There was something to the argument. The Japanese had indeed used radio deception before Pearl Harbor. Nor was radio traffic analysis infallible. A week before the December 7 raid CINCPAC had placed one Japanese carrier division in the South Pacific because the destroyers that usually guarded it were down there—yet, as everyone soon found out, this guess had been all too wrong.

But, Nimitz's intelligence men argued, this time was different. There were only isolated messages before Pearl Harbor; now there was a mountain of intelligence. And besides, there was the make-up of the Japanese force—it clearly involved a landing. They wouldn't be bringing all those troops and transports for an air raid on San Francisco.

The argument dragged on. At the bottom, it was really just the old controversy over enemy intentions or capabilities. Sacred to the Naval War College was the doctrine that all decisions must be based on what the enemy *could* do, rather than what it probably would do. Nimitz knew the risks of outguessing the Japanese as well as anyone, but, as he often told Layton, he felt the Navy's planning should put more stress on what was most likely to happen, rather than just the worst that could happen.

This time, moreover, he had a source of intelligence never dreamed of by the men who wrote the textbooks. Those intercepts gave him a priceless advantage that must not be wasted. He was sure the Japanese were coming to Midway, and all countermeasures should be based on this assumption. He stood firm—and won.

Just in time too. That key intercept of May 25 was the last message in the JN-25 code that Rochefort's group managed to unravel. Right afterward the Japanese changed their system, and everything went black. It would be weeks before the Combat Intelligence Unit began "reading" this sort of material again. Meanwhile, they could only fill in some gaps and continue to break ship-to-ship traffic—useful, but it gave no overall picture. That remained blank, but by now it was all decided. Nimitz could place his ships and planes where he wanted.

"Assume 4 CV, each with 36 VF plus 27 VSB (63 planes each) attack Balsa from short range, say 50 to 100 miles, with view of knocking out at once the air defense," wrote the Admiral in a hasty note to Captain Davis. "Visualize as clearly as possible his method of operating and OUR best counter-tactics. Give me brief pencil memo on this, and then we will discuss."*

The harried staff was bombarded with questions, often getting down to hard details, for Nimitz was not just a planner, but a careful, meticulous fighter. What would be the best positions for the 12 additional 3-inch AA guns now being rushed to Midway? Where should the U.S. carriers be placed to give the greatest support? Where should the subs be stationed after the attack began? Should Midway's planes avoid fighting the Japanese bombers and go all out for the carriers? Should more planes be based on Midway?

"The problem at Midway is one of hitting before we are hit," wrote Admiral Bellinger, submitting a search plan worked out with General Tinker of the Seventh Air Force. It called for patrolling 700 miles out every day, covering the whole 180° west of Midway. To do the job, they needed 23 PBYs . . . eight more than they already had. Endorsing the scheme on May 26, Captain Davis noted an intriguing possibility: "The plan will leave an excellent flanking area northeast of Midway for our carriers."

And they were coming in now. That same morning on the southwest horizon a single speck appeared . . . then 2 . . . 5 . . . 21 altogether, as Admiral Halsey's Task Force 16 pounded up from the Solomons. It had been an exciting trip back, full of speculation. Some, like Commander Ed Creehan, the *Hornet's* engineering officer, had a good pipe line—his old shipmate Captain Marc Mitscher tipped him off. Others could only guess. On the *Enterprise* Ensign Lewis Hopkins of Bomb-

---

* The official records are naturally full of abbreviations and code words. "CV" is Navy lingo for carriers, "VF" for fighters, "VSB" for scout-bombers. "Balsa" is a code name for Midway. For simplicity's sake, this book will usually translate such designations into layman's terms, but they seemed too much a part of the flavor of the note to do so here.

ing Squadron 6 noted that even the plane radio transmitters were wired off—it must be really big. Seamen on the destroyer *Balch* wondered why Commander Tiemroth had them working so hard rigging life lines and rescue nets—whatever it was, it looked dangerous.

The man who knew best was in no mood to see anyone. Admiral Halsey had come down with a skin disease, and the itch was driving him crazy. He tried everything—even oatmeal water baths—but nothing helped. He couldn't eat, he couldn't sleep. Completely exhausted, he now lay in his cabin, a bundle of nerves and temper.

At 11:33 A.M. the *Enterprise* entered Pearl Harbor channel, and was soon tied up at Ford Island. Dr. Hightower put Halsey on the sick list, but the Admiral—never a good patient—went over to CINCPAC anyhow. Nimitz took one look, ordered him to the hospital immediately. But first he wanted Halsey's recommendation on who should take over Task Force 16 for the coming battle. Without a second's hesitation, the normally ebullient Halsey named the man perhaps least like him in the entire Pacific fleet—the quiet, methodical commander of his cruisers and destroyers, Rear Admiral Raymond Ames Spruance.

Spruance himself had no inkling what was up. After his flagship *Northampton* made fast, he went around to the *Enterprise* to report to Halsey as usual. Only then did he find that the Admiral had been taken to the hospital. He joined the rest of the task force commanders as they sat in the flag cabin, restlessly waiting to learn who would take over.

Halsey's aide Lieutenant William H. Ashford arrived, sent by the Admiral to tip Spruance off. The place seemed a little public, so Ashford took the new commander into Halsey's bedroom and told him there. Spruance was thoroughly surprised. He was junior to several other possibilities, was a nonaviator, had never even served a day on a carrier. Yet he was used to following Halsey around the Pacific, and he'd have Halsey's fine staff to back him up.

He hurried to CINCPAC, where Nimitz formally told him of his appointment. A quick briefing followed on the Japanese advance; then the two men sat around planning the U.S. countermove. To Spruance there was only one thing to do: take the carriers and lie in wait northeast of Midway. Normally he might head northwest—straight for the Japanese—and engage them somewhere west of the atoll, but the stakes seemed too high. Even accepting that miraculous intelligence, the Japanese just might change their plans and go for Hawaii or the West Coast. Then he'd find himself caught on the wrong side of them, out of the fight and useless. He could have it both ways by waiting in the northeast: he'd be safe against an end run, and he had a marvelous chance for an ambush.

It was fine with Nimitz.

Back on the *Enterprise,* Lieutenant Clarence E. Dickinson noticed his old Academy classmate Lieutenant R. J. Oliver coming up the gangway. Oliver was Spruance's flag lieutenant on the *Northampton*—what was he doing here? It turned out he was arranging to bring over the Admiral's personal gear. One way or another the news raced through the task force: Spruance was taking over; Halsey was on the beach.

It was hard to believe. In the past six months Bill Halsey had become a part of them. From the wreckage of Pearl Harbor, he had lifted them—both the frightened recruits and the disillusioned old-timers—and given them new faith in themselves. Gradually he gave them other things too—skills, strength, endurance, spirit. They knew all this, and they loved him for it. Even now they could picture him sitting up by the bow watching take-offs—they said he knew every plane. It was almost impossible to think of being without him.

Not that they disliked Spruance—they hardly knew the man—but that was just the trouble. There were stories that he was from the "gun club"—part of the conservative battleship crowd that looked down on the jaunty aviators and their sporty brown shoes. That sounded like bad news. As one long-time machinist's mate on the *Enterprise* later explained, "We had nothing against him, but we knew we had a black-shoe admiral in our midst."

Well, they'd see. Meanwhile, they were far too busy to brood. A great sense of urgency hung in the air. People were frozen in their jobs; even Captain Marc Mitscher, slated to be an admiral, would stay on as skipper of the *Hornet*. His replacement, Captain Charles Perry Mason, came aboard as observer and reminded Mitscher, "Take good care of her—this is my ship."

The harbor was alive with activity. Fuel and ammunition barges tooted impatiently, jockeying to come alongside the ships. The destroyer *Aylwin*'s entire crew worked all night, loading and stowing fresh supplies. On the *Hornet* Machinist's Mate J. E. Hoy sweated away, shifting provisions to the kitchen. When they were one can of Spam short, the cook refused to sign for anything, and all work stopped amid angry bickering. Word reached the bridge, and Marc Mitscher exploded—unless this was settled by the time he got there, everybody would be court-martialed. The men got the point; the cook signed and the work raced on—"Mitscher was a guy you didn't fool with."

Ashore, another member of the *Hornet*'s company had a different kind of supply problem. Lieutenant Commander John Waldron, skipper of Torpedo Squadron 8, was laying siege to the Aircraft Matériel Office. He heard they had a supply of newly designed twin machine-gun mounts; now he was determined to get some for his slow, highly vulnerable torpedo planes. The guns were really meant for dive bombers, but there was something about this impassioned, almost mystical man—others noticed it too—and in the end Captain Lyon relented and gave him the guns. Waldron rushed off, so elated he forgot his flight gloves.

On the *Enterprise*, work stopped long enough May 27 for a brief ceremony on the flight deck. In a flurry of ruffles and bosun calls, Admiral Nimitz came aboard to decorate three of the pilots. Pinning the Distinguished Flying Cross on the chest of Lieutenant Roger Mehle, the Admiral paused and looked him straight in the eye: "I think you'll have a chance to win yourself another medal in the next several days."

That afternoon a new set of specks appeared on the southwestern horizon. Admiral Fletcher's Task Force 17 was coming in too. It had been a hard trip, full of suspense as the wounded *Yorktown* trailed a telltale oil slick for miles behind her. But they were safe at last, and the crew was in high spirits. They certainly didn't wish the "Old Lady" ill, but the damage from that bomb should keep her in dry dock for a long time; and after 101 days at sea they could use a little liberty. As the big carrier limped up the channel, the men could almost taste the Hotel Street beer.

A special reception committee was waiting at Dry Dock No. 1. Yard worker Cyril Williams and a crew of other hands had spent all the past night getting blocks manufactured and secured, ready to receive the *Yorktown*. They finished just in time, watching with satisfaction as the big carrier nosed through the gates.

On board, the men learned with dismay that there'd be no liberty after all. Far from it: working parties were already loading fresh supplies of food and ammunition. No one knew what was up; the ship's Marine Detachment caustically agreed, "The navigator has lost the charts to the American waters."

Even before the dock had drained, a little group could be seen sloshing around, examining the bent and crumpled plates. The yard manager, Captain Claude Gillette, conferred with his hull repair expert, Lieutenant Commander H. J. Pfingstag, and other technicians. Talking with them—in hip boots like the rest—was Admiral Nimitz himself.

It was clear the damage was very serious. The two near-misses hadn't done much—the leaks could be quickly patched —but the direct hit was another matter. It had exploded four decks down, spreading havoc for 100 feet—decks blistered, doors and hatches blown off, bulkheads ripped open, frames and stanchions twisted. It should take weeks to fix.

"We must have this ship back in three days," Nimitz told

the group. His voice was quiet, his manner very, very serious. The men hesitated, looked at one another, and finally Pfingstag gulped, "Yes, sir."

Nimitz was back in his office at the sub base by the time Admiral Fletcher checked in a little later. Perhaps it was because they knew each other so well, but Fletcher immediately sensed that his boss—normally the calmest of people—was deeply disturbed. Nimitz started off by asking Fletcher how he felt. "Pretty tired," was the answer. Nimitz nodded; yes, he understood and normally he'd send him back to the West Coast, but he couldn't do it this time. The Japanese were on their way to Midway; Task Force 17 had to go right out again.

Nimitz then poured out the details, ship by ship, of the Japanese operation. "Do you know," he added with just a touch of irritation, "they've even named the officer who is to take over the Naval Station there on August 1?"

Gradually he filled in Fletcher on everything else: Halsey was out . . . Spruance now had the *Enterprise* and *Hornet* . . . they'd be starting off soon . . . Fletcher would follow with the *Yorktown* . . . the two forces would join up with Fletcher taking over-all command as senior officer . . . then they'd lie in wait off Midway.

Fletcher understood. He had only one misgiving. The *Yorktown* had lost a lot of fliers at Coral Sea, and he was worried about the new bombing and torpedo squadrons Nimitz planned to give him. It wasn't a question of quality—he was sure they were excellent—but they hadn't worked with the ship before. Couldn't he keep his regular group, filling it out with replacements? No, said Nimitz; the old fliers needed a rest, and new complete squadrons promised better coordination.

At some point Spruance joined them, and the question arose whether the *Yorktown* could really make it. "She'll be joining you," Nimitz said firmly.

It certainly didn't look like it. The *Yorktown* now lay high out of the water. Yard workers swarmed over her, hammers clattering, acetylene torches flaring in the growing dusk. During the evening a courier came aboard, climbing over the wires and cables, and delivered a thick document to Lieutenant (j.g.) John Greenbacker, the ship's secretary. Greenbacker signed for it and thereby became the first person on board to see CINCPAC Operation Plan No. 29-42, the official blueprint setting forth all the thinking and decisions of the past two weeks.

"The enemy is expected to attempt the capture of Midway in the near future," it explained. "For this purpose it is believed that the enemy will employ approximately the following: 2–4 fast battleships: 4–5 carriers; 8–9 heavy cruisers; 16–24 destroyers; 8–12 submarines; a landing force with seaplane tenders. . . ."

This catalogue of chilling details was followed by the American answer: an outline of the tactics CINCPAC proposed to follow. Specific tasks were assigned each of the various U.S. forces. The carriers would "inflict maximum damage on the enemy by employing strong attrition tactics." As decided, they would operate northeast of Midway, hoping to catch the Japanese by surprise. Submarines would go for the enemy carriers; Midway itself would concentrate on defense and patrols; Hawaii would contribute a long-range striking force. In listing these tasks, the language was usually general (Midway's first job was simply, "hold Midway"), but there was no doubt that everybody had enough to do.

There were 86 copies of Op Plan 29-42, and as they were distributed throughout the various commands, selected officers studied the details with fascination. To those eligible to see it, the meticulous intelligence on the Japanese movements seemed almost incredible. Not knowing where it came from—and perhaps having read too many spy thrillers—the *Enterprise's* navigator, Commander Ruble, could only say to himself, "That man of ours in Tokyo is worth every cent we pay him."

A bright sun sparkled off the water next morning, May 28, as the destroyers of Task Force 16 slipped their moorings and glided single file down Pearl Harbor Channel toward the open sea. Behind them came a pair of tankers, then the cruisers, and finally the *Enterprise* and *Hornet.*

On the bridge of the *Enterprise* the "black-shoe Admiral" Raymond Spruance thoughtfully watched his first command of carriers move down the harbor. In the words of the master plan, he was on his way "to inflict maximum damage on the enemy." And to guide him he now had a last-minute Letter of Instructions just issued by Nimitz to his two commanders: "In carrying out the task assigned in Op Plan 29-42, you will be governed by the principle of calculated risk, which you will interpret to mean the avoidance of exposure of your force to attack the superior enemy forces without good prospect of inflicting, as a result of such exposure, greater damage to the enemy."

To achieve this most delicate of formulas was now up to him. At 11:59 the *Enterprise* cleared the channel, swung toward Barbers Point, and headed for those lonely waters northeast of Midway.

Back at Pearl Harbor, a rebellious but helpless patient watched from a lanai at the Naval Hospital. For the utterly frustrated Halsey, seeing them go without him was even worse than the itch.

In contrast to the antiseptic quiet of the hospital was the bedlam at Dry Dock No. 1. Hundreds of men now swarmed over the *Yorktown*—she seemed even more alive out of the water than afloat. Clouds of smoke poured up from the acetylene torches burning away her damaged plates. The clatter of drills and hammers never stopped.

Deep inside the ship Bill Bennett, the burly supervisor of Shop 11-26, bore down on his gang of 150 shipfitters. One qualification of a Navy yard boss was to be even tougher than his men, and Bennett easily met the test. He was in charge all the way as they sweated to erase the devastating direct hit.

There was no time for plans or sketches. The men worked directly with the steel beams and bars brought on the ship. Coming to a damaged frame, burners would take out the worst of it; fitters would line up a new section, cut it to match the contour of the damage; riggers and welders would move in, "tacking" the new piece in place. Then on to the next job— there seemed no end to the grind.

And it was hell down there besides—120° temperature, little light, lots of smoke. When a man looked really ready to drop, Bennett would send him topside for a sandwich and a breath of air. He himself never bothered with any of that. Occasionally sucking an orange, he worked for 48 hours straight.

All over the ship it was the same story. Ellis Clanton, chief quarterman at Shop 31, didn't leave the ship for three days, as he struggled to repair the weird assortment of fixtures that are part of a great carrier—elevator shoes, arresting gear rams and so forth. Working on the hull, Ed Sheehan grew so tired he finally fell asleep on the scaffolding.

At one point a group of welders seemed about ready to fold. Out of nowhere a naval officer appeared and asked them to gather around. The Japanese, he explained, were on their way to Midway . . . they thought the *Yorktown* was sunk . . . wouldn't they be surprised if they found her fit and ready to fight? His psychology worked; the men rushed back to their jobs.

All the night of the 28th the pace continued, the *Yorktown* spouting sparks and blue flashes as the welders worked on. It was a nightmare for the ship's crew, but few had time to rest anyhow. Gunner's Mate Jefferson Vick was typical—he spent 48 hours straight hauling bombs aboard, with only one five-hour break.

While the work went on, an odd thing was happening in nearby Honolulu. First the electric power failed in the Kahala district. Then when that was fixed, it failed in the Nuuanu Valley. The same thing happened from time to time in other parts of town. The local citizens were used to the erratic ways of the Hawaiian Electric Company, but this time was no accident. Needing extra power to run the enormous amount of repair equipment, the Navy Yard contacted Leslie Hicks, president of the company, and explained the emergency in confidence. Hicks said he thought he could help, and quietly staged "failures" in one district after another, diverting the desperately needed electricity to the Yard.

By midmorning on the 29th they had run out of time. At 11:00 the cocks were opened, the dry dock flooded, and the *Yorktown* towed back into the harbor. It was a slow, delicate job getting her out—much too slow for the tower, which kept flashing, "EXPEDITE! EXPEDITE!" Hundreds of men still worked on her; Bill Bennett's shipfitters were gone, but the electricians and mechanics were everywhere.

In his cabin Captain Elliott Buckmaster labored over a million last details. Commander Dixie Kiefer, the ship's colorful executive officer, dropped by at one point, urging the Captain to put his own personal belongings ashore. No, said Buckmaster, he was too old a sea dog for that—never get separated from your personal gear.

The work went on, ashore as well as afloat. The *Yorktown*'s landing signal officer, Lieutenant Norwood Campbell, struggled to get the new squadrons in shape for carrier landings. The pilots were mostly from the *Saratoga*. She had been torpedoed in January, and since then they had spent a good deal of time kicking around. Lieutenant Commander Max Leslie's Bombing Squadron 3 was sharp—they had spelled the *Enterprise*'s bombers on the Doolittle raid. But Lieutenant Commander Lance Massey's Torpedo 3 was rusty, and Lieutenant Commander John S. Thach's Fighting 3 was very much a mixed bag: some were *Yorktown* veterans; some hadn't seen a carrier for months; some had never served on one.

At the moment all were at Kaneohe on the other side of the island. Most still didn't know what was up, except that they were suddenly practicing a lot. But that day word began to get around. Commander Leslie took his rear-seat man, Radioman W. E. Gallagher, aside and told him they had a new assignment: they were joining the *Yorktown* and going out to meet the Japs. He didn't say where, but Gallagher was to be ready in the morning.

Saturday, May 30, dawned clear at Pearl Harbor. On the *Yorktown* the shrill call of a bosun's whistle was the first signal for many that Admiral Nimitz was coming aboard. They had won their fight to get her ready; now it was time to wish them "good luck and good hunting." Turning to Buckmaster, the Admiral said to announce to all hands that he was sorry they couldn't go back to the mainland yet. They had a job to do. But when it was over, he'd send the *Yorktown* to the West Coast for liberty, and he didn't mean peanuts.

At 9:00 the engines began turning over. Far below, yard hand Fred Rodin and his gang were still wrapping insulation around some newly installed pipes. Suddenly someone yelled down the shaft, "OK, boys, all ashore that's going ashore—we're pulling out." Rodin and his mates bolted topside—this was one trip they didn't want to make. The *Yorktown* was already gliding downstream as the last of them dropped down into a launch and bobbed off toward the shore. On she went, picking up speed as she moved down the channel. On the flight deck the ship's band—with perhaps just a touch of sly humor—lustily blared out, "California, Here I Come."

That afternoon she picked up her revamped air group—flown out as usual from the base—and by nightfall the whole task force was far beyond the sight of land. They had accomplished wonders—the *Yorktown* was there—but the odds were still long this brilliant moon-swept night. It would take more than the best intelligence, planning and determination to beat Yamamoto's huge armada. They knew it at CINCPAC too, and it had a lot to do with naming the rendezvous point where Spruance and Fletcher were slated to meet. This dot on the map—this mythical spot on a trackless ocean—they wishfully called "Point Luck."

For Lieutenant Commander Toshitake Ueno, this same moonlit night brought only bad news. As the darkened U.S. ships pounded north, his submarine *I-123* lay idle and useless off French Frigate Shoals, several hundred miles to the west. According to the final version of the Japanese plan, the *I-123* was meant to help refuel two seaplanes, up from Kwajalein, for a last-minute look at Pearl Harbor—but there would be no refueling tonight. A big American patrol plane lay anchored in the lagoon.

It was odd. When first tried in March, "Operation K" (as they called it) went off very well. Then the two big seaplanes came up from Kwajalein, refueled from the tanker-submarines, and flew on to Pearl Harbor without any hitch. True, they didn't accomplish much, but that wasn't the fault of the arrangements. The rescue sub stood by; the radio beam worked; the refueling went smoothly; and above all nobody bothered them at French Frigate Shoals.

This time was different from the start. When the *I-121*—first sub to arrive—reached the Shoals on May 26, she found a U.S. seaplane tender already sitting at anchor. Soon the *I-122* and *I-123* also came up, and the next three days were spent peeking through periscopes, waiting patiently for the tender to go away. But she didn't, and by the night of May 29 something had to be done. Tomorrow was the big day: the planes would be leaving Kwajalein during the night, planning to arrive and refuel at dusk on the 30th. As senior officer, Commander Ueno took one last look—two ships were there now—and reluctantly radioed the situation to Kwajalein. Vice Admiral Eiji Goto understood; he radioed back that the operation was postponed a day; expect the planes on the 31st.

Now it was the night of the 30th, and pretty much the same story. As Commander Ueno searched the moonlit anchorage, he couldn't see the tender, but there was no mistaking that PBY—the Americans were still there. Around midnight he again radioed Kwajalein that the place was being watched. This time the answer came from Goto's boss, Vice Admiral Nishizo Tsukahara commanding the 11th Air Fleet: the planes wouldn't be coming at all; Operation K was "suspended."

It meant there would be no reconnaissance of Pearl Harbor—

but little matter: Nimitz's ships were safely at their berths. And there they would stay, until the great attack smashed at Midway and brought them rushing out into Yamamoto's great trap.

AT PEARL it seemed strangely empty with the fleet gone, but there was still plenty of activity at CINCPAC. Coming to work that evening, Commander Layton brought along his helmet for the first time since December 7. From Rochefort's intercepts he knew this was the night for Operation K. French Frigate Shoals were under close watch, but if something went amiss there might be a lot of flak flying about. Nothing happened, of course, except that several of Layton's colleagues kidded him for bringing his helmet to work for no reason at all.

CHAPTER 3

Ready

Nobody told Admiral Nagumo that Operation K had failed. Radio silence seemed too important. So the First Carrier Striking Force plowed on toward Midway, the staff free from worry. They would get the word if "K" turned up anything useful . . . they heard no results, so there was nothing worth reporting.

Spirits were high on every ship. In the golden weather the first days out, the pilots practiced their bombing and torpedo runs, thrilling the men on deck. Watching them from the guard destroyer *Nowaki*, Commander Magotaro Koga couldn't imagine anyone beating them. "Our hearts burn with the conviction of sure victory," he scribbled that night in his diary.

Even the little things were turning out right. Through one of those happy accidents that can occur in any navy, three months of PX rations had been distributed at once—joyful bargaining filled the air. Only one man was having bad luck: first night out, Commander Mitsuo Fuchida, leader of the *Akagi*'s air group, came down with appendicitis. Now he wouldn't be able to lead the planes against Midway, duplicating his great feat at Pearl Harbor.

The weather turned sour on the afternoon of June 1— fortunately they had just finished refueling—and for the moment the flyers had little to do. Fighter pilot Raita Ogawa relaxed in the *Akagi's* wardroom while a scratchy gramophone ground out the popular song, *"Kirameku Seiza";* its lilting strains reminded them all of planes high in the sky. Torpedo pilot Takayoshi Morinaga lay in his bunk on the *Kaga* reading modern Japanese history. The *Hiryu's* assistant air officer, Toshio Hashimoto, could be found deep in a game of contract bridge. On the *Soryu* bomber pilot Juzo Mori amused himself playing a sort of bamboo flute called a *shaku-hachi.* Several others aboard liked doing this too, and they'd gather together in a corner of the flight deck, their plaintive music floating incongruously over the deck as the big carrier charged on.

Hundreds of miles to the southeast the Invasion Force lumbered along at a slower pace. On the bridge of the *Jintsu* Commander Toyama struggled to keep the 13 transports in some sort of order. The formation was quite simple—just two parallel columns of ships—but the convoy had been slapped together so quickly there wasn't time to learn the signals, and the transports had a way of straying. The troops couldn't have cared less. They practiced weapons handling and landing-craft procedures when they could, but there wasn't much room, and most of the time they were just jammed together, squatting on the open decks talking of girls and home.

Far to the rear—600 miles behind Nagumo—steamed Yamamoto's great Main Force of 34 ships. On the seven big battleships the men whiled away their free hours sunbathing, doing calisthenics and simply puzzling. The Japanese Navy always kept Tokyo time, wherever it was; now many of the new recruits, fresh off the farm, felt they were entering a strange part of the world indeed, where the sun rose at three o'clock in the morning.

On the *Yamato* Admiral Yamamoto moodily dabbed at a bowl of rice porridge. His huge appetite had finally caught up with him, and he now had a mild case of diarrhea. A more serious problem was the intelligence coming in. Starting May 29, his radio-traffic people had noted a heavy increase in U.S.

messages in the Hawaiian and Aleutian areas, much of it from aircraft and submarines. It suggested a U.S. task force might be at sea.

The disturbing signs multiplied. A U.S. submarine just ahead of the Transport Group was sending long coded messages to Pearl. Wake Island reported American patrol planes operating far out of Midway. A fresh radio traffic analysis showed 72 of 180 intercepts were "urgent"—a suspiciously high percentage. On the other hand, a new intelligence estimate from Tokyo on the 31st again placed U.S. carriers off the Solomons. It was all very baffling . . . enough to make a man wish that Operation K had worked out.

And now it appeared the submarine cordons were fouled up too. Three of the four subs assigned to the line west of Hawaii were involved in the "K" fiasco; they'd be late getting on station. Worse, all seven assigned to the cordon northwest of the Islands would also be late. They were the ones meant to take position across the Hawaii-Midway line on June 1, but fitting out took longer than planned, and now they wouldn't get there till June 3.

Should any of this information be relayed to Nagumo and the carriers? Admiral Yamamoto was inclined that way, but Captain Kuroshima was strongly opposed. As in the case of reporting on "K," he felt radio silence was too important. Besides, the *Akagi*'s own radio must be picking it all up anyhow. Nothing was done.

The question again arose a day or so later. Tokyo's radio intelligence now definitely suspected a U.S. carrier force somewhere off Midway. Once again Yamamoto was inclined to relay the word on to Nagumo; once again the "God of Operations" preached the gospel of radio silence; once again nothing was done.

Six hundred miles ahead, Nagumo's carriers steamed on. In the *Akagi*'s radio room, the operators bent low but heard nothing. The *Yamato* wasn't talking and Tokyo was too far away. With its small superstructure, the *Akagi* had a comparatively

weak wireless; it just couldn't catch those distant signals. And
now the weather was failing too. All day June 1 it grew
steadily worse—a fine rain mixed with heavy mist. The ships
plunged ahead, dim blurs in the gathering gloom.

T HE view was sharp and clear at Midway, as Commander Tanabe of the submarine *I-168* swung his periscope
toward the dazzling coral sands of the atoll. He had been
hanging around for three days now, making meticulous observations. These he carefully radioed to Tokyo, to be relayed
on to the advancing fleet.

There was much to report. Patrol boats came and went.
Some 90–100 planes landed in a day . . . including a number of
bombers. The PBYs took off at dawn, returned in the evening
—suggesting patrols at least 600 miles out. Several construction
cranes were at work: the garrison must be strengthening its
defenses.

Most of the time Tanabe stayed submerged two or three
miles offshore, his eyes glued to the periscope. Around him the
crew hopefully fingered the good luck charms that Ensign
Mochizuki had just given them all from Kameyama Shrine.
They hadn't been seen yet, but it was risky business poking
around this way; once they sneaked within 800 yards of the
beach.

At night the *I-168* surfaced and Tanabe continued his studies
with binoculars. Midway was under blackout; still it was possible to see a little. At one point he counted nine work lights
burning. Clearly something was up.

T HE past month had been a hectic one for the defenders
of Midway. They still had a long way to go, but at least they
could look with some satisfaction on what they had already
done.

Certainly it all began with Nimitz's visit. Until then the

base felt itself pretty well forgotten, except for an occasional shelling by some Japanese submarine. But that May 2 was a revelation. Nimitz was everywhere—and into everything. On Sand Island he rummaged through the underground command posts . . . he poked around the big seaplane hangar where the PBYs were serviced . . . he crawled into every gunpit of the Marines' 6th Defense Battalion. Then over to Eastern Island, twenty minutes across the lagoon. Here he examined the Marine airstrip and shook hands with all the pilots. When he finally flew off, the Marines conferred upon him their highest accolade: he was, they all agreed, a "God-damned gentleman."

About two weeks later equipment began pouring in. Commander Simard and Lieutenant Colonel Shannon had filed a list of their needs on May 7, but the first thing to come wasn't on any list at all. It was a pair of shoulder eagles for Simard—giving him a spot promotion to captain. At the same time Shannon was promoted to full colonel.

Both soon learned they'd be earning those eagles the hard way. About May 20 Admiral Nimitz's letter arrived, addressed to Simard and Shannon jointly, spelling out the Japanese plan. It was all there, every step, as far as Nimitz then knew it. Most sobering of all, he put the date at May 28—only one week away.

No one felt the pressure more than Shannon. Though under Simard, he was the Marine commander and directly responsible for Midway's defense. Next evening he called his key men together at the "Castle," an unpretentious house left over from Midway's civilian past. Here he told the group that the Japanese were coming, and outlined the steps to be taken to meet them. Adjutant W. P. Spencer then covered various matters in more detail, including instructions on what to do if taken prisoner.

At this point Marine Gunner Dorn E. Arnold, who had been in the Corps forever, closed his notebook. Shannon asked if he wasn't interested. Arnold replied that he didn't need this information since he didn't intend to be taken prisoner. He was damned if he'd end up "pulling some Japanese Pfc around in a rickshaw."

As finally outlined, Shannon's plans reflected his past. He was an old-time Marine, up from the ranks, of Belleau Wood vintage. Barbed wire, barrages, dugouts had all left an indelible impression, and sometimes it seemed he wanted to turn Midway into another Hindenburg Line. But he also had the hard-nosed tenacity that went with this kind of warfare, and that more than anything else was what Midway needed right now.

They had a good test of their spirits the very next morning. May 22 began calmly enough—Captain Simard was buried in work at his command post . . . the 81 mm. mortars were practicing on the south shore . . . Pharmacist's Mate Edwin Miller was swiping a snack from the hospital kitchen. Then suddenly it happened. A terrific explosion shook Sand Island; a cloud of dust and smoke billowed into the sky.

The Japs were here—everyone was sure of it. The men grabbed their helmets and raced for their battle stations. But it wasn't the Japs; it was far more discouraging. Some sailor, testing connections, had crossed the wrong wires and tripped a demolition charge under Midway's gasoline supply. Half the tanks, about 400,000 gallons, were gone. It damaged the distribution system too; from now on they'd have to fuel the planes by hand from 55-gallon drums.

It was enough to dishearten any one, but Captain Simard didn't panic. No heads rolled; no scapegoats; no angry recriminations. He calmly cabled the bad news to CINCPAC and asked for any help they could give. As for Colonel Shannon, airplanes were another world anyhow. "Wreck 'em on the beach," he growled, and it seemed more comforting than ever to have this tough old leatherneck as a rallying point.

They all caught his spirit. No one ever dug harder at the Marne than the 6th Defense Battalion did on Sand Island—building up emplacements, scooping out shelters, sandbagging new positions for the guns Nimitz promised. And on Eastern Island across the lagoon, the Marine airmen were digging too

—bunkers for the planes, holes to store bombs, fuses, gas and water, to say nothing of slit trenches for themselves. They were soon down to three or four hours' sleep a night.

All the while barbed wire was sprouting along the coral beaches. Major Robert Hommel strung so much his friends called him "Barbed Wire Bob." Yet there could never be enough for Colonel Shannon. It stopped the Boches; it would stop the Japs. "Barbed wire, barbed wire!" exploded a weary Marine. "Cripes, the Old Man thinks we can stop planes with barbed wire."

But they worked with little complaint, for Shannon's sheer guts had captured them all. Captain Robert McGlashan, his young operations officer, trudged 11 hours a day in the blinding sun, checking positions, checking communications, checking camouflage, checking fields of fire. Once he even took to a submarine to see how it all looked from a periscope.

Yet they still had so little, considering the size of the juggernaut hurtling toward them. They needed ingenuity too, and Captain McGlashan knew just where to turn. He went to Marine Gunner Arnold. These old-time gunners were legends in the Corps. They had been everywhere, could do anything. "Deacon" Arnold himself dated back to the Siberian expedition. Now McGlashan asked him to cook up some antiboat mines and booby traps. All it would take was an old-timer's knowledge of explosives. . . .

Actually Arnold knew almost nothing about explosives. But that didn't faze him—he once read a book on the subject. Recruiting a routine headquarters detail, he tackled the job with the kind of relish that could only come from someone not used to playing with dynamite.

He and his men located some blasting gelatin—brown stuff that looked and felt a little like dough. This they kneaded and rammed into lengths of sewer pipe. Sealing the ends with hot tar, they ended up with a sort of mammoth firecracker. Altogether they made 380 of them. These they strung together in bunches of six and planted offshore to discourage any land-

ing attempt. Electrically detonated, they made a highly satis-
factory explosion. More primitive was the impressive stockpile
of Molotov cocktails they gradually built up from Midway's
rather generous supply of empty whisky bottles.

And so the work went on, never stopping, for in a sense they
were already under siege. The guns were always manned—
meals served beside them—and the whole garrison now lived
underground. Both the Navy and Marine command posts were
dugouts near the center of Sand Island—Captain Simard giving orders by a white telephone that looked incongruously
fashionable; Colonel Shannon holding forth in a deep dugout
covered with beams and 12 feet of sand.

Every night both commanders met with their staffs to review
the day and plan for tomorrow. The Marine sessions, at least,
were often quite stormy, for the staff was perky and the
Colonel not easily moved from his favorite theories. At one
point he wanted a smoke screen, and it was quite a fracas
before McGlashan and Arnold convinced him it would draw
the Japs rather than hide the island. Another time he clashed
with Captain Simard over shifting some barbed wire long
enough to let the Navy fill a few sandbags. Touching that
barbed wire was really inviting trouble, and it finally took a
mild display of rank by the Captain before he got his sand.

In the end, of course, they always patched up their quarrels.
The staff would go off to their bunks . . . the Colonel would
gulp a last cup of coffee before turning in . . . and all would
be up again at 5:00 A.M., ready to take on another hard day.

May 25, they got some good news. First came Nimitz's
message, giving a new date for the attack. Now it would be
June 3–5—a whole extra week to prepare. Then the light
cruiser *St. Louis* tied up at Sand Island, bringing the first
reinforcements from Hawaii.

Captain Ronald K. Miller's fine battery of eight 37 mm. guns
was a welcome addition to the antiaircraft defense. Four
went to Eastern, and Miller planted the other four in the
woods on Sand Island. He was still at it when some trucks

roared up, throwing sand in all directions. A gang of men piled out, howling slogans and singing Chinese Communist songs.

Carlson's Raiders had arrived. This outfit—officially known as the 2nd Raider Battalion—was something of an experiment. Organized by Major Evans F. Carlson, its training reflected many ideas he had picked up during his days as a civilian observer with the Communist forces in North China. It had White House blessing, but its *gung-ho* philosophy smacked of indiscipline to many old Marines. To say the least, Carlson's Raiders were controversial.

But there was no doubt about their fighting qualities; and when Midway's hour came, Nimitz hurried out two companies. Arriving on the *St. Louis* along with Captain Miller's guns, "D" Company went off to Eastern; "C" joined Miller in the Sand Island woods. Both were a wild-looking lot. Bandoleers of cartridges hung from bronzed shoulders. Their pockets bulged with grenades. Their belts bristled with knives, which they flung at the trees with casual skill. Even the medics were armed—no stenciled red crosses for this bunch.

Still more help came on the 26th. That evening the big ex-railroad ferry *Kittyhawk* arrived with the guns, tanks and planes that formed Nimitz's biggest contribution. Midway could use these new 3-inchers and 20 mm. twin mounts borrowed from the 3rd Defense Battalion; it could use the five tanks too; but most welcome of all were the new planes—18 SBD dive bombers and 7 F4F fighters.

"New" was, of course, a relative term. Actually they were carrier castoffs. But they were infinitely better than the ancient relics already on hand. Until now Midway's "air force" had consisted of 16 antique Vindicator dive bombers and 21 equally antique Buffalo fighters. The Vindicators ("Wind Indicators," the Marines called them) had a tendency to ground-loop. When the pilots tried diving them earlier in the year, the wing fabric began peeling off—a hurry call went to the hospital for all available adhesive tape. The Buffalo fighters were just as inadequate. The new planes—whatever their credentials —were a vast improvement on these.

"New" in a different sense were the fliers who arrived too. Seventeen of the 21 pilots were just out of flight school. Some hadn't even had four hours' flight time since the end of their training. Nor did they know why they were here. Second Lieutenant Jack Cosley thought they were merely coming to an out-of-the-way island for further practice.

"You're just in time for the party!" called the old hands cheerfully as the newcomers unloaded their gear on Eastern Island. Second Lieutenant Allan Ringblom, one of the new dive bomber pilots, assumed this was the standard kidding he could expect from a buddy perhaps a few months ahead of him at flight school. At his first squadron briefing on May 28, he learned differently. . . .

The skipper, Major Lofton Henderson, pulled no punches. The Japs were not only coming; they were overdue. The new SBDs were assigned the experienced pilots; the Vindicators were given the green recruits. None of them had ever flown one before, and there was little time to practice. They ground-looped two the first day. The equipment was wretched too— no charts and only four plotting boards for a dozen flyable planes.

So most of the time they just waited—restless hours of cards, cribbage, and watching Midway's famous "gooney birds." A kind of large albatross, the gooneys were a graceful delight in the air, but a clumsy absurdity on the ground. They were utterly tame, fascinated all the fliers, and inadvertently caused the squadron's first casualty. In a whimsical moment Lieutenant Eke slipped one into Lieutenant Bear's bunk, and it indignantly nipped Bear's thumb getting out.

May 29 brought still more help—four Army B-26s rigged to carry torpedoes. Led by Captain James Collins, these were the first Army planes to arrive and caused quite a sensation. Everyone crowded around, but it turned out the pilots knew little more about their mission than the new Marines.

First Lieutenant James Muri had been at Hickam expecting to join the rest of his squadron in Australia. Suddenly all that was canceled and he was told to take a plane over to Pearl

Harbor instead. Three other B-26s joined his, and when they arrived there, they found a collection of Navy officers waiting for them with several very large torpedoes—the first Muri had ever seen in his life.

The torpedoes, they learned, would be slung on the planes, and the four crews briefly practiced take-offs and landings. They never tried any drops, and none of their compasses were corrected. When they started out a couple of days later, the four B-26s began by fanning out in four different directions. Fortunately a friendly patrol plane happened along and set them on the right course. No greener torpedo plane pilots ever flew a mission, but at least they got to Midway.

This same day 12 Navy PBYs also arrived—latest in a steady stream that had been building up since May 14. Like the others coming in, these men had little idea what was up, but they brought a skipper who knew a great deal indeed. Commander Logan Ramsey was one of the Navy's most colorful professionals. Physically a hulking, slow-moving man, mentally he was a genius. A great bridge player, he could do navigational problems while holding a hand of cards. He was completely unorthdox and often the despair of the Old Breed, but the patrol plane boss, Admiral Bellinger, thought the world of him and made him his chief of staff. With the Midway crisis coming to a head, Bellinger could think of no one he'd rather have out there than Logan Ramsey.

As is often the case with such men, Ramsey had a knack of attracting lively junior officers, and there was no lack of volunteers when he recruited a staff to help him. Ensign Edmond Jacoby had little idea why he was going, but with Ramsey it wouldn't be dull. As they boarded the PBY at Pearl Harbor, Admiral Bellinger came down to see them off. Knowing Jacoby wanted to be a pilot, the Admiral called out, "If you get back, I'll see you get to flight school."

"*If* I get back," thought Jacoby. "What could he mean by that?"

He found out that night almost as soon as they landed at

Midway. Captain Simard called a meeting at the BOQ, explained briefly why they were there. Then Logan Ramsey took over, filling them in on the latest intelligence: the blow at the Aleutians on the 3rd . . . the transports coming in from the southwest . . . the carriers striking from the northwest, probably on the 4th. And he told them their job. No more one-day patrolling, then two days off. Starting tomorrow, they would go out every day, 700 miles. This was the moment all their training had been leading to.

Next morning, the 30th, as the first pink trace of dawn streaked the eastern sky, 22 PBYs lumbered into the air. Some were seaplanes, some the new amphibious kind, but all looked ungainly and slow. Briefly they circled the base as they got their bearings, then headed out on the spokes of a massive arc, running from just west of south to just east of north. Midway's great search for the enemy had begun.

It was shortly after chow that noon when one of the PBYs limped back to Eastern Island, one engine out, and made an emergency landing. Then another cripple fluttered in. It seemed the Japs were also on patrol. They were down toward the southwest, flying out of Wake, snarling and spoiling for a fight. Both PBYs were riddled with bullets; from the first to land, the Marines gently lifted a gunner shot through the back.

Eight more Army planes arrived that same afternoon from Hawaii, and then another nine on May 31—all B-17 long-range bombers. There was some shuttling back and forth, but from now on about 15 were generally on hand. Led by Lieutenant Colonel Walter C. Sweeney, who invariably flew in his stocking feet, they gave a powerful boost to Midway's striking power.

As with the B-26s, the big bombers were pulled into bunkers and the crews roughed it beside them in tents . . . but that didn't stop First Lieutenant Everett Wessman from sleeping in his usual silk pajamas. The Air Force always had a flair about it.

Another welcome arrival on the 31st was the freighter *Nira Luckenbach* with some last-minute equipment and 3,000 drums of high-test gas to help replace the fuel lost when Midway's tanks blew up. It was Sunday, but nobody thought about that until a dispute erupted over extra pay for the ship's merchant crew. Word spread that she couldn't unload until Monday. Summoned to the scene, Captain Simard explained that the Japs were on the way, that the ship couldn't leave until she was unloaded, and that there'd be quite an explosion with all that gas aboard. The crew bent to it, and the *Nira Luckenbach* was gone by 7:40 next morning.

There was little more Nimitz could do; it was now up to Midway to use what it had. What steps would be most effective? In the underground Navy command post on Sand Island, Captain Simard probed for new answers every night with his staff. At some point Brigadier General Willis Hale of the B-17s would come in. He'd bring over a bottle of Old Crow bourbon; they'd set it out on the table, and the work would go on. Should the B-17s be held back as a long-range striking force, or should they be used more right now to beef up the search? How to get everything off the ground fast, when the Japs finally did attack?

Far into the night they talked and planned, while the junior officers went about their regular duties—making search assignments for the morning, writing up reports, handling communications with CINCPAC over the cable. To a communications officer this direct cable link with Pearl was a thing of beauty and a priceless asset. It meant that Midway could be in safe, instant contact with Nimitz without using radio. No risk of intercepts, no codes to break, no heavy flow of messages to start some eavesdropper thinking. To the radio-traffic analyst in Tokyo, nothing was happening on Midway at all.

It was part of the old transpacific cable system, and was what gave Midway its chief importance before the war. Now all that was gone, although oddly enough the next link westward to Japanese-held Guam was still intact. Occasionally someone in the dugout would wander over to the key and bat out an obscenity in that direction. Usually there'd be a pause, then some angry-sounding gibberish would come snapping back.

June 1, and Ensign George Fraser, the versatile young communications officer under Logan Ramsey, got a new kind of problem. Word came that a wonderful Navy torpedo plane was being added to Midway's defenses—the TBF. Six of them would be flying in that day, and since nobody would expect a plane that looked like these, he was to alert the antiaircraft batteries not to shoot them down.

"What's a TBF?" was the first question he got. There were no silhouettes, no recognition books, no trained observers. The best Fraser could do was take his cue from the familiar F4F fighter. The new plane looked, he explained, "like a pregnant F4F." The word was passed, and when the six TBFs duly appeared, not a finger touched a trigger.

It was just as well, for these men had come a long way to be in this show. They belonged to the *Hornet's* Torpedo Squadron 8, and had been in Norfolk breaking in these new planes for the carrier. They were still at it May 8, when they got orders to come to Pearl. There were 19 planes in the detachment altogether, and led by Torpedo 8's executive officer, they flew to the West Coast, then were ferried to Hawaii. They arrived on May 29—just a day too late to join the *Hornet.*

Next, a call came for volunteers to fly six of the planes to Midway. No problem here, although the men had no idea why they were going. They just set out on the 1st, happy to be led by Lieutenant Langdon K. Fieberling—a stylish, handsome, prematurely gray pilot, who was the idol of all the young fliers. None had been in combat; Ensign A. K. Earnest had never even flown out of sight of land before.

On arrival Fieberling reported to Lt. Colonel Ira E. Kimes, commanding the Marine air group. Then back to his unit with all the grim facts, plus an extra touch: don't expect any help from the U.S. carriers; they were off trying to save Hawaii.

But nothing could cool the ardor of these young men. They whiled away the time making imaginary wing guns for their TBFs. Noting that the planes with real wing guns usually had masking tape over the holes to keep the dust out, they put tape on their wings too. Then they inked "holes" in the tape where the "guns" had fired through.

Some 560 miles to the southwest, there was again some real shooting. At 9:40 A.M. a big patrol bomber out of Wake pounced on Ensign J. J. Lyons's PBY, and fifty minutes later the same Jap riddled Ensign R. V. Umphrey's plane in the next sector. Both Americans scrambled to safety—by now everyone knew the PBY was no match for any Japanese plane whatsoever.

They talked it over in the staff meeting that night at the Navy command post. But the enemy that bothered them most at the moment was not the Japanese, it was the weather. A low front was closing in to the northwest, hiding the ocean below. Under that blanket of gray almost anything could be lurking. . . .

On the bridge of the *Akagi*, Admiral Nagumo stood with his staff, silently staring into the mist. It was getting worse—changing to heavy fog—and by daybreak June 2 visibility was practically zero. Fine protection from enemy patrol planes, but hell on navigation.

Off to the left of the Admiral, Captain Taijiro Aoki conferred with Commander Gishiro Miura, his navigating officer. Miura, as always, was wearing his carpet slippers. From time to time they leaned through the bridge windows, as though the extra six inches just might help a little.

They were all concerned, for this was the day they had to turn southeast for the final dash on Midway. At the moment they were steaming in single column, able to keep in formation only because each ship trailed a marker buoy for the

next in line to follow. But this was too risky when making
a major change in course—too easy to lose some ships altogether.

They faced a difficult choice. They could slow down, hoping
for better weather before signaling the change, or they could
break radio silence and do it that way. If they slowed down,
they would upset the whole invasion timetable. If they broke
radio silence, they might give away their position and spoil
the great ambush planned for the U.S. fleet. In the end
Captain Oishi, Nagumo's senior staff officer, urged they use
low-power radio and hope for the best. They just couldn't
afford to alter the schedule—too many other units depended
on that—but the ambush was a more flexible matter. The
U.S. fleet was probably still in Pearl Harbor—anyhow it
was many days away—so a brief radio signal, even if picked
up, wouldn't do much harm.

Nagumo agreed, and at 1:30 p.m. the shortest of all possible
radio signals went out: "Course 125." On 26 ships the helms
swung over, the engines paused briefly, then picked up again,
as the First Carrier Striking Force turned southeast, now
heading straight as a javelin for Midway.

Down below there was hardly an interruption. In the *Hiryu's*
No. 1 boiler room the firemen made the adjustments chalked
on a slate in the glass-enclosed control booth. The plane
crews on the *Soryu* continued playing "Hanafuda" at 100
points a cigarette. On the *Kaga* Commander Takahisa Amagai
ran through a blackboard session on antiaircraft defense. In
the wardroom of the *Akagi* someone wound the gramophone,
and the scratchy needle once again ground out the soaring
strains of *"Kirameku Seiza."*

THE favorites were Glenn Miller, Tommy Dorsey and
Mary Martin's "My Heart Belongs to Daddy," as the U.S.
carrier *Enterprise* steamed northeast of Midway this same
2nd of June. Task Force 16 had been at sea six days now,
and life off duty was, on the surface at least, fairly routine:

all the usual phonograph records, cribbage games, bull sessions and occasional pranks. On the *Hornet* Chaplain Eddie Harp playfully swiped a much-prized case of grapefruit from Dr. Sam Osterloh; on the *New Orleans* Seaman A. M. Bagley resumed his hobby of beating Seaman F. Z. Muzejka at rummy.

On duty, the pattern seemed pretty normal too. The *Enterprise* "Plan of the Day" mechanically ticked off the chores for the 2nd: 0315 (ship's time), call the Air Department . . . 0325, early breakfast . . . 0350, flight quarters . . . 0500, launch first patrols . . . and so on, through a steady sequence of patrols out and in, watches on and off, until finally that inevitable salute to a dying day, "2049, blow tubes."

It was all very normal—yet not normal at all, for beneath the surface routine Task Force 16 seethed with a tumbling variety of emotions. "Lord! This *is* the real thing," Lieutenant Burdick Brittin breathlessly noted in his diary when the destroyer *Aylwin*'s sealed orders were opened May 29. And on the 30th his mind overflowed with awesome thoughts:

We have history in the palm of our hands during the next week or so. If we are able to keep our presence unknown to the enemy and surprise them with a vicious attack on their carriers, the U.S. Navy should once more be supreme in the Pacific. But if the Japs see us first and attack us with their overwhelming number of planes, knock us out of the picture, and then walk in to take Midway, Pearl will be almost neutralized and in dire danger—I can say no more—there is too much tension within me—the fate of our nation is in our hands.

To Brittin even the men on the tankers seemed to sense that destiny rode with these ships. They all refueled on the 31st, and as the tankers slipped astern and out of the picture, their men lined the rails, showing thumbs up for Task Force 16.

There were other emotions too as the force plowed on. For some of the pilots there was that hollow, empty feeling as they thought of absolute radio silence and all that it meant —even if an engine conked out on patrol, they could no longer ask the ship for help. Others felt a strange tingle that harked back to college and the days of the big game. On the *Enterprise* dive bomber pilot Bill Roberts was normally scared before battle—but not this time. It was too exciting: the feeling of being in on the secret, of setting a trap, of watching and waiting. Others were just plain mad. Captain Marc Mitscher had a way of getting the *Hornet*'s men "up," and this time he pulled all the stops—"They are even bringing the guns they captured from us at Wake."

For Lieutenant Richard H. Best, commanding the *Enterprise*'s Bombing Squadron 6, there was a personal worry all his own. He had a wife and child in Honolulu, and he thought of them more than once as he sat in Admiral Spruance's cabin, listening to a special briefing on the Japanese plan. The Navy, he felt, was certainly banking a lot on all this neat, precise information—what if it was wrong? He finally asked Spruance what would happen if the Japanese by-passed Midway and came straight for Hawaii.

The Admiral looked at him for a full half-minute in silence, then finally said, "We just hope that they will not."

Best said nothing more—admirals were close to God in those days—but privately he felt this was a pious hope and a rather poor basis for committing all the available strength of the United States Navy.

Actually, of course, Spruance had very good reasons for the move he was making—he just didn't care to tell them. Far from banking on "pious hopes," he was a man with a passion for facts, who insisted on every scrap of evidence before making a decision. And far from failing to think things through, he never moved without weighing every possible consequence.

Nor did his long silence before answering Best mean uncertainty; he was just considering all the factors before speaking—another Spruance characteristic. On the one hand, here was a young officer who had asked a legitimate question; on the other, he was a pilot who might fall into enemy hands. It was clear which way the scales finally went.

Dick Best wasn't the only one who had trouble grasping

this new Admiral. The whole staff found it hard to adjust. Halsey had been so outgoing; Spruance was so self-contained. Halsey was so accessible; Spruance preferred channels. Halsey paid little attention to detail; Spruance spent hours poring over charts and plotting the course. Halsey left so much to their discretion; Spruance left so little. Halsey was so free-wheeling; Spruance so precise and methodical.

Morning coffee somehow symbolized the change. In the old days everyone just slopped it down together. But Spruance —a genuine connoisseur—brought his own green coffee beans aboard. Every morning he carefully ground it himself, made precisely two cups, and then courteously asked if some member of the staff cared to join him. In the end they drew lots, with the loser getting the honor, not because they disliked Spruance but because they couldn't stand his coffee.

Yet there was much more method to this little ritual than appeared on the surface. Spruance was trying to educate himself. A man with no carrier experience, he had only a week to learn the trade before facing the greatest master of them all, Isoroku Yamamoto. In his quest for knowledge he picked the brains of his staff at coffee or anyplace else.

A great walker, he also collared them one by one and paced the flight deck with them. Searching questions probed what they did, how they did it, how each job fitted into the whole. He walked their legs off, but with his great ability to absorb detail, he was learning all the time.

The walks went on, fair weather or foul . . . as the staff soon discovered. June 1 was a wretched day, damp and foggy. Flying was out, gunnery practice called off; just the wiry Admiral and his latest victim tirelessly trudging the wet, empty flight deck. Task Force 16 was now 345 miles NNE of Midway—marking time, waiting for Admiral Fletcher and the *Yorktown*.

June 2 was another dreary day; more clouds and rain. But late in the morning two *Yorktown* planes suddenly appeared from the south. Swooping low over the *Enterprise*, they dropped a message. It was from Fletcher: rendezvous time would be 3:30 P.M. At 12:08 searchlights blinked, Task Force 16 swung around and slowly began doubling back east. Then shortly before 4:00, at exactly Latitude 32° 04′ N, Longitude 172° 45′ W, masts were sighted ahead on the horizon. The moment had come—Spruance and Fletcher were joined at Point Luck.

Task Force 17's trip out had been a smooth one—except for a single harrowing moment. As the *Yorktown* was taking on her planes from Hawaii the first afternoon out, an F4F jumped the landing barrier and plowed into the next plane ahead, killing Fighting 3's executive officer, Lieutenant Donald Lovelace.

It was a shaken group of fighter pilots who assembled in the ready room shortly afterward. They were a pickup squadron; they had never worked together; some of them had never operated from a carrier. Lovelace, an old hand, was expected to do so much to pull them together. Now, in an instant, he was gone. It was a savage blow, and none felt it worse than the squadron leader, Commander Thach. He was not only depending on Lovelace; they were also close friends and contemporaries at Annapolis.

This was no time for emotion, Thach quietly told his men, they had to do a job. Then he turned quickly to the battle coming up, and what he expected of them. If it was a matter of saving the ship, he stressed, he expected them even to ram an enemy plane. There were no histrionics—he was utterly calm. But his strength gave them strength, and they felt a new sense of being welded together. By the time he was finished, one of them later recalled, there wasn't a pilot in the room who wouldn't do anything "Jimmy" Thach asked.

Meanwhile, each of the other squadrons was also briefed, and Captain Buckmaster spoke to the whole crew over the loudspeaker. He explained he knew three days at Pearl weren't enough to complete repairs, but the Japanese were coming to Midway and the *Yorktown* was going to be there to surprise them. True to Nimitz's instructions, he then promised they'd all go to the West Coast after this "little scrap."

Cheers rocked the ship, although at least two men weren't that easily convinced. Seamen John Herchey and Bill Norton noticed there was a Royal Navy officer aboard as an observer. Superstitious in the grand manner of all true sailors, they decided that boded no good. "We will have to swim if we want to get back from this one," they told their friend Seaman Louis Rulli.

Chasing north after Task Force 16, the *Yorktown* and her escorts moved into the same dirty weather on the 31st, refueled from the same tankers all through the 1st, and now at last were ready for the same great gamble—all linked together at Point Luck.

As senior officer, Admiral Fletcher took command of both forces, and they began their quiet wait—usually closing Midway during the night, then heading off during the day. They steamed separately but within sight of each other, about ten miles apart.

As fleets go, they weren't very much, but they were nearly everything the United States had left in the Pacific—3 carriers, 8 cruisers, 14 destroyers . . . 25 fighting ships altogether. Yet a fleet at sea, even a rather modest one, is much more than ships and guns. Here it was Captain Buckmaster of the *Yorktown*, never allowing a light in his cabin after dark, so he could see at his best if called unexpectedly to the bridge. It was Lieutenant (j.g.) Bill Roberts on the *Enterprise*, trying to wade through Freud, his mind not too much on the text. It was Seaman Stan Kurka on the *Hornet*, trying to do his work in a shirt three times too big for him. It was Marine Captain Malcolm Donohoo on the cruiser *Portland*, down at this moment (of all times) with the mumps. It was Lieutenant Brittin of the *Aylwin* scribbling in his diary, "Waiting, just waiting."

Five hundred miles behind them, toward waters Fletcher had just crossed yesterday, Lieutenant Commander Tamori Yoshimatsu skillfully maneuvered the Japanese submarine

I-166. He was late—they all were late—but it should not matter. By tomorrow, the 3rd, the seven I-boats of Squadron 5 would all be on station, directly across the line from Hawaii to Midway. That should be time enough to see and report the U.S. fleet as it sped from Pearl Harbor toward its destruction.

"It is not believed that the enemy has any powerful unit, with carriers as its nucleus, in the vicinity," ran paragraph (e) of Admiral Nagumo's intelligence estimate, as the First Carrier Striking Force drove on toward Midway. The Admiral was confident, and he felt with good reason. There was no word from the sub cordon, no word from Operation K, no word from anybody—it could only mean that everything was still going smoothly.

On the bridge of the *Akagi* Admiral Kusaka studied his chief with satisfaction. It was so much better than that Pearl Harbor trip. Then Nagumo had been nervous and gloomy. Now he was his old self again—fierce, tough, the very embodiment of the *samurai* spirit.

The darkened ships rushed on, and even the weather was now breaking right. Late on the night of the 2nd the fog began to lift, and through the broken clouds an occasional star was shining.

"Is THERE *anything* we haven't done?" Colonel Shannon asked his staff as they relaxed for a moment under the stars this same June night on Midway.

There were no suggestions. By now the defenders had done everything they could imagine to beat off a Japanese landing. And if—as many of them secretly believed—the enemy finally came anyhow, they were also ready for that. Their five tanks were hidden in the Sand Island woods to make it a hot reception. Most of their codes were shipped back to Pearl Harbor; other files were burned. Sledge hammers were stored around the base to smash essential machinery. Drivers were coached to wreck their trucks, leaping out just before impact. Caches of food were buried here and there for last-ditch pockets of resistance.

They were prepared for the very end too. Taking all the left-over steel scrap, Captain McGlashan strung it along the high ground on the north side of Sand Island. When all else was gone, here the defenders would rally for Midway's last stand. It was promptly dubbed "The McGlashan Line."

On the "heights" in the center of this ridge (perhaps 30 feet, but on Midway that was a mountain) even the Navy cooks and typists would dig in. Specifically they were assigned the northeast flank, where there seemed less danger of their shooting the Marines by mistake. Of course, a landing on the north shore might still push the Marines that way, and to strengthen the leathernecks' resolve, they were warned of armed sailors lying behind them.

This last precaution was almost certainly needless. No group ever looked more ready for a fight than Carlson's Raiders did now. To the rest of the defenders they were rarely visible—just a pack of men glimpsed now and then in the woods. The naval reservists regarded them with cautious awe. They knew that it was worth a man's life to go near there after dark without knowing the password.

The Raiders were tough, and better still they worked hard. At first they had indicated that unloading ships was somewhat beneath them, but a blast from Colonel Shannon cured that. Soon they set records. More to their personal tastes, they also turned to manufacturing antitank mines. With advice from several who had been involved in the Spanish Civil War, their demolitions officer Lieutenant Harold Throneson devised a beauty—all it needed was a little dynamite, a flashlight battery and 40 pounds of pressure. Company "C" tore into the job of mass-producing them—1,500 altogether.

One of Throneson's group offered his services to a kindred soul—Marine Gunner "Deacon" Arnold, still engaged in making his own booby traps. Arnold happily added the Raider to his team, and the boy responded by devising a new antipersonnel mine. This was a sort of cigar box loaded with nails, spikes, glass and rocks with a small charge of TNT. Scattered by the dozen along the beaches, they could be exploded either electrically or by firing a rifle at a bull's-eye neatly painted on the side of the box.

Yet Midway's best hope still lay in catching the Japanese first. "Hit before we are hit," the CINCPAC planners advised, and so the 22 PBYs continued their daily runs. They were flying 15° pie-shaped sectors now—700 miles out, 700 miles back, 15 hours in the air altogether. Then a quick bite, a squadron briefing, a few hours in the sack, and the whole business all over again.

Lieutenant Commander Bob Brixner's Patrol Squadron 44 was putting in an 80-hour week; Commander Massie Hughes's Squadron 23 was matching him. Lieutenant Colonel Sweeney's B17s flew 30 hours in two days, looking for signs of that enemy rendezvous CINCPAC seemed to smell. And when the day's flying was done, they had to help service their own planes too—refueling them by hand from 55-gallon drums. They were all tired—dead tired—but somehow they carried on.

This June 2 seemed especially frustrating. If the intelligence was sound, the Japanese should be coming into range, yet there was no sign of them at all. To the northwest a curtain of fog still hid the ocean—no chance of finding anything beyond 400 miles. To the west it was clear, but despite CINCPAC's tip about the rendezvous, there was absolutely nothing to see. A specially equipped B-17 went out 800 miles; still not a ship in sight.

Wednesday, June 3, began as usual for the PBY crews— as, in fact, it did for all of Midway's fliers. Reveille at 3:00 A.M. . . . a swallow of toast and coffee that didn't go down so well . . . then to the planes by jeep and truck in the damp predawn darkness. By 3:50 motors were roaring, exhausts flaring blue, in the first pale light of another new day. At 4:15 the PBYs took off, fanning out on their assigned patrols. Fifteen minutes later the B-17s followed, not as part of the search, but just to get clear—no one wanted them caught on the ground in case of a surprise raid at dawn.

The rest of Midway's planes just waited—motors idling, pilots and gunners standing by—until they got the daily all-clear. Only when the PBYs had searched 400 miles out and still found nothing did Midway seem safe till another dawn.

This morning, as usual, there was nothing 400 miles out. But at 470 miles Lieutenant (j.g.) J. P. O. Lyle, searching to the southwest, spotted two small gray patrol boats steaming toward Midway. He investigated and got a burst of anti-aircraft fire for his pains. At 9:04 A.M. he flashed the first report of contact with enemy ships.

Farther to the west, Ensign Jack Reid piloted another PBY across an empty ocean. He had started earlier than the rest, was now 700 miles from Midway, nearing the end of his outward leg. So far, nothing worth reporting. With the PBY on automatic pilot, Reid again studied the sea with his binoculars. Still nothing—occasional cloud puffs and a light haze hung over the Pacific, but not enough to bother him. It was shortly before 9:25 A.M., and Ensign Reid was a man with no problems at all.

Suddenly he looked, then looked again. Thirty miles dead ahead he could make out dark objects along the horizon. Ships, lots of them, all heading toward him. Handing the glasses to his co-pilot Ensign Hardeman, he calmly asked, "Do you see what I see?"

Hardeman took one look: "You are damned right I do."

COMMANDER Yasumi Toyama looked up from his charts on the bridge of the light cruiser *Jintsu*. For once all the transports were keeping in column, but the destroyer on the port side forward was raising a fuss. She hoisted a signal, then fired a smoke shell. Toyama rushed out on the bridge wing, and there was no need to ask what had happened. Everyone was looking and pointing. There, low and well out of range on the port horizon, hovered a PBY.

CHAPTER 4

"Many Planes Heading Midway"

IT MUST have seemed like the whole Japanese Navy. After all those grim briefings—all those days of suspense—it was understandable that the 27 ships of the Transport Group now looked even more formidable than they were. At 9:25 Ensign Reid flashed a two-word contact report: "Main Body."

"Amplify," Midway flashed back, and for the next two hours Reid played a desperate game of hide-and-seek, darting in and out of cloud puffs, sending additional scraps whenever he could. At 9:27 he radioed, "Bearing 262°, distance 700" . . . 10:40, he noted "six large ships in column" . . . 11:00, he made out "eleven ships, course 090, speed 19." That seemed to do the job; base radio now told him to come on home.

On Midway Colonel Sweeney could hardly wait to get going with his B-17s. Captain Simard was just as anxious, but first there were some things to clear up. Where were the Japanese carriers? Nimitz's orders were, above all, to go for those carriers. None had been reported so far; the intelligence said they wouldn't come till tomorrow, and then from the northwest. Should they hold back the B-17s until they definitely appeared? That would be playing it safe.

On the other hand, Reid described this as the "Main Body."

That might well mean carriers there too. If there was any chance at all, Midway shouldn't wait. "Hit before we are hit" remained the paramount rule.

But even if the B-17s went out, where should they go? Contact reports were now coming from three different PBYs, pinpointing four different sightings to the southwest. They were all just fragments; it wasn't easy to count ships when they were shooting at you. Was Reid's contact really the big one? It was worth waiting a little while to see.

Reid's report at 11:00 A.M. settled the matter. Now it was clear he had at least 11 ships—a much bigger concentration than anyone else reported. Moreover, most of the other ships were converging that way, probably planning to link up. There was still no report of carriers, but even if there weren't any, Sweeney could go out, get back and be ready again by the time they were promised tomorrow.

At 12:30 he was on his way. One after another, nine olive-drab B-17s thundered down the Eastern Island runway and into the blue Pacific sky. With Colonel Sweeney leading in the *Knucklehead*, they roared west in loose formation. They carried only half a "pay load"—four 600-pound bombs apiece —for the range was so great they needed bomb-bay gas tanks if they were going to make the round trip.

Six hundred miles was a long way to go to drop less than 11 tons of bombs on a squirming target, but this was the first attack these young men had made. For all of them it was a new and tremendously exciting experience. Sweeney himself had been to West Point—his father was a retired major general—but the men around him were typical of the adaptable amateurs America somehow finds to fight its wars. His co-pilot Everett Wessman was a truck driver; his navigator Bill Adams a lumber salesman.

Three and a half hours went by. Then, 570 miles out and just where the Navy said to look, Sweeney made out a score of white streaks slashing the blue of the sea: the wakes of the Japanese ships. Another pilot, Lieutenant Edward Steedman, counted 26 of them, which was very good counting indeed. Contact time was exactly 4:23 P.M.

At this point Sweeney veered off, circling around the ships so as to attack from out of the afternoon sun. The white streaks stayed steady and straight; apparently no one down there yet suspected. Now the B-17s were behind the Japanese, forming into three flights of three at 8,000, 10,000 and 12,000 feet. Turning into his bomb run, Sweeney picked up his microphone and called to the planes in his own flight, "I'll go in at 8,000 feet—you follow me."

Lieutenant Wessman shuddered. He could only hope the Japanese weren't tuned in. Or if they were listening, that they wouldn't believe any foe could be so innocent of war as to broadcast his intentions in the clear.

O N THE bridge of the *Jintsu* Commander Toyama casually studied the sky with binoculars. The Japanese ships didn't have radar, and a good man's eyes remained the best defense against a surprise bombing. An attack seemed likely, too, right after the PBY spotted them, but that was seven hours ago, and nothing had happened yet. Now everything was routine again as the Transport Group continued toward Midway, plodding along in two straight columns.

Suddenly Toyama's glasses picked up nine planes flying toward them "in stately fashion." There was only time to yank the alarm before the bombs began falling. Lieutenant Yunoki gunnery officer on one of the destroyers, didn't have that much time. His first inkling was a pattern of bombs crashing down near the ship. The *Argentina Maru* was a little more alert. The alarm sounded; the bridge cranked her up to 20 knots; and at 4:38 she opened fire—one minute before a rack of bombs exploded 200 yards astern. The convoy wriggled and squirmed, smoke pouring out of the stacks and guns. Antiaircraft fire speckled the sky, but before the defense really got going the attack was already over. Still flying "in stately fashion," the nine B-17s disappeared into the northeast haze.

The Transport Group took stock. No hits, except some splinters from a near-miss on one of the freighters. With the buoyancy a fighting man always feels when he has just pulled through an engagement, the executive officer of the *Argentina Maru* dashed off his combat report, noting that all hands were in "exceptionally high spirits."

T<small>HE</small> ex-salesmen and truck drivers flying the B-17s were in high spirits too. To a man trained in banking at the University of Illinois, like Captain Paul Payne of the bomber *Yankee Doodle*, a transport at 10,000 feet could look like almost anything—he marked his target down as "hit and burning."

Taking the largest ship in the world for comparison, Lieutenant Robert Andrews said he bombed a transport of the "*Normandie* class." Captain Clemence Tokarz thought he got a battleship or a heavy cruiser. Looking back when they were 30 miles off and homeward bound, Colonel Sweeney was sure he saw two ships burning: "They were both out of column, appeared motionless and were issuing huge clouds of dark smoke which mushroomed above them."

In contrast the trip back seemed more hair-raising than bombing the Japanese. Night soon fell, and nobody was used to flying formation in the dark. There were several near-misses. It was hard, too, for an Army pilot to find a dot like Midway in the middle of the Pacific Ocean. At 7:30 Eastern Island turned on its runway lights, but for an anxious hour there was no sign of anyone. Finally, the base heard the welcome drone of distant motors, but it was 9:45 before the last planes groped their way home—Captain Willard Woodbury felt he didn't have enough gas left "to fill a cigarette lighter."

Even as they were landing, another strike was on its way out, aiming at the same Japanese force. It was the culmination of an amazing enterprise that began over 12 hours earlier at Pearl Harbor.

It must have been about three o'clock that morning when Ensign Allan Rothenburg, a young PBY skipper, was suddenly shaken awake as he lay in his bed at the Ford Island BOQ. "Get up; you're going to Midway."

"Midway to what?" was Rothenburg's sleepy reaction. His patrols in Squadron 51 never carried him in that direction, and at first he didn't even click on the name. But he pulled on his clothes, went to the field, and in the first light of dawn found his amphibian was one of four warming up. The other three were from Squadron 24, but the PBY men all knew each other, and as they briefly compared notes, it turned out none of them knew why they were going.

They took off around 7:00, landing at the Eastern Island airstrip nine long hours later. By ordinary standards this was a day's work—time for a hot meal, a good bed and maybe a stretch of routine patrols starting tomorrow. As the flight's leader, Lieutenant (j.g.) Charles Hibberd, nudged his PBY into its revetment, the crew were surprised, then, to find an enlisted man waiting for them on a tractor with a torpedo mounted on the trailer behind. It was even more astonishing when he said the torpedo was for them—that the other three PBYs would be equipped too, that all four planes were a "striking force" to go out after the Japanese fleet.

Hibberd's navigator, Ensign James Boyden, couldn't take it seriously. The PBY amphibian was a wonderful patrol plane, but it only cruised 100 miles an hour, maneuvered with stately dignity, and offered as big and inviting a target as a Pennsylvania Dutch barn. Surely no one could dream of sending it on an attack mission. Shrugging the thought off, Boyden headed for the mess hall to get a snack.

The place was crowded with other crews in flight gear—Army, Navy, Marine. The atmosphere was hushed, serious, almost gloomy. More of the new PBY men turned up, and they soon pieced together a sobering picture: a big Jap force to the southwest . . . the B-17s out bombing them now . . . the enemy sweeping toward Midway. All refreshments were on the house, creating a sort of "last supper" feeling.

A messenger came, summoning the new arrivals to the command post. They crowded into Colonel Kimes's dimly lit dugout—Lieutenant Hibberd, Al Rothenburg, the other pilots and navigators. Logan Ramsey took over the briefing. He explained they were selected to launch a night torpedo attack, and although it had never been done before, "we have to throw everything we have at them."

He went on to say it would be on a volunteer basis. If they didn't think they could do it, they wouldn't be required to go. He waited, studying their faces.

Not a word was said. Ensign Gaylord Propst grimly stared at the floor. Lieutenant (j.g.) Douglas Davis was mute, more from shock than from any burning desire to charge out on a suicide mission. Ensign Boyden silently stared back at Ramsey, trying to read the Commander's thoughts. All too clearly Ramsey's face betrayed how little he expected ever to see them again, how much he hated doing what he had to do.

The briefing continued: target, course, speed, position, technical procedures on signals and communications. Yes, it was the "Main Body"—they should look for a carrier. The attack would be led by Lieutenant W. L. Richards, the tall, redheaded executive officer of Patrol Squadron 44, already based on Midway. Outside, mechanics buckled the torpedoes onto the PBYs—one under each plane's starboard wing.

At 9:30 they took off, Richards leading the way in Charlie Hibberd's plane. It was not a graceful departure. The PBYs —laboring under the unbalanced load—struggled painfully into the air. Rothenburg, delayed by trouble with his ladder, was late getting off and tagged along after the rest.

Turning southwest, they headed into a beautiful moonlit night, flying in loose formation at 3,000 feet. On Lieutenant Davis's plane coffee was brewed and served. Taking a sip, Davis pondered his chances of coming through this night alive—and became slightly nauseated.

The hours droned by. The planes flew on, now through scattered clouds that made it difficult to follow Richards—the others had only his exhausts and a small white light on his fuselage to guide them. Rothenburg, still trailing far in the rear, lost the rest completely. Then Propst too drifted off. But just after that, at 1:20 A.M., Richards's radarman picked up some targets about seven miles away. At the controls, Charlie Hibberd calmly said he had already spotted them.

Directly ahead, bathed in the moonlight, two columns of darkened ships were steaming toward them. A ring of destroyers guarded both columns, but there was no sign that they suspected danger. Disdaining evasive moves of any kind, they held to a course that would ultimately take them straight to Midway.

Richards had Hibberd circle once to alert the others, then let down to a point off the port beam of the northern column. Now the enemy ships were silhouetted perfectly—black beads in the silvery moon path. Looking for the "carrier," he picked out a long, low ship toward the rear of the column. Charlie Hibberd began his final run-in.

The job was all his. He had to fly the plane and manipulate the torpedo director at the same time. The rest crouched at their posts, peering through the windows and blisters at the sea rushing past them. Now they were only 200 . . . 150 . . . 100 feet from the water. Still no sign that the Japanese suspected anything, but this run-in was taking forever.

"Drop that damn thing and let's get the hell out of here!" someone finally yelled. But Hibberd wasn't ready yet. At 1,000 yards he knew this wasn't a carrier after all—it looked like some sort of merchant ship—but they hadn't come this far for nothing. On they roared, now only 50 feet off the sea. At 800 yards Hibberd finally released the torpedo, rammed the controls forward, and the PBY heaved up and over the target as a few scattered shots blazed out. Looking back, the man at the waist hatch saw a muffled explosion followed by a second and clearer flash. It looked like a hit, and they were home free.

Lieutenant Davis was close behind. But he didn't like his position, turned away, circled and came on again. Starting his second approach, he too flew straight up the moon path toward a ship in the rear of the north column. He too faced no return fire as he raced in, now at 50-75 feet.

But they certainly saw him. The target veered hard to starboard and put on speed. Too late to do anything about that; just get as close as possible. At 200 yards Davis released the torpedo almost dead astern of the ship. He had a fleeting glimpse of her thrashing screws and rudder jammed hard to starboard.

A blaze of antiaircraft fire erupted as he pulled up with full power over the stern of the ship. On the port waist gun Machinist's Mate Ted Kimmell fired back at the forest of masts, funnels and ventilators directly below. In seconds the whole convoy seemed to be shooting at them. Strange pink and red tracers ripped the night; shrapnel and machine-gun fire raked the PBY. One blast smashed through the nose bubble, shattering Navigator J. I. Foster's goggles, but miraculously not hurting him. They picked up 58 bullet holes altogether . . . but they too were home free.

Now it was Ensign Propst's turn. Though he had lost Richards on the way out, he found the Japanese anyhow. He circled down on their port side and, like the others, attacked up the moon path. It proved to be another of those low, harrowing run-ins. At one point he almost rammed one of the escort. "Don't run into that destroyer!" someone yelled. They hopscotched over it, skimmed on in, releasing at 800 yards. Then with everything bent to the fire wall, Propst did a mad, climbing turn to the left. Co-pilot B. L. Amman had a brief glimpse of a flash that looked like a hit, as the whole Japanese fleet opened up. To Propst it was "Coney Island on the 4th of July."

They caught some shrapnel, once exchanged shots with a prowling Japanese seaplane. But with a little luck and a friendly cloud, they too managed to get clear and were home free.

Only Rothenburg missed the show. Lost early in the game, he kept on course but never found the others again. By the time he reached the scene, the attack was in full swing. Tracers laced the sky, and there was absolutely no chance to get near enough for a successful run. Hoping for an opening, he milled around for 30 minutes. Finally—his gas half gone—he broke off and headed home, winding up a thoroughly frustrating evening.

On the transport *Argentina Maru*, Commander Yonai never expected an attack at night. It was astonishing the way those big PBYs came in from nowhere. Commander Toyama was just as surprised on the escort flagship *Jintsu*. After a hectic day, he was finally relaxing in the operations room—even time for an action meal of rice balls—when a destroyer flashed the first warning.

As the bugle blared general quarters over the loudspeaker, Toyama rushed out on the bridge. He was just in time to see a big, black enemy plane come skimming across the water. Then another . . . and another. Antiaircraft fire exploded everywhere, but they were gone as suddenly as they appeared.

Happily there was little damage. The tanker *Akebono Maru* —bringing up the rear of the north column—caught a torpedo in the bow, killing 13 and wounding 11. The transport *Kiozumi Maru* lost a few men from strafing. The other ships weren't touched, but Admiral Tanaka spent some anxious moments worrying whether the *Akebono Maru* could continue. Finally word came that she could make 12-14 knots—more than enough to keep in line. Still intact, the convoy plodded on toward Midway.

All this was promptly radioed to the *Yamato*, where Admiral Yamamoto's staff reacted with considerable surprise. It was all very puzzling—first, getting sighted at nine o'clock that morning . . . then the B-17s . . . and now this torpedo attack. Certainly nobody expected the Americans to move so quickly. In fact, Captain Kuroshima had hoped they wouldn't find the convoy at all until after Nagumo's attack on the 4th. Here they were a day too soon, already lashing at the transports 600 miles out.

The question again arose whether to relay all this news to Admiral Nagumo, now starting his final run-in, but once again it was decided radio silence was just too important. Nothing must give those carriers away.

Perhaps more thought might have been given to the matter, but too many things were happening. In all its complexity the great operation was beginning to unfold. On May 31 midget subs had staged a brief, diversionary raid at Diégo-Suarez, Madagascar . . . then on June 1, others raided Sydney Harbor . . . and now in the early hours of June 3 Admiral Hosogaya's Northern Force launched its major attack against the Aleutians. Long before Admiral Yamamoto sat down to breakfast, he got the welcome word that the *Ryujo*'s bombers had plastered Dutch Harbor.

At 8:00 he detached an important part of the Main Force in a pre-arranged plan to back up this effort in the Aleutians. Vice Admiral Shiro Takasu took his flagship *Hyuga*, three other battleships, two light cruisers, a handful of destroyers and headed for northern waters. But not too far. His "Aleutian Screening Force" would hover halfway between the Northern Force and Yamamoto himself—ready to jump either way, depending on how the U.S. fleet reacted. The Commander in Chief continued east with the rest of the Main Force, now about 500 miles astern of Nagumo's carriers.

Nagumo himself was less than 700 miles from Midway, girding for his final dash. At 6:07 A.M. Captain Masanao Oto's five oilers dropped astern. The carriers inched up to 12 knots. No more right now—it was folly to go any deeper into patrol plane range than necessary during daylight hours. But by 3:00 P.M. the Admiral had to make his move if he was going to launch tomorrow at dawn. The engine room telegraphs rang, and the First Carrier Striking Force leaped forward at 24 knots.

Down in the *Akagi*'s engine room Commander Yoshibumi Tanbo watched the great turbines respond. How he loved that place. He even took his meals there—rice balls with pickled plums amid the hot oil and pounding machinery. Topside, working parties were rigging stacked hammocks and coils of rope to protect the most exposed equipment from flying shrapnel. Overhead there were still plenty of clouds, but the weather was steadily improving, and at 7:30 Admiral Kusaka stood on the bridge watching the last rays of a magnificent Pacific sunset.

A crash of gunfire shattered the evening calm—the escorting cruiser *Tone* began blazing away with her antiaircraft batteries. Three fighters roared off from the *Akagi* to investigate, and the whole task force scanned the sky. At 7:40 the *Tone*'s blinker explained she had spotted about ten enemy planes, but then lost them. Fourteen minutes later the *Akagi*'s fighters returned after a fruitless search. Clearly some lookout was getting the jitters.

Not so the fliers. The months of solid victory had built that rarest kind of confidence—the faith that lets a man rest easily the night before a battle. The *Kaga*'s pilots turned in early, and when the air officer Commander Amagai checked a little later, they were all fast asleep. On the *Soryu* Juzo Mori inspected his bomber one last time, then went to bed as usual with his mother's picture by the pillow.

By midnight the Striking Force was less than 340 miles from Midway—about 110 from the launching point. At 2:30 A.M. on the 4th a lookout on the *Akagi* sounded another alert—a "light" from an enemy plane on the starboard beam. Another flurry of excitement; another false alarm. It wasn't the first time in history a sailor had been fooled by a star.

Admiral Nagumo knew better. The halfhearted Americans weren't about to cause any trouble at this point. Later they might be goaded into action. His intelligence estimate explained it nicely: "Although the enemy lacks the will to fight, it is likely that he will counter attack if our occupation operations progress satisfactorily."

"LOGAN, I just know I can get them," Massie Hughes urged in his deep Southern drawl as he talked with Commander Ramsey in the Midway command post dugout. It was around 3:00 A.M.; word had come through that the PBYs had hit the Japanese force hard; and now Hughes wanted to take some more PBYs and finish them off. He was a real fighter—an aggressive little middleweight boxer from Alabama —and sitting still was always hard for him.

Ramsey was gently discouraging. It was now clear that this was only the Transport Group, that the Sunday punch was coming from the carriers hidden under those clouds to the northwest. He explained all this, but still it was difficult; they were only a few years apart at Annapolis, and he didn't want to make it a question of rank. But he remained firm, and beyond tactical grounds there was another reason: Ramsey wanted Hughes to take over if anything happened to himself during the coming attack. He didn't want to risk killing the next-in-line chasing a group of transports.

Not that Ramsey didn't appreciate the difficulty of just waiting. "I feel like a June bride," he remarked, "I know it's going to happen, but I don't know what it will be like."

They all felt the same. It was a tense night, for everything was turning out exactly as the intelligence boys had said— first the raid on Dutch Harbor . . . then the invasion force discovered to the southwest . . . now, according to the same script, they'd really get it in the morning from that big force of carriers.

Intelligence said they'd be coming in on a 320° bearing; so it was a serious group of PBY pilots who studied their patrol sector assignments that evening. When Lieutenant

Howard Ady of Squadron 23 checked the blackboard at the Sand Island BOQ, he saw he drew 315°. That meant he'd be flying out on 322½°, back on 307½°. As far as he was concerned, he was "elected."

After briefing, the usual bull session. Squadron 23 had a great collection of talkers, and tonight there was an extra treat: John Ford, the distinguished movie director, was on hand. In an imaginative stroke, Nimitz had sent him out to film whatever might happen. Now he was in the middle of everything, exasperating the supply people but delighting everyone with his tremendous enthusiasm. Far into the night he helped ease the tension with tales of glamorous Hollywood.

"Oh, my God—now I've got a movie-ite!" was Captain Simard's somewhat quaint reaction when Ford first appeared, but he too was soon won over, and now the problem was where to put this celebrity and still keep him alive. Simard finally decided the best place would be the upper part of the main powerhouse on Sand Island. It was relatively well protected and at the same time offered a superb vantage point. From there Ford could take his movies and at the same time give the underground command post a useful running account of what was going on.

This solved, Captain Simard's preparations were practically over. Everything had been done that could be done—even a touching talk to the navy yeomen and pharmacist's mates chosen to make the last stand. With great feeling in his voice, Simard wished them all "good-bye and good luck."

Nearly everyone now seemed resigned to "another Wake Island"—that base's capture remained a bitter memory. The officers removed their insignia to keep Japanese snipers from picking them off. In the harbor the PT boat crews prepared to make the landings as expensive as possible. One of the squadron's officers had always refused to buy GI insurance; that afternoon he asked for the full $10,000 worth. Sorry, he was told, no forms available.

The Marines were grimly determined. Captain McGlashan

carefully burned most of the remaining classified documents. The men in the gun positions swapped chilling bits of scuttle-butt—the Japs had a marvelous new landing barge that could drop a gate right over the reef . . . the big blow would be a night gas attack. Carlson's Raiders busily armed themselves with a new weapon—the 14-inch screwdriver that was part of a PT boat's standard equipment. As one of the Raiders ex-plained, it was "good for the ribs, if you know what I mean."

One and all, they continued working on Midway's defenses to the end. On Sand Island men were still placing the last mines on the northwest beach in the early evening twilight. At Eastern, "Barbed Wire Bob" Hommel anchored his last concertinas offshore after dark. Private Joseph E. Love, norm-ally relegated to garbage collection and the gooney bird burial detail, found himself stringing telephone lines until nearly midnight.

It was after 12:00 when Colonel Shannon and Captain McGlashan finished one last tour of inspection and trudged back to the command post. McGlashan was satisfied: he felt that come what may, the Marine garrison had done all it could.

The fliers were ready too. During the evening Colonel Kimes called a meeting of all the personnel in Marine Air Group 22. "This is it, boys," he said, and not knowing how things would turn out, he simply told them, "Give it all you've got, and good luck to you all."

The fighter pilots in Squadron VMF-221 would need all the luck they could get. The seven F4Fs seemed so pitifully few, the 16 Brewster Buffaloes so hopelessly obsolete. Major Red Parks, the squadron commander, knew how long the odds were. Normally he was an aggressive, intelligent extrovert, not too concerned with psychology or the vulnerabilities of mankind. He would rather slit his throat than admit to any-thing that might be construed as longing for solace. Tonight was different. As he sat with his executive officer Captain Kirk Armistead in the Eastern Island snack bar, he seemed very serious and disturbed. Armistead tried to cheer him up, saying something like, "By this time tomorrow it'll all be behind us."

"Yeah," Parks gloomily nodded, "for those of you who get through it."

The outlook wasn't much brighter for the dive bomber pilots in Squadron VMSB-241. During the evening Major Henderson called them together and gave them a few of his thoughts. He said he knew how poor the equipment was; the flight tomorrow would be strictly a voluntary proposition. However, he was taking off as soon as the enemy fleet was within range, and the others could follow him if they wished. Henderson was like a father to most of the squadron, and there was little doubt what they'd do.

"Sleep in your clothes tonight,'" Captain Richard Fleming, one of the pilots, told his rear-seat man Corporal Eugene T. Card. "They may come in at any time, so be ready to turn out."

Card was ready. He had gone over his machine gun once again. He checked and rechecked the radio frequencies and various dial settings. He even stocked the plane with cans of corned beef and pineapple juice in case they were forced down at sea. Now if only the Japs would attack or go away —anything, as long as they did something.

The young Navy pilots "on loan" from Torpedo 8 were ready too. During the day they kept posted on the various sightings and strikes; they knew their turn would soon be coming up. But Ensign Bert Earnest felt he had a good omen. Walking alongside the Eastern Island runway just after dark, he found a two-dollar bill. He carefully tucked it in his wallet, hoping that any powers it had would help bring him through.

The B-26 crews remained utterly casual. Probably nobody is less informed than an Army flier at a Navy base (unless it's a Navy flier at an Army base), and these men were no exceptions. Lieutenant Muri had yet to learn of any enemy sighting, still had only the haziest idea why he was at Midway.

That evening as he and his crew sat beside their plane, a Marine private wandered by who knew just as little. The private was happy, said he was about to go Stateside on leave, and demonstrated a "gooney-bird dance" which he planned to introduce back home. The crew laughed and clapped, agreed that it would soon be all the rage. They hadn't a worry in the world.

By the end of the day, seven more B-17s had arrived from Hawaii—a final "gift" from Admiral Nimitz. Altogether, some 120 planes now jammed the base, along with 11 PT boats, 5 tanks, 8 mortars, 14 shore-defense guns, 32 antiaircraft guns, and 3,632 defenders. For two tiny islets in mid-Pacific—one two miles long, the other about a mile—it all added up to quite a show. Midway, as one Marine put it, "looked like an asparagus patch."

Even so, they felt very much alone. In some cases the defenders were warned they were strictly on their own; in others they just assumed it. Only a few knew there was any chance for help from the outside. One of these exceptions was Ensign Jacoby, Logan Ramsey's aide in the command post. Jacoby wasn't making the big decisions, but he listened a lot, and nothing intrigued him more than the talk about Point Luck.

For Admiral Fletcher on the *Yorktown*, it just didn't add up right. Ensign Jack Reid's contact report, intercepted by the carriers, clearly said "Main Body," yet it was the wrong direction. According to Nimitz's briefing, the carriers should be coming down from the northwest, and certainly the intelligence had been right so far about everything else—Dutch Harbor was hit exactly on schedule.

"That is not repeat not the enemy striking force," warned a radio message that soon arrived direct from Nimitz, ending all doubts on the matter. CINCPAC's signal went on to stress that only the Invasion Force had so far been sighted, that the carriers would still strike from the northwest tomorrow.

Task Forces 16 and 17 continued marking time, cruising slowly north under gray, broken clouds. On the carriers the fliers went over their planes, checked the firing circuits, cleaned their charts and plotting boards for tomorrow's data. The fighter pilots saw that their guns were loaded bullet by bullet. The bomber and torpedo pilots once again went over their signaling and firing procedures with their rear-seat men. No relationship was closer—and none more of a life-and-death matter—than the teamwork between these two. The crew captains fussed over the planes, and when there was nothing more to be done, polished them one more time. Woe to the mechanic on the *Yorktown* whose maintenance work didn't come up to Leading Chief V. J. Feigenbutz's standards. The old chief had a passion for Bombing Squadron 3 and a volcanic vocabulary to express it.

All afternoon Fletcher and his staff waited for word that Nagumo had been sighted, but nothing ever came. At 7:50 P.M. he changed course to the southwest. This would take him to a point about 200 miles north of Midway at dawn. Assuming Nagumo was still following the script, the U.S. carriers would be in perfect position for launching a surprise attack on the Japanese flank.

The ships steamed on into the night, dark forms cutting a calm, moonlit Pacific. If the battened ports and hatches suggested inactivity, that was deceptive, for there was plenty going on. It has been said that running a carrier for an air group was a little like running a hotel for a crowd of conventioneers, and this was never truer than the night before a major strike.

On the *Enterprise* the supply officer, Commander Charles Fox, faced a hundred extra problems feeding and servicing the ship. Tomorrow, most of his men would be at battle stations far from their regular jobs—the day's needs must be met in advance. Spares and plane parts were brought up from below; battle rations prepared and packaged. In the kitchen the cooks turned out stacks of sandwiches, and no less than 10,000 spiced ginger cookies.

The fliers themselves had little to do but wait . . . and think about tomorrow. There was no single, dominant mood. Every man had his own private mixture of feelings. For Ensign Charles Lane, a young but experienced dive bomber pilot on the *Yorktown*, it was not a feeling of fear exactly, but apprehension and regret that he might not return. On the *Enterprise* Lieutenant Bill Roberts felt a strange sense of excitement. It was the element of trapping the Japanese, he thought, that made this time so different. Ensign Thomas J. Wood on the *Hornet* bubbled with high spirits. Like the rest of the ship's pilots, he knew nothing of combat, had never even had a chance to learn about fear. He was young, aggressive, and boasted to anyone who would listen that he personally would sink the *Akagi*.

The dive bomber pilots, at least, shared one thing in common. They were ready. They had trained months for this, worked hard, now felt prepared to give a really decent account of themselves. The new men, in particular, yearned to go out and show what they could do.

Not so, some of the older torpedo pilots. They had been around too long to be carried away by the excitement. By now they had been in enough scrapes to know that even the finest spirit can't make up for poor equipment. And they knew these TBDs were death traps—the 100-knot speed, the slow rate of climb, the wretched torpedoes.

None knew the truth better than Lieutenant Commander Massey, skipper of the *Yorktown*'s Torpedo 3. Lem Massey was a shambling, lovable character who enjoyed good company and went out of his way to find it. Tonight he recruited a couple of nonfliers in the squadron and brought them into his cabin. Bringing out a bottle of scotch (illegal but not unknown on carriers), he told them how long the odds were against the squadron. He probably shouldn't be talking this way, he said, but he just had to share his gloom with someone. When they went out tomorrow, he didn't see how they'd ever get back.

Another man who knew about these torpedo planes was John Udell Lane on the *Enterprise*. He was a rear-seat man in Torpedo 6, and he too had a premonition of what tomorrow offered. Visiting a friend's compartment, he talked long and sadly of his home in Illinois. Putting on a favorite record of soprano Miliza Korjus, he moodily played it over and over again.

Against this almost bittersweet mood of resignation, the blazing spirit of the *Hornet*'s brand-new Torpedo Squadron 8 seemed all the more striking. Lieutenant Commander John Waldron was a hard-driving taskmaster with a fierce passion for getting at the enemy. Whenever the big day came, he was determined to be ready. He drilled his men mercilessly, ran their legs off, fought for extra equipment—anything to win. "If we run out of gas," he once remarked, "we'll piss in the tanks."

He also knew how to blow off steam. The squadron parties that he and his wife Adelaide gave in Norfolk were famous. Then he put aside his toughness, royally entertained the young ensigns, and sometimes allowed a deep streak of tenderness to shine through. There was the night when he took Ensigns Jim Cook and Corwin Morgan to a darkened room where his children were sleeping: "Cookie, you and Morgan look in this room. Did you ever see such pretty little girls?"

The following morning he'd be all business again, pounding away at his tactical theories. They were often unorthodox. Ensign George Gay considered him "foxy"; Waldron himself lightly referred to his extra intuition, thanks to a streak of Sioux blood. In any case, he hammered home his ideas till, as Gay put it, "We could almost look at the back of Commander Waldron's head and know what he was thinking."

His men griped a lot—no one else had to work that hard —but they believed in him completely. Soon they were a compact, closely knit team as fiery and determined as their skipper. They ran laps around the flight deck and did group calisthenics, while the other fliers hooted and loafed. They tucked knives in their belts, wore shoulder holsters, and didn't give a damn about the taunts of "Circus" and "Mexican Panchos."

And all the time they worked. There wasn't much chance to fly, but no squadron ever spent more hours in the ready room. Waldron was a fanatic on detail, and he'd go over the smallest point again and again. Like a schoolteacher, he'd toss sharp, unexpected questions at any pilot who seemed to be daydreaming.

This night of June 3 the briefing stressed one of the skipper's favorite subjects: the proper angle of attack on a hard-turning target. As usual he was all business, but when the meeting broke up, he turned almost shy as he handed out a final mimeographed message along with his plan of attack:

Just a word to let you know I feel we are all ready. We have had a very short time to train and we have worked under the most severe difficulties. But we have truly done the best humanly possible. I actually believe that under these conditions we are the best in the world. My greatest hope is that we encounter a favorable tactical situation, but if we don't, and the worst comes to worst, I want each of us to do his utmost to destroy our enemies. If there is only one plane left to make a final run in, I want that man to go in and get a hit. May God be with us all. Good luck, happy landings and give 'em hell.

Torpedo 8 drifted back to its quarters. Most of the men puttered, read or played records. Ensign Abercrombie won $45 at poker. Waldron himself wrote a tender note to "Dearest little Ann," one of his children, and endorsed a small check to his father-in-law. He had already written Adelaide everything he could say: ". . . I love you and the children very dearly and I long to be with you. But I could not be happy ashore at this time. My place is here with the fight."

Only Ensign Gay was still busy. As navigation officer he was attending to the last-minute job of getting some charts run off for the rest. Finally it was time to turn in, but he found it hard to sleep. Bulletins on the battle were beginning to come in . . . the PBYs were out making their midnight attack. Gay felt "a little bit nervous, kind of, like before a football game."

Throughout the fleet others had the same trouble. On the

Enterprise Dick Best slept "like a baby," but more were like Lieutenant Dickinson of Scouting 6, restlessly visiting back and forth, talking the night away. One thing was true of them all. As Lieutenant Jim Gray, skipper of Fighting 6, has put it: "It is doubtful that there were any atheists in *Enterprise* on the night of 3 June 1942."

Through the night and into the first hour of June 4, the U.S. force steamed on, always edging southwest toward Midway. On the *Yorktown*'s bridge Admiral Fletcher's staff were "biting their nails" wondering why the Japanese carriers were still unreported—they should be well within Midway's range by now. "After a battle is over," Fletcher later remarked, "people talk a lot about how the decisions were methodically reached, but actually there's always a hell of a lot of groping around."

He finally decided to launch a search to the north at dawn, just in case the enemy might be sneaking down that way. Certainly they were out there somewhere; everyone knew that by now. Belowdecks, Seaman Melvin Frantz slipped down to his locker and switched his money to his wallet: "By tomorrow night I might be swimming."

Up in sky control on the *Enterprise* the assistant gunnery officer, Lieutenant Elias Mott, restlessly flicked on a portable radio. Wherever it happened to break out, he knew battle would be joined in the morning. Maybe a little music and news from home might help. Honolulu came in strong and clear: the news said a leading entertainer had just been commissioned a lieutenant commander. Mott bitterly snapped it off—"That's all I need from home tonight."

Actually, "home" was taking things far more seriously than Lieutenant Mott thought. The Army had never completely given up thinking that the real Japanese target was the West Coast, and tonight was a time of great jitters. Leaves were canceled; West Coast radio stations were silenced for a while; a nine-minute "blue" alert was sounded in the San Francisco Bay area. Radar had picked up an unidentified target 60 miles off the Golden Gate. Whatever it was, it soon faded away, but not the feeling of fear and alarm.

To get early warning of any assault, the Navy's Western Sea Frontier Command established a picket line of patrol boats and yachts 400 miles off the California coast. Ashore, the Fourth Army and the Western Defense Command urged the public to report immediately any Japanese seen wearing the uniform of an American soldier. There was little chance of mistaken identity, because all Japanese-Americans in uniform had been shifted to other areas, except three men on special duty at Fort Ord.

Conditions were even more tense in Hawaii. By now every one knew "something was up," and the wilder rumors had a big Japanese fleet heading straight for Pearl Harbor. Army patients were discharged from the hospital at Schofield in anticipation of battle casualties. The Civilian Defense Volunteers were called to duty. General Emmons urged all women and children living in downtown Honolulu to evacuate to a safer place. A strange silence seemed to hang everywhere—a mixture of hope and fear.

At Pearl Harbor the Marine guards manned the machine guns atop the concrete pillars of the Navy Yard gate. Trucks were parked as roadblocks across the entrance before dark. On all ships the gun crews were at their posts.

Shortly after dark there was an A-1, all-out "red" alert. All repairs came to a stop. Workers manned machine guns on the shop roofs: others stood by the fire hoses. The yard was completely blacked out and sealed off. When the grave-yard shift came they were told to go home; the swing shift, caught by the alert, sat around in the shelters. They tried to sleep or smoked and talked about the coming invasion.

Behind blackout curtains, the CINCPAC staff worried the night away. Commander Layton found himself thinking of the people he knew on the other side. He wondered what an old friend like Takashi Kanoe was doing right now.

O<small>N THE</small> *Hiryu* Commander Takashi Kanoe paused briefly before the ship's shrine outside Captain Kaku's cabin, then hurried on to the bridge. As executive officer, this was Kanoe's battle station, and looking down, he could already see the planes warming up in the pre-dawn darkness.

Below decks the ship was springing to life. The fliers were up at 4:00 and had breakfast on trays in the ready room. Normally they had just an action meal before battle, but this time they got the full treatment—rice, soybean soup, pickles, everything. And to top it off there were dry chestnuts and cold *sake*—a traditional combination served from the earliest times to Japanese warriors entering battle.

The *Hiryu*'s air officer, Lieutenant Commander Susumu Kawaguchi, had never heard of such a breakfast. All this symbolism suddenly made him take Midway far more seriously. In his final briefing, he made a special plea, urging the pilots to "put their nerve into it."

Beyond that, there was little to say. The men were all veterans, knew their jobs perfectly, and Kanoe had complete faith in their leader Lieutenant Joichi Tomonaga. A tough, silent, hard-drinking man, Tomonaga was an expert torpedo plane pilot. He had seen no action since Pearl Harbor and was champing at the bit. When he said good-bye to his wife at Beppu, he seemed particularly glad to get aboard the *Hiryu* and head for battle. Kanoe noticed this, and when Fuchida came down with appendicitis, he immediately thought of Tomonaga as the ideal man to take over. Kanoe put it to his old Academy classmate Commander Minoru Genda, who was Nagumo's operations officer, and the matter was quickly settled.

The briefing over, the pilots headed for their planes. Overhead a few stars lingered in the sky. It was still quite cloudy, but the eastern horizon glowed orange, promising clear weather ahead.

On all the carriers the scene was much the same . . . yet as varied as human nature. On the *Soryu* CPO Mori and his friends engaged in the nervous banter that fighting men find useful at such times. "You're going to get it today," someone told Mori. "No, you're the one," he retorted exactly as expected. Then they turned to joking about who would end up with each other's savings accounts. On the *Kaga* serious, thoughtful CWO Morinaga quietly adjusted his *senim bari* around his waist. According to ancient tradition, its thousand stitches—each sewn by a different well-wisher—would give him divine protection.

On the flagship *Akagi* a wobbly Mitsuo Fuchida struggled topside to see them off. Then Commander Genda arrived on the bridge in pajamas; he too had been sick, down with a wretched cold, but was determined to be on hand today. And no one could have been more welcome. Admiral Nagumo depended enormously—some said too much—on the brilliant mind of his operations officer. On practically any subject Nagumo accepted Genda's recommendations without question. Indeed, cynics referred to the striking force as "Genda's fleet." But his appearance at this moment was a shot in the arm for them all. In a rare display of sentiment by that dour old sailor, Nagumo threw his arm around the Commander's shoulder.

"All hands to launching stations," blared the *Akagi*'s loudspeaker.

"Start engines."

A sudden roar, and the soft gray of dawn blazed with unexpected color. Exhausts flared white . . . wing lights flicked on, red and blue . . . floodlights bathed the yellow flight deck. "Commence launching," ordered the bridge, and the air officer Commander Shogo Masuda swung his green signal lamp in a great arc over his head.

Lieutenant Shirane's Zero crawled forward . . . gathered

speed . . . thundered down the deck and into the air. Eight
more fighters followed, then 18 dive bombers. As Lieutenant
Chihaya's plane flashed by, he had his canopy open and
waved to the cheering men on deck.

The other carriers were launching too, their planes orbiting
slowly around the fleet till they were all in formation. From
the *Hiryu's* bridge, the ship's only passenger watched with
more than academic interest. He was Lieutenant Commander
Asaichi Tamai, appointed to command the air wing of the
new naval base to be established at Midway.

By 4:45 they were all formed up and on their way—36
level bombers from the *Hiryu* and *Soryu;* 36 dive bombers
from the *Akagi* and *Kaga;* 36 fighters, 9 from each carrier.
Heading southeast, they soon faded into the brightening sky.

All was quiet again on the carriers, but not for long. Orders
went out to prepare the second attack wave—Nagumo's insurance policy in case a U.S. fleet unexpectedly turned up. In
total strength these reserves matched the force now winging
toward Midway. The main difference lay in the arming. This
time the level bombers would carry torpedoes, and the dive
bombers would switch to armor-piercing missiles for use
against ships. It all added up to 36 dive bombers from the
Hiryu and *Soryu;* 36 torpedo planes from the *Akagi* and *Kaga;*
and, again, 36 fighters from all four carriers.

In the first rays of the morning sun, the elevators brought
the new planes up . . . flight deck crews wheeled them into
position . . . mechanics shackled on the torpedoes. The pilots
stood by, loafing and relaxed. It seemed almost a waste to hold
back so many good men this way—Lieutenant Takashige
Egusa on the *Soryu* was the finest dive-bomber pilot in the
Navy—but Nagumo wanted to be safe. Anybody could bomb
an island, but a moving ship took skill. As long as there was
any chance of the Americans appearing, however unlikely, he
wanted to have his best men available.

On the same unlikely chance, he had also ordered search
planes to scout generally eastward for 300 miles. There were

only seven of them—a motley collection from five different ships—and they had to cover an arc of 165°, but nobody was taking this effort too seriously. Nagumo remained convinced that there were no U.S. carriers around, and Genda had a reputation for always slicing reconnaissance rather thin. Every plane used for patrol work meant one less for the slashing attacks that were his specialty.

Today the search also had a ragged start. The planes were meant to leave at 4:30, same as the Midway strike, but it didn't work out quite that way. The cruiser *Tone*, which was contributing her No. 1 and No. 4 float planes, had catapult trouble, and that held her up awhile. But finally all was fixed, and at 5:00 A.M. the *Tone's* No. 4 plane—last of the seven to leave—soared eastward into the sunrise. It was a half hour late, but to Lieutenant Takeda, the *Tone's* hard-working air officer, that shouldn't make very much difference.

I⊤ was breakfast as usual—almost—in the *Enterprise* wardroom, as the U.S. fleet hovered 200 miles north and slightly east of Midway. Although only 1:30 A.M., Steward Collins had everything ready. Lieutenant Best had his invariable shirred eggs . . . Lieutenant Gray had his "one-eyed sandwich"—an *Enterprise* specialty consisting of a slice of toast holed to accommodate a fried egg.

For some of the old hands it seemed like any other day. But for others it was different. Lieutenant Commander Wade McClusky, leading the *Enterprise* Air Group, felt the usual quips were missing; a hushed note of expectancy hung over the room. On the other hand, Commander Fox sensed a note of nervous gaiety. In any case, as supply officer, Fox knew for a fact that appetites were below par.

As McClusky sampled his scrambled eggs, he was surprised to see Lieutenant Commander Gene Lindsey slide into the seat beside him. Skipper of Torpedo 6, Lindsey had cracked up coming in the other day. Fished out of the Pacific with a badly wrenched back, he was meant to be sidelined indefinitely. Now here he was, not only up but planning to fly in a spare torpedo plane. When one of his pilots asked how he felt, Lindsey obliquely replied, "This is the real thing today, the thing we have trained for, and I will take my squadron in."

Breakfast over, the pilots drifted off to their ready rooms. There was one for each squadron on every carrier, and they looked more like classrooms than anything else—rows of seats with writing arm attached, a blackboard up front for the latest dope on position, wind, course, target and the all-important "Point Option" where the ship could be found again after a strike. There was also a teletype machine that clacked out bulletins which were projected on a screen.

At the moment there was little on the blackboard and the teletype was silent—Nagumo's force still hadn't been found. On all three carriers the pilots hauled out their plotting boards from drawers under their seats, checked a few odds and ends, then sat back and waited. Cards and paperbacks appeared. Seats were adjustable, and a man like Ensign Whitey Moore of Torpedo 8 was soon leaning back, grabbing a little extra sleep—he could never get enough.

Commander Waldron slipped down to the *Hornet's* wardroom for morning coffee with Commander Ed Creehan, the ship's engineering officer. They were old Annapolis classmates, and this was a daily custom. Today Waldron was in an exalted mood—Torpedo 8 would at last have a crack at the enemy. He said he was going to "get a Jap carrier" or he wouldn't be back.

The minutes crawled by. On the *Yorktown* Ensign Charles Lane of Bombing 3 decided to leave behind his Clemson ring and Hamilton watch in case he didn't return. On the *Enterprise* Commander McClusky began assembling his flight gear in the little office he used outside the squadron ready rooms. At this point his regular rear-seat man stumbled in to report he had just broken his glasses. Of all times. McClusky put in a hurried call to Bombing 6 for a spare gunner who didn't need glasses, and in a few moments a bright-looking lad named Chochalousek appeared. He had no combat experience, but he was just out of aerial gunnery school—welcome news on this particular day.

The U.S. force continued southwest—the *Yorktown* trailing about ten miles behind the *Enterprise* and *Hornet*. On the *Yorktown's* bridge Admiral Fletcher still wondered where Nagumo could be. He had sent out his "just-in-case" search to the north, but there was no word from that direction. No word from the Midway planes either.

LIEUTENANT Ady was an hour out of Midway now, and still no sign of the Japanese. "Elected" to patrol the all-important 315° segment, so far he was having a milk run. The big PBY droned on, the long rays of the rising sun lighting the broken clouds ahead.

Then around 5:10 a small seaplane came whistling along from out of the west. It was on an opposite course and didn't swerve an inch—just hurried on toward Midway about 120 miles away. Ady radioed the single word "aircraft," then followed it up with a longer description.

To the crew in the PBY, it meant only one thing: the Japanese fleet must be close. On they flew through occasional squalls. By 5:30 the weather was clearing "upstairs," but there were still some cloud banks near the water. As Ady approached one of these, two aircraft carriers burst through from the other side—just 20 miles away and steaming directly toward him. It was, he thought, like a curtain going up at the theater.

In the next patrol sector to the south, Lieutenant William Chase had also spent an uneventful first hour. His PBY was flying about 15 minutes behind Ady's, but the sunrise, the clouds, even the coffee were much the same. Then around 5:40—probably just after Ady discovered his carriers—Chase found something too. There to the north was a huge formation of fighters and bombers flying toward Midway. Standard procedure called for a carefully encoded contact report, but this was no time for that. In plain English, he shot off a fast warning: "MANY PLANES HEADING MIDWAY. BEARING 320, DISTANCE 150."

"THAT's him!" Relief, excitement, elation, anticipation were all mingled together in Admiral Spruance's first reaction, as news of the contact reached him on the flying bridge of the *Enterprise*. It was the same on the *Yorktown*, where Admiral Fletcher thankfully realized the long wait was over.

So the Japanese carriers were found . . . but where? The first brief contact reports were agonizingly sketchy. Task Forces 16 and 17 were both tuned to the PBY frequencies, so there was no delay, but there was certainly confusion. For one thing, the fact was quickly lost that two different PBYs were reporting two different sightings; messages were mixed together, making for inconsistencies. More important, there was nothing yet on enemy course and speed—absolutely vital for launching an attack.

LIEUTENANT Ady was doing his best. After that electrifying discovery of the carriers, he veered to the left, circling slowly around the Japanese fleet. He used the clouds as much as he could, sending back bits of information as fast as he gathered it: "5:34, enemy carriers" . . . "5:40, ED 180, sight 320°" . . . "5:52, two carriers and main body of ships, carriers in front, course 135, speed 25."

That was enough. Somehow the full picture didn't reach the *Yorktown*'s bridge until 6:03, but once in hand Admiral Fletcher lost no time. At 6:07 he signaled Spruance, "Proceed southwesterly and attack enemy carriers when definitely located. Will follow as soon as search planes recovered."

Task Force 16 plunged forward at 25 knots. On all ships

general quarters began sounding—at 6:15, the harsh staccato of the buzzer on the *Enterprise;* at 6:26, the urgent clang of the *Hornet's* gong. It varied from ship to ship but the effect was always the same: the scrambling, the pounding of feet, and always in the background the insistent clamor of the alarm itself.

ON SAND ISLAND the powerhouse whistle blasted away; the siren on Eastern added its wail. Private Love, just lining up for chow, dropped all thoughts of breakfast and raced for his antiaircraft battery. Lieutenant Donald Cooksey, 6th Battalion dental officer, rushed to his first-aid post, well aware of Colonel Shannon's sharp reminder, "A dead or wounded doctor is no damn good to me." In his Eastern Island dugout Captain W. M. Bell, platoon leader of I Battery, recalled an old Marine dictum that it was an officer's duty to look calm and well-groomed at all times. He carefully shaved, dressed, and sipped a glass of pineapple juice before going to his platoon.

Confusion was everywhere along the Eastern Island runway. When the first contact reports came in around 5:30, the Marine CP ordered all planes to start engines. Enemy bombers were said to be only 100 miles away. But when minutes went by and nothing appeared on radar, new orders went out: cut engines. Then at 5:53 Navy radar broke in: "MANY BOGEY AIRCRAFT BEARING 310°, DISTANCE 93."

This was it all right, and as the siren went off at 5:55 new orders went out to get going. But by now some of the pilots had cut engines; others were still warming up and couldn't hear the alarm. The CP truck raced along the runway, its own siren shrieking, Captain Bob Burns shouting to everyone to stand by for take-off.

At least the B-17s were no problem. They had gone out as usual at dawn, but instead of merely using up gas, this morning they had been ordered to attack the Japanese transports again. Now the new threat changed everything. Captain Simard radioed Colonel Sweeney to divert his bombers to the carriers sweeping down from the northwest. At the same time, orders went out to the PBYs on patrol: stay clear of Midway; after completing mission, go to French Frigate Shoals, or one of the outlying reefs.

But there were still 66 planes at Midway; none must be caught on the ground. At 6:00 the 26 fighters began taking off. One of them soon returned with engine trouble, but the other 25 climbed toward the northwest. Major Parks led the way with two divisions; Captain Kirk Armistead followed with the rest, heading out on a slightly different bearing as a hedge against radar error. About 30 miles out they were all ordered to orbit. They would not have long to wait: at 6:04 Navy radar put the "bogeys" only 74 miles away.

Next it was the six TBFs's turn to take off. Captain Burns raced up in his jeep and spoke to Lieutenant Fieberling. The skipper sent a mechanic running to each plane; he scrambled on the wing and yelled above the roar of the motors, "320°, 150 miles out!" One by one the TBFs thundered down the runway, rising gracefully despite the torpedoes. It was 6:10, and radar had the Japanese 47 miles out.

Now the four B-26s. Major Jo K. Warner, the Army liaison man, drove up and gave Captain Collins the dope. But as the crews scrambled into their planes, Lieutenant Jim Muri still wasn't sure what this was all about. He only knew he had a torpedo, a position, and there was some "target" out there. Rolling down the runway, he hoped it would be a nice, fat, easy merchantman.

Only the Marine bombers were left. Major Benjamin Norris went first, taking out his 12 decrepit Vindicators. One immediately returned when a cowling blew off. The squadron's skipper Major Henderson brought up the rear, leading the relatively new SBDs. By now there was no field organization left —no radio, no briefing officer, no directions. Just a wild scramble to get into the air. But Joe Henderson somehow knew what to do, and his young pilots were more than willing to follow. At the last minute two of the SBDs broke down, but the other 16 took off. Colonel Kimes fixed the time at 6:15; some put it a few minutes later. In any case it was none too soon—at 6:16 the radar had the Japanese at 29 miles.

With the last planes gone, an overwhelming silence hung over Eastern Island. Men crouched quietly in the gun pits, the slit trenches, the observation posts—all eyes fixed on the empty blue sky to the northwest. It was almost hypnotizing, and at E Battery Captain James O'Halloran sharply reminded his lookouts that there were other sectors too—that the Japanese had been known to pull some surprises.

In the shelters and dugouts hundreds of other men quietly waited, hidden by sand and camouflage. As WO Bill Lucius hurried toward his slit trench near the mess hall, Major William Benson called out from the command post dugout: "Bill, I have the best dugout on the island, as well as the best communications equipment. Why don't you stay with me?"

"I was so scared at Pearl Harbor," Lucius replied, "that I hardly saw the Japanese planes; I don't want to miss them now."

From the piers and moorings a small flotilla of boats slipped into the lagoon between Eastern and Sand. Lieutenant Clinton McKellar neatly dispersed his 11 PTs. Boatswain Olivier carefully positioned his collection of launches, all loaded with machine guns and rifles. Chief Boatswain's Mate Stanley Engels took his tug *Tamaha* and tied up to an old sunken scow that looked like the last thing the Japanese would want to bomb.

In the dugout hospital on Sand Island Pharmacist's Mate E. B. Miller began boiling coffee on a hot plate. It was far too strong to drink; he was making it for a "Murphy drip," an old-fashioned remedy used rectally in treating shock.

At the command post Captain Simard couldn't resist temptation. He should be in the dugout by now, but he hung back —fascinated like so many others—straining his eyes to the northwest. Logan Ramsey kept urging him to get under cover.

On the upper decks of the powerhouse Simard's "movie-ite" John Ford was searching the northwest too. He was now equipped with cameras, film, binoculars and a phone direct to the CP. His vantage point was perfect, but so far there was nothing to see. In fact Midway looked deserted—nothing moving—just a lazy, peaceful tropical island.

Outside Colonel Shannon's command post the Marine guard, Pfc Ed D. Winslow, stood watch by the doorway. It was a distracting assignment this morning. The radar station was hard by, and as the Japanese drew closer, someone kept calling out the miles. Inside, the radar operators watched closely as two sets of blips—one enemy, one friendly—swept together just beyond the horizon.

CHAPTER 5

"Hawks at Angels 12"

LIEUTENANT Hashimoto knew they were getting close from an outlying reef he sighted below. Riding as observer in Lieutenant Tomonaga's lead plane, he pointed it out to the attack commander.

The trip in had been uneventful; one *Hiryu* bomber turned back with engine trouble, but something like that always happened. The other 107 planes carried on, the bombers in two separate V-of-Vs, the fighters flying cover above them. At 6:16 CPO Juzo Mori, leading his three-bomber division from the *Soryu,* sighted a dark blot on the glittering horizon—Midway.

Next instant two of the *Hiryu's* bombers, flying just ahead of his own, suddenly burst into flames. Mori, Hashimoto—everybody—looked up just in time to see several American fighters swooping down on them, guns blazing.

"TALLYHO! Hawks at angels 12 . . . supported by fighters." Captain John Carey was the first to spot them, and in the verbal shorthand of the Marine fliers, his words told the others that he had spotted the Japanese coming in at 12,000 feet. All 25 fighters converged on the scene.

Carey didn't wait. Leading his three-plane division of F4Fs, he made a wide turn and dove at 90° on the enemy formation. His guns hammered away at a Japanese section leader; it fell out of line burning. Captain Marion Carl and Lieutenant Clayton Canfield followed Carey down; Canfield set his sights on the third plane in the third section; it exploded in flames.

Major Parks piled into the melee with the rest of his group. Most of the Marines got in one good pass; then as they climbed for a second run, the Zeros tore into them. Bullets ripped Lieutenant Carey's cockpit, smashing both his legs; a 20 mm. cannon shell tore Canfield's wing flaps to shreds. Parks himself went reeling into the sea.

Captain Armistead, arriving with his division a few minutes later, fared little better. After one pass at the bombers, he saw three fighters climbing toward him, steep and fast. For a second he thought they were Marines, but no such luck. Cannon and machine-gun shells blasted him out of the fight.

Seeing a Zero on his tail, Lieutenant Darrell Irwin tried to escape by diving. He plunged down from 16,500 feet at 300 miles an hour . . . pulled out at 3,500—the Zero was still there. Down again, this time out at 500 feet—the Zero was still there. He finally crash-landed what was left of the plane—with the Zero still there.

Captain Herbert Merrill caught it from above and behind. At 8,000 feet he lost partial control. Then two more hits, and the gas tank blew up in his face. He bailed out, but his worries weren't over. He had heard the Japanese often strafed parachutists; so he didn't pull the ripcord for another 3,000 feet. Finally he hit the water a couple of miles offshore, got rid of his chute and inflated his Mae West. Midway looked a long way off—how could he swim that far? Then he thought of home and his new baby twins, and began to try.

Occasionally a trick worked. When Marion Carl couldn't shake off a Zero, he suddenly cut the throttle, threw his plane into a skid, and the Jap raced by. Captain William Humberd couldn't shake his Zero either, finally turned and gave it a burst head on. The Zero staggered and fell into the sea.

Usually the Japanese were much too clever—and sometimes had a trick of their own. When Lieutenant William Brooks saw two planes dogfighting at one point, he went over to help the American. Both planes turned on him—he had been fooled by a sham battle between two enemy pilots. Brooks finally escaped with 72 bullet holes in his plane.

But it wasn't deception, skill or even numbers that made the big difference. As the Marine fighters fluttered down to the sea, or staggered back toward Midway, it was clear that the greatest Japanese advantage lay in the Zero itself. The Marine pilots were astonished. Like most Americans, they had been taught to think of the Japanese as an imitative people who couldn't do much on their own. Now here was a fighter that could outclimb, outrun, outmaneuver any plane the U.S. had. If it was also highly vulnerable, they rarely had a good enough shot at it to find out. Even the F4Fs were completely outclassed, and the ancient Buffaloes—as Lieutenant Charles Hughes sadly remarked—"looked like they were tied to a string while the Zeros made passes at them."

For their part, Nagumo's pilots also got a surprise. They too had some fixed ideas about their enemy. Like most Japanese, they believed Americans had little heart for fighting and would quickly fold once the going got rough. Yet here the Marines were, hurling themselves into battle with a spirit worthy of the *samurais*. They also showed better tactics than expected; Hashimoto, for one, was amazed how they dived from overhead so unexpectedly.

Anyhow, Lieutenant Suganami's Zeros now had everything under control, and the attacking force continued on. Under "Organization No. 5" they would strike in three waves: first, a dose of level bombing by the *Hiryu*'s and *Soryu*'s units; next the *Akagi*'s and *Kaga*'s dive bombers would come; finally the fighters from all four carriers would strafe anything left.

The *Hiryu* and *Kaga* would concentrate on Sand Island; the *Soryu* and *Akagi* on Eastern. Still in two V-of-Vs—with the fighters re-forming above—the whole force curled around the atoll and began its final run from the north.

To Pfc Philip Clark at D Battery, they looked like three wisps of clouds far out on the horizon. To Pharmacist's Mate Miller, up from his dugout for a look, they seemed more stretched out in a single line. But there was no doubt they were coming on fast. At 6:29 the radar fixed them at eight miles . . . 6:30, Battalion said fire when within range . . . 6:31, all guns opened up.

A dozen black puffs erupted 200–300 yards behind the advancing planes. At D Battery Sergeant Evitts, who knew more about fire control than all the brass, cranked in an arbitrary adjustment. A single string of bursts left the main group and "walked through" the formation, setting one plane on fire. Then another blazed up, but kept flying in flames for an interminable period. As it fell a great cheer went up; even the men deep in the Navy command post could hear it. At the entrance Captain Simard watched transfixed, while Logan Ramsey urged him again and again to get under cover: "Skipper, this is no place for you to be."

At 6:34 the planes were directly overhead. On Sand Island Sergeant Jay Koch studied them through the F Battery telescope as the bomb bay doors opened and the first bombs dropped out. He felt a moment of terror as he wondered where they were going to hit.

High in the powerhouse John Ford didn't see them unload, but assuming the seaplane hangar would be one of the first Japanese targets, he already had his camera trained on it. He was right. A stick of bombs hit home, spewing fragments in all directions. Ford not only filmed the scene, but perhaps too smart for his own good, he caught a load of shrapnel in his shoulder. Stunned for a moment, he was soon back on the job, shooting pictures and phoning his blow-by-blow account to Captain Simard's command post.

Another stick of bombs crashed down on D Battery. Captain Jean Buckner didn't see them coming . . . never knew what extra sense made him yell over the command phone, "Take cover." But he did, and his men ducked just in time—except Corporal Osa Currie, hanging on at the exposed height finder. He fell fatally wounded.

Yet war is a matter of wild contrasts. The same moment on Eastern Island found Warrant Officer Lucius dodging a barrage of knives, forks, cigars and cigarettes, as the first bombs there smashed the PX and mess hall. And even before the dust settled, one old-timer ran out from his shelter and gathered in all the cans of beer he could carry.

Now it was 6:40, and the dive bombers' turn. To Carpenter's Mate William Schleis, battling a fire on the roof of the seaplane hangar, it looked as though every plane was diving directly for him. Huddling against a heavy beam, he put his hands over his face, but peeked through his fingers and saw how it came out. The bombs just missed.

No such luck at the powerhouse on Eastern. It was a small building, heavily bunkered, but that didn't help. A perfectly aimed bomb landed squarely on the roof, wiping out the inside completely.

Major Benson's command post got it next. Seeing it go, Warrant Officer Lucius thought of the Major's invitation to spend the attack there, where it was "safe." Now Lucius was untouched in his slit trench, and Benson's CP was lost in dust and smoke. He rushed over to help, but it was too late—his friend was already dead in the rubble.

In a way it was hardest on the men underground. They could only listen and wonder. In the first-aid dugout on Sand Island, Pharmacist's Mate Miller tried to concentrate on his Murphy drip, while the light bulb blinked and swayed. Smelling the coffee, Lieutenant Commander A. E. Ady, the doctor in charge, cheerily announced he would like some. It wasn't fit to drink, but this seemed a brave attempt to keep up morale; so Miller poured them each a cup. They stood up and solemnly toasted each other. Then hanging onto a stanchion as the dugout rocked with explosions, they tried to drink it down. Still going strong, Dr. Ady launched into a series of jokes. Miller—now as sick as he was nervous—vaguely heard him ramble on, "Well, that reminds me of the old fat woman in Arkansas. . . ."

Outside, it was the Zeros' turn. In they swept—strafing the oil tanks, the gun pits, anything that moved. One fighter came so close to D Battery that Captain Buckner yearned for a full-choke shotgun. Another skimmed by F Battery as Sergeant Carl Fadick ducked low . . . but not low enough. A bullet smacked into the back of his helmet—then miraculously came out the front without even scratching him.

A man could be unlucky too. When a Zero swooped down on *PT 23* out in the lagoon, a bullet entered the bell of the boat's bull horn, made a 370° turn, and hit a machine gunner in the back while he was shooting at the plane.

In Colonel Shannon's command post a phone began ringing. It was some quartermaster who noticed that in the confusion no one had yet raised the American flag—shouldn't it be up? It was a morning of a million problems, but here was one where the answer was easy. "Yes," said Captain Mc-Glashan, "run her up!"

Pfc Billecheck, a handful of others raced out to the pole . . . snapped on the flag . . . and heedless of the Zeros streaking by, raised the colors for all to see.

The men fought back with everything they had. Not just the regular antiaircraft guns, but small arms too. Anything. "Deacon" Arnold used a Browning automatic rifle. A sailor at the Sand Island Fire Station had a Colt .45. At E Battery on Eastern, Pfc Roger Eaton popped away with his 1903 Springfield.

Of course, they usually missed . . . but not always. A Zero

staggered over the southwest tip of Sand Island, fell in a blazing heap 50 yards from H Company. A dive bomber caught another blast, careened wildly down—almost taking out the water tower—and crashed by the entrance to Captain Simard's command post.

But there was little anyone could do about the Zeros shooting at the few Marine fighters left. They were usually too far away. The men at E Battery watched helplessly as one Buffalo, returning with a badly sputtering engine, went after a circling strafer. The Marine, coming in quite low, tried to climb up under the Japanese. The Zero simply stood on its tail and executed a beautiful loop. A few short bursts, and the Buffalo fell in the ocean.

Two Zeros went after another Marine fighter off the northern edge of Eastern Island. The Buffalo began burning, and the pilot bailed out. The Zeros followed him all the way down, blazing away as he dangled in his chute . . . then strafing the sea where he landed.

Somehow a few of the Marine fighters limped home. Shot in both legs, Captain Carey "proved the hard way that you could fly an F4F with just the stick and no rudder." Lieutenant Canfield's flaps were gone, and when he touched ground his landing gear collapsed. Sliding to a stop, he dived into a trench while a Zero slashed away at the abandoned plane.

A crippled Buffalo came in low, a Zero in hot pursuit. With a last effort the Marine climbed a few feet, forcing the Japanese even lower. Every gun on Eastern Island seemed to open up. The Zero wavered, then slammed down burning on the runway. As it skidded along, Pfc Clester Scotten had a fleeting, indelible glimpse of the pilot throwing his arms over his face. Then he was lost from sight in the flames.

But the one they remembered best of all was the really "hot" pilot who wasn't content with bombing and strafing. Sweeping in alone, he turned bottoms-up and stunt-flew the runway upside down. He nearly got away with it. For long seconds the Marines watched in amazement, too surprised even to fire. Then the spell broke, and guns opened up everywhere. The antiaircraft finally got him, and he spun off into the lagoon.

LIEUTENANT Rokuro Kikuchi knew the end had come. The antiaircraft guns had found the range; now his horizontal bomber was bathed in fire and falling out of line. He pulled back the canopy and waved a last good-bye to his friends from the *Hiryu*.

The ground fire was far worse than expected. Not especially accurate—it rarely was—but the tremendous volume was enough to throw everyone off a little. Lieutenant Tomonaga's lead bomber took a near-miss at the moment of release, jarring the plane and hurting its accuracy. More serious, another burst punctured the left-wing gas tank.

Looking down, Lieutenant Hashimoto was fascinated by the activity below—especially the little PT boats that scurried around like water bugs on the ponds back home. But above all he noticed one thing: there were no planes left at Midway. The Japanese had attacked an "empty target." It reminded him of the way a snake sheds its skin; here the snake had crawled away, leaving only the cast-off skin behind.

Well, they must make the best of it. As planned, the *Hiryu* and *Kaga* units concentrated on Sand Island while the *Soryu* and *Akagi* took care of Eastern. If one could forget there were no planes, the results were not at all bad. Lieutenant Hashimoto's own squadron got a good hit among the oil tanks on Sand, and Lieutenant Ogawa's dive bombers really pasted the seaplane hangar. On Eastern, CPO Mori at first feared his bomb had missed—it seemed to land in some bushes —but a great explosion went up; so maybe he did some good after all.

By 6:48 they'd done all they could and were on their way to their rendezvous point. A few Zeros lingered, perhaps looking for some last easy kill, but by 7:01 they too were gone—disappearing, as they had come, into the northwest.

For Pfc Morris McCoy at E Battery, the sudden silence was worse than the bombs and the gunfire. Major Warner, the Air Force man, had never known such an eerie quiet. No sound whatsoever, except the occasional wail of a tern, or the mournful honk of a gooney bird.

In the dugouts the men waited . . . and waited . . . then cautiously began to emerge, blinking in the bright morning sun. Almost the first thing Ensign Jacoby saw was the wreckage of the Japanese plane that crashed near the entrance of Captain Simard's command post. The pilot's body was lying nearby, a symbolic Rising Sun flag tied around his waist. It was the very first "enemy" Jacoby had ever seen, but with the foe right before him, his mood was empty of hate. It was just another man, whose teeth were pushed in the way his would have been, had the tables been somehow reversed.

The all-clear sounded at 7:15, and Midway began to pick up the pieces. On Eastern Island Colonel Kimes radioed his VMF-221 pilots: "Fighters land, refuel by divisions, 5th Division first."

There was no answer. Kimes tried again. Still no answer. After trying several more times he began to understand, and new orders were sent: "All fighters land and reservice."

One by one they straggled in—six altogether. Added to the four that crash-landed during the raid, it meant only ten had survived the fight . . . and only two of these were in shape to fly. VMF-221 was virtually wiped out: of the 25 planes that took on the Japanese, 23 were shot down or put out of action.

"It is my belief," Captain Philip White observed in his action report, "that any commander that orders pilots out for combat in an F2A-3 [Brewster Buffalo] should consider the pilot as lost before leaving the ground." Understandably bitter, yet a commander must fight with what his country gives him.

In any case, VMF-221 was gone. Nor was that all. The thick black smoke rolling skyward told the story on Sand Island's fuel tanks, and the seaplane hangar was burning too. The Navy dispensary was a total loss; other buildings like the parachute loft were badly damaged. In the shell of the laundry, a five-gallon glass water cooler stood majestically intact amid the rubble and shredded shirts.

On Eastern the CP, the powerhouse, the mess hall and PX were all demolished, but what really hurt were the gas lines. True, they were always breaking down, but now some bomber had finished them for good—just when they were needed the most. Colonel Kimes shuddered to think of the bucket brigade he'd have to organize to refuel those thirsty B-17s.

Casualties were a happier story. Colonel Shannon's reproduction of the western front had paid off well. Thanks to all his sandbags and dugouts, there were only 11 dead and 18 wounded among the islands' defenders.

Best of all was the way they handled their planes. Only one was caught on the ground—an obsolete biplane used for utility work. The only other aircraft lost was a decoy plane made of packing crates and tin roofing. Dubbed the "JFU" ("Jap Fouler-Upper"), it played its role to perfection.

So they were still in business. But Midway's biggest fear lay in what was yet to come. When would the Japanese be back? What would they bring next time? Were the battleships and transports just over the horizon, waiting to close in? Even the cheerful Dr. Ady, casting aside his jokes and bad coffee, grabbed a Springfield rifle and headed for the beach.

T wo miles offshore a highly interested observer enjoyed the morning's events—the antiaircraft puffs, the diving planes, the column of smoke rolling up. Commander Tanabe was still watching Midway from the Japanese submarine *I-168*. He was, of course, at the periscope, and from this vantage point he gave the crew a running account of the whole attack. They were overjoyed, and a great cheer rang out when he described the fuel tanks blowing up.

Leading the air strike, Lieutenant Tomonaga knew better. It didn't matter that the damage was great; it didn't matter that the losses were small. What did matter was Midway's air strength . . . and that was still intact. Somehow the Americans had suspected something and cleared the field. Well, they couldn't stay up forever. Soon they'd have to land and refuel. . . .

At 7:00, as the Japanese planes turned for home, Tomonaga radioed the First Carrier Striking Force: "THERE IS NEED FOR A SECOND ATTACK."

CHAPTER 6

The Target Attacks

COMMANDER Genda wasn't surprised by Tomonaga's
call for another attack. From an earlier message he rather
suspected it might be necessary. And as Nagumo's operations
officer, he had no hesitation recommending the step.

The Striking Force had been at sea more than a week, and
not a word of warning about any U.S. ships. The morning's
search planes had been out two hours, and they hadn't found
anything either. Even the *Tone*'s No. 4 plane—the late one—
must be on its return leg by now. With no sign of the American fleet, it was folly to hoard the reserve air strength any
longer. They should use it to finish off Midway.

Admiral Kusaka hesitated. Nagumo's chief of staff was
always prepared to carry out a second strike—*if* the U.S.
Navy wasn't around. So far everyone had assumed it wasn't, but
nobody really knew. Until now it hadn't been crucial. If
wrong, they could adjust—but no longer. These were the only
reserves. He suddenly felt "a little like a hunter chasing two
hares at once." There was the United States fleet to catch . . .
now there was this call for another go at Midway.

As he talked it over with Genda and Admiral Nagumo, the
Striking Force raced on toward a point about 140 miles
northwest of Midway. Here it expected to start recovering

Tomonaga's planes a little after 8:00 A.M. The force was steaming in regular battle disposition: the carriers formed a sort of square box—*Akagi* leading on the right, followed by *Kaga; Hiryu* leading on the left, followed by *Soryu*—with the screen of battleships, cruisers and destroyers deployed around in a large, loose circle.

The crew were all at battle stations . . . had been since 5:32 when the *Nagara* first sighted that PBY. They never managed to shoot it down—or another that joined it—and plenty of contact reports must have gone back to Midway. Now there was nothing to do but wait and watch. On the *Akagi* alone, 20 lookouts stood on top of the bridge scanning the sky.

At 7:05 everything seemed to happen at once: a destroyer up forward hoisted a flag signal; the *Tone's* main battery opened fire; the *Akagi's* bugler began sounding the air-raid alarm. . . .

Ensign Earnest understood that the six TBFs would rendezvous, link up with the Marine bombers and fighters, and all go out together—but it wasn't that way at all. Once clear of Midway, the dashing Lieutenant Fieberling turned northwest and led his torpedo planes straight for the Japanese position.

About five minutes out there was a moment's excitement when they met an enemy fighter inbound for Midway. The Japanese made a single pass and continued on. The TBFs didn't even shoot back; they too had other business. Still, here was the enemy. Feeling they had been "blooded" and passed the test, Earnest and Ensign Charles Brannon, flying alongside, exchanged a salute, playfully spoofing the squadron's clenched-fist insignia.

They hurried on. For nearly an hour nothing happened—just a quiet trip at 4,000 feet through occasional puffy clouds. Around 7:00 Earnest noted what looked like a nondescript steamer plodding along below. Then another . . . then no end of them. He never saw anything like it. They were literally spread all over the ocean. In the distance he could make out two carriers steaming side by side and behind them still more ships—too far away to tell what they were. He had little time to drink it all in. Even as he called out the contact, his turret gunner Jay Manning warned that enemy fighters were closing in. At the same moment Lieutenant Fieberling signaled, and they all headed full throttle toward the two carriers. It was a long way down to 150 feet, with the Zeros snapping at them all the way.

At the second enemy pass, Manning's turret gun stopped firing. Working the tunnel gun, Radioman Harry Ferrier looked back over his shoulder. He was horrified to see Manning's body slumped at his post. In all his 18 years, Ferrier had never seen death before, and here in a single shattering instant he was staring right at it. All at once, he felt very scared and old.

He turned back to his own gun, only to find it useless. By now the TBF's hydraulic system was shot away, dropping the tail wheel and blocking his field of fire. Another burst raked the plane, and a bullet tore through the bill of the baseball cap he was wearing. It creased his scalp, and he fell back dazed.

In the cockpit Ensign Earnest was having his own troubles. First the radio went . . . next the compass . . . then the controls began to go. He glanced out the canopy—large holes appeared in the wing. A sliver of shrapnel caught his right jaw and there was blood everywhere.

At 200 feet he was still boring in, when another burst got the elevator wires. The stick went limp; nothing responded, and Earnest was sure this was the end. There was no hope left of getting the carrier—no hope of coming out alive—but he still had rudder control, and he would do something with that. He gave it a hard kick and swerved toward the only Japanese ship near him, a three-stack light cruiser. He let the torpedo go.

Now he was down to 30 feet and steeling himself for the crash. At this point some instinct made him put his hand on the wing tab—perhaps to adjust for hitting the water— and to his surprise the plane responded with an upward lift. In a flash he realized he could fly the plane this way, even if the stick was gone. As he later put it, "Suddenly it was a brand new ball game."

He zipped up and away from the scene. The Zeros, having written him off, were gone. Looking back, Earnest couldn't see what had happened to his torpedo or to the other TBFs. He was all alone. He had no compass, no radio, and was on the far side of the Japanese fleet. But he hadn't come this far to give up now. He headed for the morning sun, as Ferrier —the old man at 18—crawled up through the wreckage and nestled down behind him.

C LOSE behind the TBFs—so close he could see them going in for their attack—Captain Collins led his four B-26s. They too had flown out on their own: no rendezvous, no plans to work with the TBFs, B-17s or the Marines. They simply got their target and here they were.

The first thing Lieutenant Muri saw was some smoke on the horizon . . . then many destroyers . . . and there went his hopes for an easy morning. Studying the situation, he plucked a Chesterfield from a can he kept at his feet and put it in his mouth.

He was still fumbling for a match when a horde of Zeros appeared from nowhere. Captain Collins held his course, heading for the carriers he could now see at the center of the Japanese formation. Trouble was, the carriers were too well protected on the near side. It was necessary to curl around to their starboard to get a good crack at them. And that meant hedge-hopping a whole line of escorting destroyers.

But it had to be done. Veering to the left, Collins led his group over the escort, through a curtain of antiaircraft fire.

Then hard to the right again, and straight for the carriers. As they raced in at 200 feet, an unknown voice yelled out in one plane, "Boy, if mother could see me now!"

There was no formal attack plan—not even time for assignments—the four planes just made a mad rush at the leading carrier. Collins alternately climbed and dropped, throwing the Japanese aim off, and Muri did his best to follow. Now they were in the middle of the formation; as Muri's co-pilot Lieutenant Pete Moore glanced quickly around, every ship seemed a solid sheet of gunfire. The Japanese gunners would shoot at the water to see where the bullets hit. Using the splashes as tracers they would "walk" their fire right into the B-26s.

But they came on anyhow. Collins finally released at 800 yards and zoomed away to the right. Muri came hard behind, with the Zeros flying right into their own fleet's line of fire in a desperate effort to stop him. Bullets smashed the Plexiglas turret; a ricochet clipped Sergeant Gogoj's forehead.

Muri shouted to Moore to release the torpedo. But the improvised switch was something that Rube Goldberg might have invented—a trigger, a cable, a plug with innumerable prongs. Moore frantically squeezed the trigger, twisted the plug, still couldn't tell whether the torpedo was gone.

"Is it away?" Muri kept shouting.

"How the hell do I know?" Moore answered.

Keeping one hand on the controls, Muri fiddled with the plug and trigger too. They never felt the welcome surge of the plane rising, relieved of the torpedo. Later they learned that at some point they had indeed released it.

Right now, they could only hope, and there wasn't much time to do that. They were almost on top of the carrier. Banking hard, Muri flew straight down the middle of the flight deck. His bombardier Lieutenant Russ Johnson grabbed the nose gun and strafed in all directions. They had a brief, vivid glimpse of white-clad sailors scattering for cover.

Pulling out, Muri caught a fleeting glimpse of Lieutenant

Herbie Mayes's plane boring in too. It came all the way, almost hit the carrier, careened into the sea alongside. None of the group ever saw what happened to the fourth B-26.

No time to look, either. The Zeros were diving at them again. They riddled the landing gear, the fuel tanks, the propeller blades, the radio, the entire top edge of one wing. They wounded Pfc Ashley in the tail turret and Corporal Mello at the side guns. With an extra surge of effort Mello crawled up to the cockpit, covered with blood, to report the plane was on fire and "everybody's hit back there." Lieutenant Moore scrambled back, put out the fires, gave sulfa to Ashley and manned a gun.

At one point Muri thought to himself that the plane was really gone, and he'd rather splash than be shot down in flames. He moved to ditch the ship, but as sometimes happens, an extra ounce of reserve spirit seemed to grasp him and hold back his hand.

Finally the fighters broke off. Heading for Midway, Muri realized he still hadn't lit the cigarette he put in his mouth just when the Zeros struck. But it was almost too late now. In his excitement, he had bitten it in two and swallowed half of it.

Thinking back, it was ironic that the only moment he felt safe was when he was directly over the Japanese carrier. Flying down her flight deck, he was simply too close to be shot at. Even so, it was anything but comforting to see that large Japanese battle flag streaming from her mast. After all those newsreels, here it really was. Nothing ever looked bigger.

LIEUTENANT Ogawa couldn't get over how big the white star looked on those B-26s. So much larger than he expected. Until these American torpedo planes appeared, he had spent an easy morning policing the skies above the Striking Force with two other Zeros in his unit. The PBYs were

The target. Midway Islands, looking west, as seen just before the war. Eastern Island lies in the foreground; Sand Island to the rear. Although the whole atoll amounted to only three square miles of dry land, its capture was the goal of one of the mightiest fleets ever assembled. The Japanese armada totaled some 190 ships altogether.

Author's collection

Navy Depart

The Japanese commanders. Adm
Isoroku Yamamoto (left) was the l
liant Commander in Chief of the
perial Combined Fleet. A dai
gambler, he wanted Midway pa
to strengthen Japan's defenses,
mainly to lure the weakened U
fleet into all-out battle. Vice Adm
Chuichi Nagumo (above) would p
vide the spearhead of the thr
Everything depended on his Strik
Force of four powerful carriers.

e U.S. commanders. Ad-
ral Chester W. Nimitz
bove, left) guided the des-
y of the U.S. Pacific Fleet,
sed at Pearl Harbor. Stand-
; with him is Rear Admiral
ymond A. Spruance, who
Task Force 16. Rear Ad-
ral Frank Jack Fletcher
ght) handled Task Force
and was in tactical com-
nd during the battle.

The *Akagi* (above) was flagship of Admiral Nagumo's powerful Striking Force. She and the *Kaga* (below) were huge, unwieldy ships, originally laid down as battle cruisers. Their horizontal funnel arrangement made for miserable living conditions; smoke was constantly seeping into the crew's quarters. They were, nevertheless, great sentimental favorites within the fleet.

The *Hiryu* (above) and *Soryu* (below) rounded out Nagumo's force. Although somewhat smaller than the other two carriers, they were faster, more powerful, and much larger than generally thought. On all four ships the pilots played *shogi,* wrote letters, and relaxed in utter confidence as the fleet pounded steadily closer to Midway.

Thanks to a brilliant job of code-breaking, the American high command was thoroughly aware of the Japanese plans. Reinforcements were rushed to Midway, and the Marine defenders dug in for a last-ditch fight. Here a sun-baked gun crew at E Battery, 6th Defense Battalion, practices during the tense wait before the attack.

Army B-17s were an important addition to Midway's defenses. It was hoped these tough, long-range bombers would give Midway a striking power of its own. Bearing jaunty names like *Yankee Doodle* and *Knucklehead*, they reflected the exuberance of the young men who flew them. Here one is taking off from Eastern Island.

Lieutenant Commander John C. Waldron, skipper of Torpedo 8, typified the fierce determination of all the torpedo pilots at Midway. Against the heaviest odds, they recklessly drove home their attacks. Including those based on the atoll, 42 out of 51 torpedo planes were lost in strikes against Nagumo's carriers.

The day's fighting began with the Japanese attack on Midway itself. As over 100 planes bombed and strafed the base, famed movie director John Ford filmed the action. The above shot is taken from the superb documentary that resulted. Below is the destruction on Sand Island photographed immediately after the attack.

At sea the U.S. fleet quietly waited in ambush. First on the scene was Task Force 16, led by the carrier *Enterprise*. This view (not taken at Midway) was snapped from a dive bomber just taking off.

The other carrier in Task Force 16 was the *Hornet*, new and with an air group not yet tried in combat. These ships were soon joined by the *Yorktown* at a rendezvous symbolically called "Point Luck."

June 4, 1942. The Japanese carriers have been located, and on the *Enterprise* Torpedo 6 prepares to take off. Only four of these planes ever came back. The *Hornet* and *Yorktown* torpedo squadrons took even greater losses during the morning's action.

The *Hornet*'s Torpedo 8 was virtually wiped out: all 15 planes lost, 29 of 30 men. Of the pilots in this squadron picture, only one survived: Ensign George Gay, fourth from left, front row.

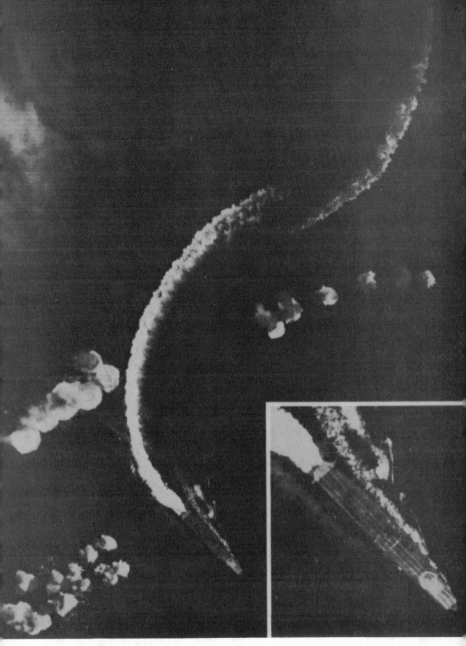

Meanwhile the Japanese carriers were coming under heavy attack. Here one of them (probably the *Hiryu*) dodges bombs dropped by the B-17s. Close-up shows her flight deck, including two Zeros by the portside island. Later the U.S. Navy dive bombers struck, knocking out three carriers within an incredible six minutes.

Navy Department

The U.S. fleet was soon attacked too. Around noon the *Yorktown* was hit by dive bombers

The *Yorktown* survived the dive bombers but not a second attack, this time by the *Hiryu's* torpedo planes. Hit twice, she lost all power and listed 26° to port. Revenge was swift—the *Hiryu* soon paid the price—but not before the *Yorktown* was abandoned and out of the fight.

Navy Department

On the morning of June 5 the *Yorktown* was still afloat. Efforts to salvage her failed the following day when the Japanese submarine *I-168* pumped two more torpedoes into her hull.

At 5:00 A.M. June 7 the *Yorktown* finally rolled over and sank. This picture of the end, believed never before published, was taken by her boiler division officer, Lieutenant (j.g.) Charles Cundiff, from one of the stand-by destroyers.

Courtesy of Charles R. Cundiff

Navy Department

All through June 5-6 the U.S. fleet pursued the fleeing Japanese. Above, Navy dive bombers attack the heavy cruisers *Mogami* and *Mikuma*. Below, the shattered *Mikuma*, photographed by Lieutenant (j.g.) Cleo J. Dobson shortly before she sank on the 6th.

Navy Department

Courtesy of Shizuo Fukui

The wreckage of Japanese hopes. The smoldering hulk of the *Hiryu* wallows in a calm sea in the early hours of June 5. These pictures were taken from a Japanese scout plane sent by Admiral Yamamoto to investigate the situation. The lower photo, published here for the first time, clearly shows how the carrier's forward elevator was hurled against the front of the bridge.

Courtesy of Shizuo Fukui

gone—at least temporarily—and they had little to do but orbit with similar units from the other three carriers.

Then unexpectedly Ogawa's No. 2 man began firing his machine guns to attract attention. Ogawa looked and saw two separate flights of torpedo planes approaching through a hole in the clouds. The rest of the Combat Air Patrol saw them too, and Zeros began diving from all directions. Most piled into the leading flight of six TBFs; the rest, including Ogawa's unit, headed for the other four American planes: the B-26s with the big white stars.

The carrier crews watched in excitement as the Zeros methodically picked off the TBFs. On the *Akagi* a storm of hand-clapping went up with every splash. It was almost like a theater audience watching a superbly skillful performance —which in a sense it was. None of the TBFs got close enough to make an effective drop, and five of the six were shot down well clear of the carriers.

With the B-26s it was another matter. The Zeros got on them, but they had more speed than anyone guessed, and they really knew how to use it. One of them fell, but the others kept coming . . . right at the *Akagi*, leading the right side of the box formation. But the *Hiryu* was in danger too, and on both ships men watched breathlessly as the torpedoes dropped. Happily they were very slow. The *Hiryu*, especially, dodged them easily—some sailors even picked one off with a machine gun.

The highly exposed *Akagi* had more trouble. At 7:11 Captain Aoki gave her a hard right rudder, heading into the approaching planes. As the first one dropped, he made a full turn to escape a torpedo to starboard, then another full turn to escape a second torpedo to port. All within two minutes.

More was to come. As the B-26s pulled out, heavy strafing ripped the *Akagi*'s deck, killed two men, knocked out the No. 3 AA gun, cut the transmitting antenna. And just when it looked as if the danger was over, the last B-26 didn't pull out at all: instead it hurtled straight for the *Akagi*'s bridge. No one saw

how it could miss. Admiral Kusaka felt sure they were done
for. He instinctively ducked as the plane came right at him.
But it didn't hit: it cleared the bridge by inches, cartwheel-
ing into the sea just off the port side. The whole bridge let
out a yell of relief that meant the same in any language:
"Wow!"

A shaken Kusaka found himself strangely moved. He thought
only Japanese pilots did things like that. He had no idea
who this steadfast American was, but there on the bridge
of the *Akagi* he silently said a prayer for him.

To the practical eye of Lieutenant Ogawa, it was really
not a very professional effort—any of it. There was no coordination between the TBFs and the B-26s . . . the torpedoes
were dropped too far out . . . the planes all approached from
one side. No wonder they didn't hit anything.

Yet the attack accomplished more than Ogawa knew. It
ended all doubts about a second strike on Midway. That was
where these planes came from—Nagumo needed no more
convincing. At 7:15 the Admiral ordered his second attack
wave to rearm: the torpedo planes to shift over to bombs,
the dive bombers to switch from armor-piercing to instant-
contact missiles. This was relatively easy for the *Hiryu* and
Soryu—they were supplying the dive bombers this time—
but on the *Akagi* and *Kaga* it meant a back-breaking job.
The air crews rushed forward, lowered the torpedo planes to
the hangar deck and began making the switch. It was a frantic scene: they hoped to get the second wave rearmed and
into the air before Tomonaga got back.

They were hard at it when a startling message arrived from
the *Tone's* No. 4 plane, now on the dog-leg of its 300-mile
search to the east. At 7:28 it reported: "Sight what appears
to be 10 enemy surface ships in position bearing 10 degrees
distance, 240 miles from Midway. Course 150 degrees, speed
over 20 knots."

Surface ships. So they were out there after all . . . and
well within striking range. If Chuichi Nagumo had been more

of a philosopher and less of an admiral, he might have pondered the fate that put the *Tone*'s plane a half-hour behind schedule. If there had been no catapult trouble—if only it had been on time—he would have known about this American fleet before Tomonaga asked for another strike at Midway. Then there would have been no doubt about his course: go for the ships right away. But as matters stood, it was no longer that easy. His torpedo planes were now belowdecks, being reloaded with bombs.

The Admiral shuffled his plans as best he could. He suspended the second strike on Midway, and at 7:45 signaled new orders to the Striking Force: "Prepare to carry out attacks on enemy fleet units. Leave torpedoes on those attack planes which have not as yet changed to bombs."

Next step would depend on what the Americans had out there. The *Tone*'s pilot was exasperatingly vague. "Ten surface ships" certainly didn't say much. Were there any carriers? If so, they must be hit right away. If not, maybe this enemy force could wait. Over half the torpedo planes were already switched to bombs: if the Americans had only cruisers and destroyers, Admiral Kusaka felt it might be better to go through with the second strike on Midway, then go after the ships. But to decide, they must know what they were up against. At 7:47 Nagumo brusquely radioed the search plane: "ASCERTAIN SHIP TYPES AND MAINTAIN CONTACT."

Despite their quandary, there was no reason to panic. They had plenty of strength; all they really needed was a little time. Time to switch back to torpedoes and armor-piercing bombs, if there were carriers around. Time to finish changing to land bombs, if they were going to hit Midway again. Time to regroup the ships scattered by the enemy torpedo attacks. Time to replenish and tighten up the air patrol. Time to recover Tomonaga's planes. And, above all, time to think and plan intelligently, without too many twists and unexpected pressures.

Nagumo was still waiting for more details from the *Tone*'s

plane when, at 7:50, the *Soryu's* air cover unit suddenly reported "about 15" single-engine dive bombers coming in from the southeast.

CORPORAL Eugene Card felt as though a bar of ice-coated lead were in his stomach. One consolation: in three hours it would all be over, one way or another. It was also good to have Captain Fleming flying the plane—a man so cool he took a nap during the on-again, off-again confusion at Midway just before VMSB-241 set out on its mission to bomb the Japanese carriers.

Now at last they were on their way, with Captain Fleming serving as navigator for the 16 SBDs led by Major Henderson. The other planes in the squadron—the 11 old Vindicators —would come separately under Major Norris. They were just too slow to operate with the rest.

Henderson's group had enough problems already. Thirteen of the 16 pilots had never flown an SBD until a few days ago. Ten of them had been in the squadron only a week; they hardly knew each other and had little time to practice together. Like Card, most of the gunners were inexperienced. It was because of their greenness as a group that Major Henderson decided not to dive-bomb the Japanese, but to glide-bomb instead. It required less skill—but no less courage, for the planes would be exposed that much longer.

Heading for the enemy position, they kept in tight formation at 9,000 feet except for Henderson himself. He flew detached, herding them along like an industrious shepherd dog. Craning his neck, Card could see the rest of the planes, stepped down in a giant staircase. Feeling a surge of new confidence, he looked over at Lieutenant Al Tweedy's plane and gave Tweedy's gunner, Sergeant Elza Raymond, the old four-oh sign. Raymond grinned and waved back.

Around 7:50 Lieutenant Daniel Iverson swung by and pointed down to the left. Card looked but couldn't see anything. Fleming broke in on the intercom: "We've made contact. There's a ship at ten o'clock." Card looked again and sure enough, beneath a large hole in the clouds he saw a long, slender, black ship. It was heading for Midway and making knots.

The SBDs continued on, the clouds rapidly breaking up. Through the holes he could see more and more of these slim black ships, all heading in the same direction. Then a sight he would never forget. Through a large clear space he saw four carriers almost side by side, and near them a battleship with a pagoda-like superstructure. He watched utterly fascinated as the carriers turned in unison and began launching planes.

At 7:55 Henderson's voice came calmly over the radio: "Attack two enemy CV on port bow. . . ." The SBDs began circling down.

"Here they come!" Captain Fleming yelled over the intercom. Card caught a glimpse of two streaks of smoke flying past the starboard wing; then a fighter flashed by, climbing almost straight up. Lieutenant Harold Schlendering, flying nearby, had a longer look and wondered at the odd white smoke rings made by the Zeros' guns. As the first shell fragments slapped into Lieutenant Tom Moore's plane, Moore thought to himself, "Here comes a hunk of the Sixth Avenue el."

Major Henderson's left wing began to burn. He fought it all the way, but he was soon out of control, plunging toward the sea. Off to the right, Corporal Card saw fragments from some other plane tumbling over and floating back like leaves in a breeze. A parachute blossomed out, but there was no time to see who it was.

Captain Elmer Glidden took over the lead, heading for a bank of clouds that might give greater protection during the descent. The Zeros hounded them all the way, while the Marine gunners did their best to fight back. Corporal McFeeley, flying with Captain Blain, grew so excited he fired through the tail of his own plane. Private Charles Huber found his gun hopelessly jammed, but Lieutenant Moore told him to aim it at them anyhow. Huber did, and put on such a panto-mime of resolution that the Zeros kept a respectful distance.

Lieutenant Doug Rollow's rear-seat man Reed Ramsey tried a different sort of guile. He knew that the Japanese liked to capitalize on the Marines' careless habit of throwing empty ammunition cans overboard. Whenever a Zero saw this, it would quickly close in, since it took about 30 seconds for the Marine to reload. Ramsey decided that two could play this game. With his gun fully loaded, he threw out a beer can. As usual a Zero rushed over—and Ramsey got a hit at point-blank range.

Soon they had other troubles. Corporal Card heard some-thing go "Wuf!" (It sounded, he later stressed, just the way a person would say "Wuf" in a normal voice.) Then he heard it again, and again. Big, black, soft-looking balls of smoke began to appear. It meant that they were now within anti-aircraft range too.

A moment's relief when they hit the cloud bank—then worse than ever when they broke out on the other side. At 2,000 feet they nosed down and began their final run. Now there was nothing between them and the enemy, twisting and turning below.

Face to face with the Japanese carriers at last, every man had his own most vivid impression. For Lieutenant Moore it was the brilliant Rising Sun insignia on the flight deck. For Lieutenant Rollow it was the scattering crewmen. For Lieu-tenant Iverson it was the solid ring of fire that encircled the flight deck as every gun blazed away.

Captain Fleming cut loose with a blast of his own, saw a whole gun crew topple over. Facing aft from his rear-seat position, Corporal Card could see very little, but he could hear more than enough. To the "wufs" of the antiaircraft there was now added the steady crackle of small-arms fire. The SBD lurched—"Somebody threw a bucket of bolts in the prop." Small holes appeared all over the cockpit and a thousand needles pricked his right ankle. Swooping in, the Marines made their drops—Rollow at 400 feet . . . Schlendering at 500 feet . . . Fleming at 300 feet. There were ten of them left altogether. Columns of smoke and water billowed up, nearly hiding the carriers from view. It was a conservative pilot indeed who didn't think he got at least a near-miss.

Then away, skimming the waves to make it harder for the Zeros and the ships' guns. Nosing down to a few feet above the sea, Lieutenant Rollow suddenly faced huge towers of water shooting up in front of him. He was heading directly for the main battery of a Japanese battleship. He yanked the stick back and the SBD popped to 2,000 feet. As he tried to get his controls set again, a Zero came by. That should have been the end, but nothing happened. Apparently out of ammunition, the Japanese pilot merely gave him a casual wave.

Captain Fleming was running into still more trouble. Pulling out from his drop, another "bucket of nails" hit the prop. Something hard kicked Corporal Card's left leg to one side, and more holes appeared all over the cockpit. Then as the plane leveled off, Card caught his only good look at the carrier —a "writhing monster" bristling with fast-firing guns, all pointing straight up, a steady jet of flame pouring from each.

The ice in his stomach had melted; hot anger was boiling up. The plane was hit; he was hit; he couldn't see how they'd ever get out of this alive; the only hope was they'd take a few Japanese with them.

COMMANDER Fuchida couldn't understand why those American planes came in that way. They were too low for dive bombing, too high for torpedoes. Those long shallow dives gave the Zeros a field day.

But certainly they never wavered. Concentrating on the *Hiryu* off to port, one after another they swooped in and dropped. Teiichi Makishima, a civilian newsreel photographer on the *Akagi*, watched with dismay as the *Hiryu* disappeared in a dense cloud of black smoke. It took forever, but finally she emerged. She was still at full speed, her white bow wave glittering in the sun. The men watching from the *Akagi* let out a shout of relief.

On the *Hiryu* it had been a frantic minute as Captain Tomeo Kaku tried to outguess the swooping planes. At 8:08 the ship was completely bracketed by four bombs. At 8:12 another near-miss landed just off to port. Down in the engine room Ensign Hisao Mandai shuddered as the ship took a terrific jolt. Topside they got a dose of strafing too—four men killed, several more wounded.

As Commander Amagai watched from the *Kaga*, his own ship's lookout suddenly shouted, "Enemy planes, quarter!" The warning came none too soon. A final three U.S. bombers —either a separate division or planes somehow diverted from the main target—glided in from the port quarter, dropping three bombs just off the stern of the ship.

Then it was over. The Striking Force had done it again: a third American attack smashed with hardly a scratch to themselves. Satisfying, but at the moment Admiral Nagumo had other matters on his mind. He still needed to know what sort of ships the *Tone's* No. 4 plane had seen. All during the American glide-bombing attack he waited for some sort of answer. At 7:58 the search plane finally came on the air again, but it still didn't identify the enemy ships. It merely reported that they had changed course from 150° to 180°.

The whole staff fumed. What could they do with that, unless they knew what they were up against? At 8:00 an exasperated Nagumo needled the pilot again: "Advise ship types." At 8:09 he finally got an answer. A new message from the *Tone's* plane reported: "Enemy is composed of five cruisers and five destroyers."

So there were no carriers. Relief swept the flag bridge. The intelligence officer Commander Ono said he knew it all the time. Admiral Kusaka felt it would now be safe to get on with the second strike at Midway.

But this brought up a new complication. The three American attacks did no damage, but they certainly disrupted the fleet. The neat box formation was gone; the carriers were spread all over the place. To cover them adequately, many more fighters were needed. As Lieutenant Shindo, commanding the Combat Air Patrol, used up his reserves, he began drawing on the fighters assigned to the second attack wave. Now there were none left to support any strike it made.

Of course it could be remedied. All they needed was a little time to regroup the fleet—reassemble that compact box formation—then a little more time to refuel the fighters that would be freed from the air umbrella. The staff was still discussing it when at 8:14 the *Tone*'s port guns opened up—signaling a brand-new danger from the sky. . . .

"WE SHOULD be sighting them now," said Lieutenant Bill Adams, the lumber salesman turned navigator, as Lieutenant Colonel Walter Sweeney led his 15 B-17s toward Nagumo's position. It was 7:32, and more than an hour had passed since they were diverted from another blow at the transports to hitting the carriers instead.

Adams couldn't have timed it better. Next moment Colonel Sweeney pointed through the broken clouds, and there in the distance were the white wakes of many ships. To Captain Don Kundinger, piloting one of the planes, it was an astonishing sight: "a panoramic view of the greatest array of surface vessels any of us had ever seen—they seemed to stretch endlessly from horizon to horizon."

But which were the carriers? Leading the group in, Sweeney looked hard . . . saw nothing. It was all so difficult. None of these Army fliers had any experience in ship identification. Broken clouds were everywhere, making it still harder to see. Ships would pop out, then disappear again before anyone could get a decent look.

Most important of all, there was this matter of height. After several close calls attacking the transports at 8,000 feet,

Sweeney felt his men would be sitting ducks if they tried to do the same against carriers. So now they were coming in at 20,000 feet—quite a distance for an inexperienced eye to pick out anything.

But they could see the Japanese were busy. Enemy ships were turning in evasion maneuvers. Yet no antiaircraft fire was coming their way. It took some extra squinting, but finally the Army fliers understood. There, far below, Major Henderson's glide bombers were going in.

The B-17s continued searching. Then suddenly Captain Cecil Faulkner spotted something. Beneath a thin wisp of clouds steamed a ship—not an ordinary ship, but one with an oblong shape, a flat yellow deck, a Rising Sun insignia painted in the middle. Then he saw another like it . . . then two more. There was no doubt what they were.

No time to lose. Sweeney was far ahead, probing the northwest, so Faulkner signaled the other two bombers in his unit, and they left the formation to attack on their own. By now Captain Carl Wuertele had also found the carriers, and so had Captain Paul Payne in the *Yankee Doodle*. It was Payne who finally got the word to Sweeney, still searching to the northwest. The Colonel told him to start attacking and hurried to the scene with the rest of the planes.

Officially the strike began at 8:14, but it was a more ragged affair than that might suggest. The three-plane elements bombed pretty much on their own, and in several cases the planes attacked individually. But what they lacked in finesse they made up in enthusiasm. As the *Hel-En-Wings* unloaded its bombs, Captain Wuertele's crew whooped in triumph.

The Japanese gunners replied immediately, and the very first round exploded just to the right of Sweeney's plane, smashing the co-pilot's window. To the co-pilot Lieutenant Wessman, it underlined the wisdom of such high-level bombing. "From then on," he recalled, "all of us were sorry we stopped at 20,000 feet."

Next some Zeros appeared. Three ganged up on Captain

Faulkner, ripped his fuselage, disabled his No. 4 engine. Another dueled with Captain Payne but never really closed for a fight. The Zero pilots always respected the B-17, and today was no exception.

It all added up to a hot ten minutes, but no serious damage. The only casualty was Captain Faulkner's tail gunner, who suffered a wounded index finger.

The Army fliers were jubilant. The price seemed small indeed. The carriers looked finished. Captain Faulkner thought his group got at least two hits; Captain Wuertele and Lieutenant Colonel Brooke Allen each claimed one. Colonel Sweeney's own crew were no less optimistic: they felt sure all eight bombs were on target, and the carrier's stern rose up most convincingly. A shrewd student of human nature, Sweeney cut back on all these claims in his official report, but he felt at least one of the carriers must have been hit.

CAPTAIN Aoki watched with dismay from the *Akagi*. There were so many columns of water around the *Soryu* he couldn't see her at all. He thought she might well be sunk. The *Hiryu* was in trouble too, also lost in spray and smoke. Everyone was of course firing back, but the B-17s were too high to bring down. The Striking Force would just have to sweat it out.

None found it harder than the fliers returning from the Midway strike. They arrived back, by chance, just at this moment. Waved off their carriers, they orbited uselessly around, praying that the bombs would miss. For Lieutenant Tomonaga there was an extra problem: he was very low on gas, thanks to the hit that holed his wing tank at Midway.

By 8:20 the danger was over. The B-17s flew off; the *Soryu* and *Hiryu* emerged untouched; and the orbiting planes waited for the signal to start landing. On the *Akagi* Admiral Nagumo had good reason to feel satisfied. Four times the Americans had attacked; four times they were beaten off. For over an hour the Striking Force had taken everything the enemy could give—and every ship remained intact.

At this moment a new message arrived for Nagumo from the *Tone*'s No. 4 plane, still shadowing the U.S. task force: "The enemy is accompanied by what appears to be a carrier bringing up the rear."

This was a stunning surprise. The last thing anyone expected. Originally—when the *Tone*'s plane first reported the American force—Admiral Kusaka had half-suspected there might be a carrier out there. But that was 52 minutes ago. Surely if there was one, the pilot would have seen it almost right away —nobody could miss anything that big for long. Yet the fellow had sent several messages since then, and never a hint of a carrier. Now here he was saying there was one after all.

No more thoughts about a second attack on Midway. They must strike that carrier instead. The only question was when. Should they attack immediately? Or should they wait till they switched the second wave back to torpedoes and armor-piercing bombs? Or until they recovered Tomonaga's planes? Or until they refueled the fighters that had been flying air cover? Or maybe some combination of these possibilities?

Nagumo's staff had barely posed these questions when one more unexpected development occurred. Still another group of American planes—the fifth that morning—was sighted flying toward them.

I⊤ ALL seemed remote and unreal to Lieutenant Ringblom, approaching at 13,000 feet with Major Norris's group of 11 Marine Vindicators. Just out of flight school, fresh from the states, it was hard to believe that here he was, flying against a real enemy. He was too inexperienced to appreciate his predicament either, pitting this ancient plane against the First Carrier Striking Force.

But his education was beginning. At 8:17 he sighted the Japanese ships through the broken clouds, and almost immediately three Zeros turned up. They seemed to be toying with the Vindicators as they nonchalantly did vertical rolls right through the formation.

Getting down to business, one of them poured a few bursts into Lieutenant Daniel Cummings's plane, last in the Marine group. Cummings heard his gunner stop firing and called to him, but there was no answer. Nor could one have been expected. Private Henry I. Starks of Springfield, Illinois, was really a mechanic, not a gunner. But during the great build-up Colonel Kimes had run out of gunners, and Starks had volunteered. When he climbed into Cummings's plane that morning, he had never fired a machine gun in the air, and had only been in the plane three times. He had no chance to learn to be a good shot, or even protect himself, but he died, giving his best.

As more Zeros arrived, Major Norris led his men on a fast shallow dive toward some clouds. On the far side was a line of ships—no one could say what type. Sweeping down into the overcast, he radioed his order to attack and calmly instructed every one that the way home would be 140°; expect to get there around 9:00.

Bursting out of the clouds at 2,000 feet, Norris found a battleship and cruiser directly below. There was also a carrier on the horizon, but the Japs were throwing everything at him, and he figured he could never reach it. Picking the battle-ship instead, he peeled off into a much steeper dive. Everyone else followed.

Plunging down, Lieutenant Ringblom had a fleeting impression of orange gun flashes all over the ship. Tracers whipped by; balls of black smoke everywhere. To his astonishment, he saw identical round holes, about six inches in diameter, appear in each of his ailerons. Some enemy gunner had fused the shells for the wrong altitude, and they had passed right through without exploding.

One after another the Marines released at 500 feet, then skimmed away, hugging the water for protection. Pulling out, Lieutenant Sumner Whitten found himself between two lines of Japanese ships. All were firing hard, some aiming their main batteries at the sea to make a wall of water that might slap down low-flying planes. To his gunner, Sergeant Frank Zelnis, Whitten was staying around much too long—he seemed to be almost sight-seeing. Zelnis finally called out, "You dropped your bomb; let's get the hell out of here before we get hit."

Still sticking close to the water, the Marines headed for home. For 20 minutes Lieutenant Ringblom was never higher than 50 feet above the sea. A Zero trailed behind, making occasional passes, but Ringblom somehow escaped. Certainly it must have been luck, for he tried no tactics at all. He flew a straight steady line all the way. He was now much better educated in war, but still too scared and ignorant as a pilot to even look back.

CAPTAIN Tamotsu Takama handled the *Haruna* beautifully. The Americans pressed home their attack, yet the old battleship managed to dodge everything. Two near-misses were logged at 8:29, but the damage control officer Lieutenant Commander Yoshino reported they were nothing to worry about.

On the *Akagi*'s bridge, Admiral Kusaka once again felt a surge of relief. For the fifth time they had come safely through an American attack. And what a variety! Torpedo planes, B-26s, B-17s, those curious glide bombers. And as if these weren't enough, a submarine was reported to be poking around too. It all made Kusaka think of *Hiruko-Daikokuten*, the legendary Japanese demon with three heads and six arms.

It was hard to concentrate on other matters, but a new message from the *Tone*'s No. 4 plane made it more imperative than ever to do something about that American carrier lurking to the east. At 8:30 the search pilot reported two more cruisers a little to the west of the ships sighted earlier, and trailing them by perhaps 20 miles. It suggested the possibility of an additional enemy task force. Yet most of the second wave were still equipped with land bombs; the torpedo planes were still belowdecks; Tomonaga's force was still waiting to come in; the fighters were still low on fuel. What was best to do?

"Consider it advisable to launch attack force immediately," signaled Rear Admiral Tamon Yamaguchi from the *Hiryu* shortly after 8:30. Yamaguchi was leading the Second Carrier Division (*Hiryu* and *Soryu*), and he found it incredible that Nagumo had done nothing yet. He knew what *he* would do: strike immediately with everything that would fly. Whether they carried the right kind of bombs, whether they had torpedoes or not, whether they had fighters or no fighters—nothing meant as much as getting in that first blow.

His reaction was predictable. Yamaguchi was one of those aggressive young leaders who embodied the new spirit of the Imperial Navy. Hand-picked from the start, he had been carefully brought along every inch of his career—including duty in Washington and graduate courses at an American university (in his case, Princeton). Now gossip had him someday succeeding the great Yamamoto as Chief of the Combined Fleet. Even so, in the strait-laced Japanese Navy it took a rare degree of independence—and exasperation—to indicate so openly his impatience with his chief.

He was willing to take that risk too. Flashed by the *Hiryu*'s blinker, his message was quickly picked up by the destroyer *Nowaki* . . . relayed to the *Akagi* . . . and delivered to the Chief of Staff Admiral Kusaka.

No, thought Kusaka, it would just be throwing away planes to follow Yamaguchi's advice. Launching an attack immediately meant sending the bombers alone, for the fighters had all been used up protecting the carriers, and to send bombers without fighter support was really inviting disaster. Look what had happened to the unescorted American planes during the past hour and a half.

Instead of going off half-cocked, it would be far wiser, he felt, to delay a little and do the job right. First, recover both Tomonaga's planes and the second-attack-wave fighters that had been diverted to combat air patrol . . . next, rearm and refuel them all. And while that was going on, they could also be switching the second wave back to torpedoes and armor-piercing bombs. With proper coordination, they could then launch everything at once for an all-out assault on the U.S. task force. This was his recommendation to Admiral Nagumo.

In the end, as always, Nagumo turned to Commander Genda. What did he think? Genda was most concerned about the planes just back from Midway, now orbiting above the carriers. They had been in the air four hours—all were nearly out of gas. They should be recovered before anything else was done—and that included launching this new attack.

If Tomonaga's planes splashed with empty tanks, scores of top pilots would be lost, affecting not only Midway but the whole schedule of operations planned for the months ahead. On the other hand, it would delay matters only 30 minutes to recover this force. Then they could go ahead with the second attack, supported by such fighters as might be ready at that time. So he too was against Yamaguchi's recommendation.

As usual when Genda spoke, there was no dissent.

"Here we go again," laughed Commander Shogo Masuda, air officer on the *Akagi*, as orders came to clear the flight deck and rearm once more. On all four carriers the hangar deck crews, in T-shirts and shorts, swarmed over the planes, unloading the bombs they had just put on. Dollies rolled up with the torpedoes and armor-piercing bombs again, and the job began of shackling them back in place. There was no time for routine procedures—or even precautions. As the land bombs were taken off, nobody took them back to the magazines. They were simply rolled out of the way and left lying on the deck.

With the flight decks cleared, the four carriers turned into the wind. At 8:37 signal flags flew from every mast, telling Tomonaga's planes to start coming in. On the *Hiryu* a bomber wobbled down to a one-wheel landing, the pilot passing out as it rolled to a stop. Though shot in the leg by an American fighter, Lieutenant Hiroharu Kadano had somehow managed to keep formation, make his run and get back anyhow.

Another bomber circled the *Kaga*, its landing gear still up. The crew waved red flags, everything, at the pilot, but he seemed so slow to understand. Finally he did get the point, lowered his wheels and came on in. When the plane stopped, they found Air Petty Officer Tanaka half-conscious and shot in the head. Spirit alone must have carried him back.

And, of course, there were those who didn't get back at all— 11 altogether.

Climbing down from his bomber on the *Soryu*, CPO Juzo Mori joined the other pilots on the flight deck just below the bridge. They stood around swapping experiences, while the division commander Lieutenant Abe went up to report to Captain Yanagimoto.

Nobody had time to listen. All the officers were busy preparing to attack the American carrier. The Midway report could wait. On the *Soryu* the air officer simply told CWO Tatsuya Otawa that he better get something to eat right away . . . he'd be needed again soon enough.

Even Lieutenant Tomonaga, commanding the whole attack, found it hard to make his report. Going to the *Hiryu*'s bridge with Lieutenant Hashimoto, he found both Captain Kaku and Admiral Yamaguchi absorbed in plans for the new strike. Shrugging off Nagumo's blunt rejection of his advice, Yamaguchi was now trying to get the *Hiryu*'s and *Soryu*'s horizontal bombers (just back from Midway) reloaded with torpedoes. They could then serve as still another attack wave against the U.S. task force.

It was no time to listen to a battle report. He quickly drafted Tomonaga and Hashimoto into the new project, and they rushed off to set the wheels in motion. Hopefully they could have the planes rearmed, refueled and ready to go again by 11:00.

On the *Akagi*, Admiral Nagumo breathed more easily. The box formation was tightening up again, gradually releasing the extra fighters from air cover duty. They were now being refueled and resupplied with ammunition. The shift back to torpedoes was well under way. The Midway strike planes were coming in smoothly. The *Chikuma* was going to send out four search planes to replace the *Tone*'s No. 4 plane, and thus keep a firm eye on the enemy.

Meanwhile the *Tone*'s pilot was still on the job. At 8:55 he radioed, "Ten enemy torpedo planes heading toward you," but this made little impression. Nagumo was too busy planning his own next step. At the same moment the *Akagi*'s blinker was flashing a confident message from the Admiral to the rest of the Striking Force: "After completing homing operations, proceed northward. We plan to contact and destroy the enemy task force."

Nagumo also radioed his intentions to Admiral Yamamoto, coming on with the Main Force about 450 miles to the rear. Telescoping his exchanges with the *Tone*'s plane into one over-simplified paragraph, Nagumo reported: "Enemy composed of 1 carrier, 5 cruisers, and 5 destroyers sighted at 8 A.M. in position bearing 10 degrees; distance 240 miles from AF. We are heading for it."

Everything was falling into place. Shortly after 9:00 the last of Tomonaga's planes were recovered, and at 9:17 the Striking Force made a 70° change in course to the northeast. To save time the ships did not turn in formation, but swung left in their tracks—thus the "box" of carriers now found the *Hiryu* leading the *Akagi* on the right side, the *Soryu* leading the *Kaga* on the left.

Admiral Nagumo was nearly ready. All ships had reported; everything was set. The second wave would conform to Organization No. 4: 18 torpedo planes from the *Akagi*, 27 from the *Kaga;* 36 dive bombers from the *Hiryu* and *Soryu;* 12

fighters from all four ships—3 from each. He would have preferred a few more Zeros, but overall this promised the "grand scale air attack" he wanted. He would launch promptly at 10:30. Yamaguchi might fret, but it was so much better to take a little longer and do the job right.

Suddenly at 9:18 a destroyer near the *Tone* began laying a smoke screen. Then the *Tone* herself did the same. Plane-sighting signals fluttered from one ship after another. Engine room telegraph bells rang for maximum battle speed. Along the eastern horizon, about 20 miles away, the *Chikuma*'s lookout counted 16 torpedo planes. He was one off—there were 15—but his confusion was understandable: there wasn't much time to count. These planes were coming straight in—without splitting or swerving—hurtling themselves directly at the First Carrier Striking Force.

CHAPTER 7

"Pilots, Man Your Planes!"

SWEEPING toward the Japanese ships, Ensign George Gay watched their sharp turns, the smoke pouring out, and decided they must already be under attack. It looked as if the 15 planes of Torpedo 8 were late.

They were far from late. Yet Gay's fears were natural. It had been a morning full of tense waiting, false starts, and finally a late launching from the *Hornet*. Yet this too was understandable, for the top command was still groping for the right decisions on the skimpiest information.

Racing southwest at 6:30, Task Force 16 had nothing to go on except those first contact reports—growing colder every minute. Spruance's staff could listen to the PBY traffic, but there was nothing in since 6:02. The other best source—Midway itself—they couldn't pick up at all. The fleet and the base were on entirely different frequencies, so there was no direct way to get anything reported by Midway's Army and Marine pilots. Everything had to be relayed by Pearl—a slow, hit-or-miss process. Nor could Task Force 16 ask any questions—radio silence limited the fleet's efforts at self-help to eavesdropping.

But cold information is better than none, and assuming the Japanese would continue to close Midway as last reported,

Spruance's chief of staff, Captain Miles Browning, urged that the attack be launched at 7:00 A.M. Browning, inherited from Halsey, was a difficult man—almost impossible to get along with—but there was no doubt about his mind. He calculated that Nagumo would then be 155 miles away—just within effective striking range. That meant a long flight to the target —practically no safety margin—but it was all-important to attack at the earliest possible moment. The key to everything was surprise . . . to hit the Japanese before they discovered the U.S. force.

Spruance understood. Originally his own inclination was to launch at 9:00. Task Force 16 would then be about 100 miles away, and this would allow a certain margin of error for the planes to find the enemy, strike and get back home. But Browning was his man on this, and if the chief of staff said 7:00, he would follow that advice.

Still, it was a tough decision. The fighters had a combat range of only 175 miles, the torpedo planes not much more. There would be little leeway for maneuvering, even less for fooling around in case of navigational errors. Many of the planes were bound to splash—hopefully the destroyers could rescue the crews—it was a risk that had to be taken.

At the same time, Spruance took another risk, equally daring: he would hit the Japanese with everything he had. It was a temptation to hold something back, for the contact reports mentioned only two of the four enemy carriers meant to be present. Perhaps the others were lurking somewhere else. But CINCPAC's intelligence said they were bunched together, and it was all-important to hit hard. Spruance decided to take his chances.

The *Enterprise* would attack with 33 dive bombers, 15 torpedo planes, 10 fighters; the *Hornet* with 35 dive bombers, 15 torpedo planes, 10 fighters—everything available. Only a handful of scouts and fighters were left to fly antisub and combat air patrols. That too was cutting it thin, but here again was a risk that had to be taken.

Meanwhile the pilots waited restlessly in the various squadron ready rooms. Five hours had passed since that 1:30 breakfast, and nobody's disposition was noticeably improved. Nor did it help to have two false alarms that sent everyone trooping up to the flight deck, only to be ordered back below.

But on one of these false alarms an odd thing happened. As the members of Scouting 6 stood up to go, they unaccountably shook hands all around. They were quite surprised at themselves, for studied casualness was an unwritten law. Maybe this time was different after all.

Things seemed more normal when the order was canceled, and they trooped back to the ready room, griping about the bridge. More waiting, more fidgeting. . . .

Then around 6:45 the teletype machines began clacking again. Once more the men got out their pencils as the "talkers" went to the blackboards and chalked up a new set of data: enemy position based on 6:02 contact report . . . heading . . . speed . . . Point Option where their own carrier could be found again. The pilots busily scribbled away, hunched over their plotting boards like schoolboys taking a final exam.

"Hope you're ready," a flier on the *Hornet* said to Gus Widhelm, one of Scouting 8's jauntier characters. "*I'm* ready," Widhelm replied, "I only hope the Japs are."

On the *Enterprise* many of the fighter pilots added an extra twist to getting ready—they were lining up at the water cooler. The theory was to drink up now; if shot down, they could last that much longer before thirst became a problem.

"Pilots, man your planes," for the third time this morning the traditional summons came over the loudspeakers. On the flight decks of both the *Hornet* and the *Enterprise* the starters whined, the motors sputtered and roared, the blue exhaust smoke washed back in the light morning breeze. The two carriers veered apart—the *Hornet* and its escorts falling out of line, the *Enterprise* group continuing on course. Then at 7:00 both ships swung sharply into the wind (this morning not enough and from the wrong direction), and the launching began.

The fighters and bombers were already taking off when the men of Torpedo 8 left their ready room. As they zipped up their flight jackets, tightened their yellow Mae Wests, and pulled on their helmets, Commander Waldron gave them a few final words. He said he thought the Japanese ships would swing around once they discovered U.S. carriers present; they would not go on to Midway as everyone seemed to think. So don't worry about navigation; he knew where he was going. "Just follow me. I'll take you to 'em."

Climbing the ladder to the flight deck he turned to his young navigator Ensign Gay, reminding him to "keep on my tail." Then up to the bridge for final instructions, stopping by the chart house long enough to assure his friend Commander Frank Akers that he'd take the squadron all the way in. His exchange with Captain Mitscher was very brief—neither was given to oratory. As the Commander promised to "get hits," Mitscher gently put his hand on Waldron's shoulder.

Across the water the *Enterprise* planes were taking off too; the plan was to rendezvous above the carrier, then fly out together in a single, coordinated strike. The dive bombers left first at 7:06—climbing, circling, forming into ever larger groups. Taking off like that, a flier's heart always thumped a little faster, but it also had its secret pleasures. As one pilot has remarked, "To get off a carrier deck, one does have a lot of mechanical preparation on deck and a never-failing audience, which means that the beginning of every strike involves fulfillment of Walter Mitty dreams. I'd say the actual take-off forced one into some self-confidence and bravado, unlike the infantry situation where no one was watching."

Orbiting high above the *Enterprise*, Lieutenant Commander Wade McClusky, leading the carrier's whole Air Group, waited for his torpedo planes and fighter escorts. Fifteen minutes . . . a half-hour went by, and still no sign of them. Impatiently he studied the flight deck far below: "Action seemed to come to a standstill." Meanwhile he was using up desperately needed gas, just circling and waiting.

There were many reasons for the delay. Spruance's decision

to throw a "full load" at the enemy had its price—no more than half the planes could be on the flight deck at once. Also, there was a last-minute change in the bomb load on some of the planes; that took time too. In addition, a torpedo plane broke down. But above all, there was the problem of inexperience. Carrier operations might be an old story to the Japanese, but the Americans were still just feeling their way. Confusions of all sorts were bound to occur while the U.S. Navy got "on-the-job training" in this new business of carrier warfare.

At 7:28 there was a new complication. Spruance's radar picked up something suspicious; then the *Enterprise*'s forward gun director, with its powerful range finder, sighted it for certain—a Japanese seaplane lurking on the southern horizon. It hung there much too long to hope it had missed them. No doubt about it: they had been spotted.

The chance for surprise seemed gone—with the planes only half launched. Still, there was no thought of calling off the operation. As Miles Browning pointed out, the Japanese would be locked in their present course at least till they recovered their Midway strike. But it was more important than ever to get going fast.

By 7:45 Spruance felt he could wait no longer. The *Enterprise*'s fighters and torpedo planes were still on deck, but the launching had dragged on long enough. He'd just have to give up the plan for a coordinated strike and send out what he had—the rest could follow. The ship's blinker flashed to McClusky, "Proceed on mission assigned."

As the dive bombers headed southwest, Lieutenant Jim Gray's Fighting 6 was already taking off. Then it was Torpedo 6's turn. The injured Gene Lindsey hobbled over to his borrowed TBD. The plane captain had to help him climb in, but the skipper was as determined as ever to lead his squadron. They left at 8:06.

On the *Hornet* John Waldron's Torpedo 8 was leaving about the same time. For George Gay and the other "boot" ensigns it was all a brand-new experience. They wondered how hard it would be taking off with that "pickle," as they invariably called the torpedo. Not only had they never done it before, they had never even seen it done. For all that, it turned out to be easy, and they too were heading out at 8:06.

But if this suggested that the *Hornet*'s and *Enterprise*'s air operations were in any way coordinated, that would be misleading. This was another art America had yet to learn. Here, neither Air Group knew what the other was doing, much less what the *Yorktown*'s planes were up to. And while the two torpedo squadrons were indeed leaving at the same time, the circumstances were entirely different. The *Enterprise*'s Torpedo 6 was chasing after its dive bombers; while the *Hornet*'s Torpedo 8, although last off, was actually leading its group.

Captain Mitscher's idea was to send his slow torpedo planes ahead, while the faster bombers and fighters were climbing to rendezvous high above the ship. These could then catch up en route, and all would attack together. Fine in theory, but risky too. With the torpedo planes below a thousand feet and the rest of the squadron at 19,000, it would be easy to miss connections.

So now Torpedo 6 and Torpedo 8 were each heading out alone—separately yet close together—with very little to choose between them. One difference lay in the courses they took. Torpedo 6—under the meticulously correct Gene Lindsey— was flying exactly as prescribed. His course was 240°, or generally southwest. Torpedo 8, on the other hand, was veering off to the right, flying a more westerly course. The unorthodox John Waldron had said to forget navigation—just follow him—and he meant it. Another difference lay in the number of planes. Torpedo 6, short one TBD, had only 14; while Torpedo 8 was at full strength with all 15 on hand.

Looking down from above, Lieutenant Jim Gray watched 15 torpedo planes join up and set out with no escort. As skipper of Fighting 6 it was his job to protect Torpedo 6. Not knowing the squadron was short a plane, he decided these unescorted TBDs must be his. He took station over them and continued to climb.

This was in line with an arrangement he had with Lieutenant Art Ely, operations officer of Torpedo 6. Shortly before take-off, they had agreed that Gray would fly high enough to protect not only the torpedo planes but the dive bombers too. After all, it was the bombers that took the big beating at Coral Sea. But the torpedo planes weren't neglected; if they needed any help, Ely was to radio, "Come on down, Jim."

As they continued on, Gray noticed another torpedo squadron flying behind him and heading more to the southwest. For a while he tried to cover them too, but the gap grew steadily wider. Finally he gave up and concentrated on those below. He didn't realize it, but the others were the 14 planes of Torpedo 6—the squadron he was meant to cover.

Directly below, the 15 planes of Torpedo 8 lumbered on—oblivious of the fighters above, of navigation, of everything except the determined man who led them. Waldron had his planes flying in two rough Vs; there were six sections of two and one section of three bringing up the rear. He, of course, was leading; Ensign Gay was flying the last plane in the last section.

Around 9:00 Waldron opened up on the intercom to warn they were being watched. Gay looked up and saw a Japanese seaplane trailing them in the distance. It finally broke off and Torpedo 8 continued on, wondering what sort of reception committee the seaplane's radio might recruit. At the moment, there was nothing in sight—Torpedo 8 was all alone between the empty blue sea and the broken white clouds.

High above the clouds, and a little to the south, the *Hornet*'s 35 dive bombers and 10 fighters overtook Waldron's squadron and continued on to the southwest. Whether it was due more to the clouds or the diverging course no one would ever know, but the rendezvous had failed. Torpedo 8 continued on alone.

About this time Waldron put his planes into a long scouting line. It was nearly time they sighted something, and this might make it easier. Soon, over his right wing, he saw two columns of smoke rising from beyond the horizon. He swung to the right, waggling his wings for the others to join up again. By 9:20 they were there, skimming the waves, going full throttle toward Nagumo's outer screen of cruisers and destroyers.

"He went just as straight to the Jap fleet as if he'd had a string tied to them," George Gay later recalled. Pardonable license. If the enemy forces weren't exactly where Waldron expected to find them, they were close enough. But there's a limit to Sioux intuition, and the Commander's reasoning was somewhat off. Nagumo had indeed turned north, but only a minute or so before Waldron got there. There was a different reason why the Japanese were far short of the position estimated by Spruance's staff. Nagumo was short because he had spent so much of the past two hours dodging the planes from Midway.

In any case, Waldron had found them, and as Torpedo 8 roared closer he could soon make out three carriers already turning in evasion moves. Picking out the one to his left—southernmost of the three—he drove on in. The carrier threw out a curtain of antiaircraft fire. Waldron then shifted to the central carrier instead—it was smaller but looked easier to reach.

The rest of Torpedo 8 swung with him—Ensign Grant Teats, the lumberjack . . . Ensign Harold Ellison, the insurance man . . . Ensign Bill Evans, the Wesleyan intellectual . . . all of them. Outnumbered amateurs, they never faltered, but they had so far to go—the carrier was still nine miles off.

Without warning 10, 20, no one knew how many Zeros came raging down at them from somewhere high above. These fighters knew their business—they concentrated on the leading planes of Torpedo 8. The very first Zero picked off a TBD on the far left. Waldron came on the radio, asking his rear-seat man Horace Dobbs whether it was "ours or theirs." Gay, who had all too good a view of the proceedings from his position at the rear, broke in to say it was a TBD.

Torpedo 8 continued on, with the Zeros diving again and again. The rear seat men did their best to fight back, but even the new twin mounts were no match for the Japanese. The Zeros were just too fast, the TBDs just too slow. Waldron again opened up on his radio, trying to reach Commander Stanhope Ring, leading the rest of the *Hornet*'s planes: "Stanhope, from Johnny one, answer." But there was no answer.

The Zeros kept pounding, and more planes fell. Yet Waldron had one satisfaction: he was at last ramming home an attack, right down the enemy's throat. It was what everything had been leading to all these months—all that training, all that psychology—it was what his whole life was all about. Now that the big moment had come, there was a touch of fervor in the broken phrases that crackled over his radio: "Watch those fighters . . . See that splash! . . . How am I doing, Dobbs? . . . Attack immediately . . . I'd give a million to know who did that."

Then he got it too. A burst of flame—a brief glimpse of him standing up in the blazing cockpit—and he was gone. Then another went, and another. It was always the same: that sheet of flame, the blur of erupting smoke and water, the debris swirling by to the rear. Watching planes fall in these early battles, young Americans often thought of the old war movies they had seen. But this wasn't like those movies at all. George Gay could only think of the time he was a boy and tossed out orange peels from the back of a speeding motorboat.

Soon there were only three TBDs left—Gay and two others. Next instant the others were down and there was only Gay. Bullets slashed into his plane and rattled against the armored back of his seat. His gunner Bob Huntington was hit, and Gay felt a sharp pain above his left elbow. He fumbled with his torn sleeve; the bullet was spent, and he easily pressed it out. Not knowing what else to do with it, he put it in his mouth.

Incredibly the plane was still flying. And now he was by the destroyer screen, heading straight for the carrier. He was coming in on her starboard side, and as he drew near, she turned hard toward him, hoping to offer less of a target. Instinctively (or, more accurately, thanks to all those blackboard sessions), Gay pulled out to the right, cut across the carrier's bow, and swung back to the left. Now he was coming in on her port side.

All the ship's guns were firing. The air around him was black with antiaircraft bursts, but Gay kept boring in.

At 800 yards he pressed the release button. Nothing happened—the electric connections had long since been shot away. He couldn't use his left hand, so he jammed the stick between his knees and yanked at the manual release. The plane gave a welcome surge; the "pickle" was on its way.

Now to clear out. He was much too close to turn away. Those guns would pour into the plane's belly at point-blank range. So he did the only other thing he could do. He kept on coming.

Flying "right down the gun barrel" of a big pompom up forward, he hopped across the flight deck, did a flipper turn and flew aft along the starboard side. It was a wild moment as he swung by the island below bridge level—"I could see the little Jap captain up there jumping up and down raising hell."

Scooting by the afterpart of the flight deck, he had a glimpse of a sight that made him yearn for a heavy machine gun up forward. The deck was full of planes, clearly being rearmed and refueled. Gas hoses were scattered all over the place, and a few incendiary bullets could have started an inferno.

For a split second he felt an urge to crash into the whole mess, but then he decided things weren't that bad. The plane was still flying; he felt pretty good. Maybe he could get out of this, come back and hit them again someday. He dropped down close to the water and headed astern of the carrier.

The Zeros weren't about to let him get away a second time. A string of them poured down from above, and the second or third one caught him. An explosive shell carried away his left rudder control, flash-burning his leg. Nothing worked any more, and Gay pancaked hard into the ocean. The fifteenth and last plane of Torpedo 8 was gone.

Circling high above, Lieutenant Jim Gray was having a comparatively uneventful morning. Fighting 6 had little trouble following those 15 torpedo planes most of the way. Like most fighter pilots, he left the course to the planes he escorted; after all, they had an extra man. So now he just "followed the crowd," which he still assumed to be Torpedo 6.

As the time drew near when they should be sighting the Japanese, Gray began to worry about Zeros. It would be hard to protect both McClusky's dive bombers (whenever they appeared) and those torpedo planes far below. Then, as if in answer to a prayer, he saw a low-lying cloud bank directly ahead. Fine. The torpedo planes could use this for cover, as they did at Coral Sea, and he could concentrate on keeping the upper area safe for the dive bombers. If anything went wrong below, there was always the prearranged signal with Torpedo 6 that would bring him rushing down.

Shortly after 9:00 the 15 torpedo planes disappeared under the clouds and Gray saw them no more. But it was easy to guess they must have made contact, for soon afterward he sighted the white feathers of the Japanese wakes at the far edge of the overcast. Fighting 6 began circling above, watching for Zeros, wondering where McClusky was, occasionally catching a glimpse of the ships below. The torpedo attack must be going well; no one called the magic words, "Come on down, Jim."

As Ensign Gay's TBD smacked into the sea, the right wing snapped off, and the canopy hood above his head slammed shut with the impact. The plane began filling with water. Gay desperately tugged at the hood. He was scared. The Japanese were one thing, drowning was another.

Somehow he finally yanked it open. Climbing out, his first

thoughts were for his rear-seat man Bob Huntington—there had been no word from him since he said he was hit. The plane was sinking fast, but Gay made a dive anyhow to try and pull him out. The wreckage sank too soon.

Gay inflated his Mae West and looked around. The plane's rubber boat bobbed up, deflated and in its bag . . . then the black cushion Huntington used to kneel on while working. Gay tucked the boat under his arm, and recalling stories of Zeros strafing helpless pilots in the water, he pulled the cushion over his head and kept as low as possible. From this unusual vantage point, he settled down to a front-row view of the First Carrier Striking Force in action.

At 9:36 the *Akagi* ordered cease-fire; the fighters were bringing down the last of the U.S. torpedo planes. They had given the *Soryu* quite a scare, but beyond that nothing. To the critical eye of the experts on the Striking Force, the American tactics were very primitive. Surprisingly, they had no fighter escorts. Nor did they split their attack, as the Japanese had learned to do. They foolishly kept in a single unit and simply hurled themselves at the *Soryu*. Bunched together, they were easy to shoot down. Their torpedoes (the men on the *Soryu* thought they saw four) passed harmlessly by the carrier.

So a sixth American attack had been beaten off. But there was little time for self-congratulation, for at 9:38—just two minutes after the *Akagi*'s cease-fire—a new enemy flight of 14 torpedo planes was sighted, steadily boring in from the south.

The smoke, the distant wakes were farther north than Gene Lindsey expected. Fortunately, Torpedo 6 was flying at 1,500 feet—below the clouds yet high enough to catch those first telltale traces 30 miles away.

Lindsey signaled, and the 14 planes made a wide swing right so that they approached the target from about due south. The Japanese were heading west at the moment, and their formation was extremely loose—they were apparently under, or had just been under, a heavy torpedo plane attack by somebody.

But where were all the *Enterprise's* own planes? Jim Gray's fighters were meant to be on hand, yet no one had seen them all the way out. And the disappearance of Wade McClusky's dive bombers was even more baffling. They left first, were faster, should be here waiting. But they too were nowhere in sight. Gene Lindsey just didn't have the gas to wait around. He would have to go it alone.

Picking the closest carrier, he began his approach about 9:40. He was off his target's port bow—an excellent position—and at 20 miles he split his planes, seven and seven, hoping to come in on both sides.

There was only one thing wrong with his theory: the planes were TBDs. The manual might say they went 134 knots, but 100 was closer to the mark these days. With the carriers going 25-30 knots, it took a long, long while to close the gap. All the more so, since the Japanese skipper cleverly kept his stern to the planes, forcing them into an ever wider arc to get in a bow shot. And this was necessary because a 30-knot ship could easily dodge a 33-knot torpedo at any other angle. It all added up to a 20-minute approach.

The Zeros made good use of the time. Starting about 15 miles out, 25 of them swept down, making pass after pass at Torpedo 6. The rear-seat men fired back as best they could; the pilots just hunched low and hoped. They couldn't dodge; they couldn't maneuver; everything depended on keeping course. Pablo Riley . . . Tom Eversole . . . Gene Lindsey himself went down one after another in flaming cartwheels. Others went too, but the rest kept coming—slowly, ever so slowly, edging around toward the bow of the turning carrier.

The antiaircraft was there too; they had a 15-minute dose of it. As usual, it caused little actual damage, but it did have a jarring effect. It forced the planes out a little more, making that long circuitous journey that much longer.

They never did reach a decent launching position, but that didn't keep them from trying. At 9:58 the remaining TBDs finally turned in and began a desperate run on the carrier's port quarter. The big ship—so far away for so long—suddenly seemed overwhelmingly near. Lieutenant Ed Laub found he could make out the planes on her flight deck . . . next instant he could even see their propellers turning.

And that was close enough. At 500-800 yards he released, felt that lift to his plane, and raced to get clear. Three other TBDs did the same; the remaining ten were gone.

It was all over soon after 10:00 A.M. For more than 20 minutes the men of Torpedo 6 had pitted themselves against the entire First Carrier Striking Force. They had, of course, their prearranged signal for help—"Come on down, Jim"—but there's no sign it was ever used. Perhaps it was sent but never received; perhaps Art Ely was shot down too soon; perhaps Gene Lindsey didn't know about it; or perhaps, having seen no sign of Fighting 6 all the way out, he just assumed there was nobody up there.

High above the broken clouds, Fighting 6 restlessly orbited at 20,000 feet. Still no sign of the torpedo planes, but if they needed help, they'd call. Meanwhile Jim Gray was more and more worried about McClusky's dive bombers. Where were they anyhow? He circled, looking to the south; no luck. He tried a few radio calls; no answer.

He glanced at his gas gauge—and got a shock. It stood about half where it normally did after two hours' flying. This meant Fighting 6 couldn't do much even if the dive bombers came. They no longer had the gas to mix it up with the Zeros.

At 9:52 Gray again tried to contact McClusky. He reported he was over the target, but running short of fuel and would soon have to go back to the ship. No answer. At 10:00 he tried again, this time summing up the situation as far as he could see it: the enemy fleet had eight destroyers, two battleships, two carriers . . . course north . . . no combat patrol. Still no answer.

By now he had little gas left for anything at all. Maybe he should strafe the Japanese carrier he could see clear of the clouds. On the other hand, that would take him down too low to use the *Enterprise*'s homing device to return to the ship. All things considered, the gains from a strafing run just didn't seem worth the risk of running out of gas. As Admiral Halsey once said, the fighters' first job was to protect the fleet.

Gray decided the sensible thing to do was go back for more fuel. A few minutes after 10:00—just about the time Torpedo 6 was making its final, lonely dash at the First Carrier Striking Fleet—Fighting 6 headed for home.

IT TOOK all Captain Okada's skill to keep the *Kaga's* stern to this new group of American planes. At one point he had to use hard-left rudder to avoid some torpedoes on his starboard quarter, then go immediately to hard-right rudder to dodge another set to port.

But the job was done. By 10:00 everything seemed under control, and the Striking Force hurried northeast at 24 knots. Admiral Nagumo still planned to strike the American carrier at 10:30, and the time had come to close the enemy.

Nagumo also sent a new message to Admiral Yamamoto, reviewing the morning's events. He briefly reported his attack on Midway, the futile attacks on him by shore-based planes. He again told how a U.S. task force, complete with carrier, had been found. "After destroying this," he reported, "we plan to resume our AF attack."

He didn't mention the two TBD strikes he had just received, or perhaps he assumed they were shore-based too. After all, what did it matter? He had hurled back seven separate American attacks. Admiral Nagumo was more than satisfied.

ENSIGN Thomas Wood was beginning to realize he might have to eat his words. Back in the wardroom he had boasted that he, personally, would sink the *Akagi*, but the *Hornet's* 35 dive bombers and 10 fighters had been searching for an hour now, and it looked more and more as if they might not find the Japanese fleet at all, much less sink the flagship.

It was all very baffling. Commander Stan Ring had led his planes exactly as directed—239°, 155 miles—but nothing had gone quite right. First, they didn't link up with Torpedo 8 on the way out. Topping that, when they reached the interception point around 9:30, there were no ships in sight.

Yet they must be somewhere. Were they to the right, off to the north? This would be the case if they had unexpectedly changed course—and carriers had a way of doing that. Or were they to the left? Had they already passed by the interception point and were now between the *Hornet*'s planes and Midway? Maybe not as likely, but a far more harrowing thought. The whole point of the battle was to defend the base. Stan Ring swung left and headed south. Scouting 8, Bombing 8, Fighting 8 all followed along.

By the time they reached Kure—the tiny atoll 60 miles west of Midway—it was clear there were no Japs in this direction. But they had made their choice, and now they were stuck with it. They milled around, hoping for some helpful word over their silent radios, while their gas dropped ever lower.

Finally Ring decided it was useless. They would have to return to the *Hornet*. There they could refuel and start all over again. The group broke up, and each squadron headed back on its own. It would be up to others to stop Nagumo this morning.

ENSIGN Bill Pittman was getting more and more worried. The *Enterprise* dive bombers had been out more than two hours—and still no sign of the Japs. By now his gas gauge was touching the halfway point, yet here was Wade McClusky continuing to lead them "all over the Pacific."

Pittman, a young pilot in Scouting 6, was flying wing on

McClusky. Across the way Dick Jaccard was flying the other wing, and behind these three, stepped at various levels, followed the other 28 SBDs of Scouting 6 and Bombing 6. They were all still there with two exceptions—both forced to drop out with engine trouble. Tony Schneider looked as if he might be the next to go—his engine was smoking badly, eating up gas. Yet he kept perfect formation, as though he had all the fuel in the world.

Ensign Pittman figured they were almost at the end of their rope. He glanced across at Dick Jaccard, who was also wondering when—or if—the "old man" would ever turn back.

Wade McClusky flew on, sure he had made all the right decisions, yet understandably wondering why nothing better had come of them. Just as instructed, they flew out on 240°, distance 155 miles—yet when they reached the interception point at 9:20 the sea was empty. Not a ship in sight. He checked his navigation; no mistake there.

Nor could it have been the weather. The day was beautiful. Just a few puffy clouds below—certainly nothing that could hide the whole Japanese fleet. And all the way out he used his binoculars; he couldn't have passed them unsighted.

Yet they must be somewhere. To the left, between himself and Midway? No: allowing for a maximum advance at 25 knots, McClusky felt certain they hadn't already passed. Then they must be to his right—gone off to the east or west, or most likely, turned around.

He decided to fly a "box" search, covering as much of this area to the right as he could. First he kept on to the southwest for another 15 minutes. The other pilots dutifully followed, wondering what the skipper was up to. Radio silence made it all a guessing game.

At 35 miles there were still no signs of the Japanese. McClusky was convinced they couldn't be any farther down this way. So he turned right, to the northwest, and began flying the reverse of Nagumo's course. The rest of the planes turned too, the pilots still wondering.

Now McClusky's big problem was how far he could go. The planes had been in the air a long time. They had climbed, heavily loaded, to 20,000 feet. The less experienced pilots were probably using more gas than himself—and he was using plenty. He decided to keep flying northwest until 10:00, then turn northeast before making the final, dreary decision to give up the hunt and go back to the *Enterprise*.

The 31 planes flew on. No sign of anything, left or right. The gas gauge in Tony Schneider's plane dropped toward empty.

WHILE the dive bombers from the *Hornet* and *Enterprise* searched in vain, Admiral Fletcher on the *Yorktown* was by no means idle. He had sent Task Force 16 on ahead, while he picked up his planes scouting to the north. But by 6:45 they were recovered and the *Yorktown* was pounding after the *Enterprise* and *Hornet*.

Fletcher's problem was how best to support the other two carriers. Should he throw everything at the same target they were attacking? Or should he hold something back? He was still bothered by the fact that the PBYs had reported only two enemy carriers. There should be four; that meant two others were somewhere. The *Yorktown*'s planes were all he had left to get them. He decided to hold back for a while, hoping time might throw a little more light on the situation.

But time revealed nothing. There was no further news from the PBYs, and if anyone else was sending reports, the information was not getting through. Around 7:00 word came that the *Enterprise* and *Hornet* were launching; the *Yorktown*'s pilots grew more and more restless.

The squadron leaders got together for a final conference. They quickly reviewed how they could carry out their attack, whenever and wherever it happened. It would be a coordinated job, with Fighting 3 going in first to strafe; then Bombing 3 and Scouting 5; and finally Torpedo 3. Hopefully the early planes would cripple the target enough for the slow-moving torpedoes to do their job. As for when they could start, the key decision lay in Commander Thach's lap—his fighters had the shortest range. Thach said he was willing to go at 175 miles, which Leslie felt was "really giving a lot." It left practically no safety margin at all.

To save as much fuel as possible, the *Yorktown* Air Group commander, Oscar Pederson, suggested an arrangement somewhat like that on the *Hornet.* He proposed that the squadrons rendezvous along the way. The torpedo planes would go first; the rest would catch up.

The discussion turned to the interception point. According to the last contact report, Nagumo was heading straight into the wind for Midway. This was ideal for air operations, and he'd probably stick to this course as long as possible. At the same time, the contact report was now very stale, and the *Yorktown's* air officer, Commander Murr Arnold, felt the Japanese wouldn't get too close on their first strike. He and Pederson decided to allow for a maximum enemy advance; then if the planes found nothing at the interception point, they'd turn northwest and fly the reverse of the Japanese course.

Meanwhile Admiral Fletcher fretted on the bridge, hoping in vain for some new report pinpointing those missing enemy carriers. Finally at 8:38 he decided he could wait no longer. After all, he was a target too. The Japanese now knew the Americans were around, and any moment their dive bombers might come screaming down from the sky. He certainly didn't want to get caught with all his own planes on deck.

Yet the missing carriers still bothered him. Only a month ago at Coral Sea he had been fooled in a situation like this. Acting on a bad contact report, he had thrown his whole Air Group at the little escort carrier *Shoho,* while the big *Zuikaku* and *Shokaku* lay undiscovered within range. It was just luck they hadn't clobbered him. He didn't want to run that risk again. As always, a battle remained this eternal business of groping.

In the end he decided he could have it both ways. He'd send off Bombing 3, Torpedo 3 and six planes from Fighting 3. But as an ace in the hole, he'd hang on to Scouting 5 and the rest of the fighters. The stay-at-homes didn't take it easily, but Fletcher was firm.

While the brass debated—and the pilots fidgeted—the rear seat men once more checked the planes spotted on the flight deck. This was now an old story to Radioman Bill Gallagher, who rode with Max Leslie, skipper of Bombing 3. When the time came, the "old man" would tell him everything he needed to know, and sometimes a little bit more.

This morning he went to the plane as usual when general quarters sounded. He knew the *Yorktown* was out here on serious business, but he didn't know of any plans for attack this particular day. That wasn't his job. But he checked and rechecked everything (that *was* his job) and stood by while the plane captain warmed up the motor. Then more waiting. Sooner or later they'd either secure, or Mr. Leslie would come up from the ready room. This time they didn't secure. At 8:40 the loudspeakers blared the familiar call, "Pilots, man your planes."

As the pilots poured out on deck, Gallagher climbed into the plane, and in a few seconds Leslie joined him. Swinging aboard, the skipper said something about a "Jap contact." But he didn't mention carriers, and Gallagher still had no idea exactly what they were gunning for. Yet after years of service, a man could smell out situations, and he certainly sensed that this was "it."

At 8:45 Lem Massey's 12 torpedo planes roared into the sky. Then Max Leslie led his 17 dive bombers off. Lieutenant (j.g.) Paul Holmberg, following right behind the skipper, caught his slipstream and almost spun into the water. An added difficulty was the big 1,000-pound bomb he carried— it was the first time he had ever taken off with such a load.

For 12 minutes the bombers climbed and circled high above the *Yorktown*, then started off after the torpedo planes. Finally at 9:05 Jimmy Thach's six fighters followed. As they pulled out, the men on the ships of Task Force 17 waved them on, and the cruiser *Astoria*'s blinker signaled a parting salute: "Good hunting, and a safe return."

Less than five minutes out, Jimmy Thach was startled by an enormous explosion erupting in the water just ahead of Fighting 3. There were no ships around; it could only come from a bomb accidentally released by somebody "upstairs."

High above, Commander Max Leslie shook his fist in wild frustration. He had just signaled the squadron to arm their bombs, but when he threw the new electric arming switch in his own cockpit, some faulty connection released the bomb instead.

He banged on the side of the plane—his standard method of signaling Bill Gallagher in the rear seat—and wondered aloud whether they had time to go back and reload. Gallagher, with an enlisted man's healthy distrust of brass, said they'd probably be kept on the ship if they did. Leslie said he certainly didn't want that, so on they flew.

A few minutes later a second bomb went, as another pilot tried to throw the electric switch. This was too much. Leslie now committed the dangerous sin of breaking radio silence long enough to warn all pilots not to use the new device—go back to the old manual way instead. For his own peace of mind, happily he didn't know at the time that two more pilots had lost their bombs the same way. Bombing 3 still boasted 17 planes, but only 13 of them now had anything to drop on the enemy.

For Leslie, the leader, it seemed especially ironic. The others were mostly young reservists, but he had studied and practiced for twenty years for just this climactic moment—and now this: he was en route to the enemy without a bomb.

Yet it never occurred to him to drop out. A dive bombing squadron is an intricate mechanism, requiring split-second timing to do its job properly. Bombing 3 was used to Leslie and his way of operating. No matter how skillful, another man taking over now might upset their coordination just enough to throw everything off. So Leslie was determined to lead his squadron anyhow; he would be the first to dive, just as though he still had his 1,000-pound bomb.

Far below, Jimmy Thach flew on—his aplomb mildly upset by those four explosions that rocked the sea around him. About 9:30 he caught the reassuring sight of Lem Massey's torpedo planes flying directly ahead. Fifteen minutes later Leslie's SBDs caught up with them too.

They flew on together, in a sort of vertical formation. At the bottom, of course, were the torpedo planes sticking to 1,500 feet . . . next the fighters, keeping low enough to cover them . . . and finally the dive bombers—a wedge of tiny specks at 16,000 feet. Except for some cumulus along the horizon, most of the clouds had now disappeared. Just occasional white tufts in a world of sparkling blue.

At 10:00 the sharp eyes of Lem Massey picked up three columns of smoke rising from beyond the northwest horizon, some 30-40 miles away. Torpedo 3 immediately turned right, climbing a little to get a better look. Fighting 3 and Bombing 3 swung too, although neither yet knew what Massey had seen.

Max Leslie again risked breaking radio silence, asked Massey in code if he had sighted the enemy. No answer. They flew on, and at 10:05 Leslie found out for himself. First the smoke; then Bill Gallagher pointed out the wakes of ships perhaps 35 miles dead ahead.

About 10:15 Leslie lost track of the torpedo planes. They were somewhat ahead, 14,000 feet below, and between the distance and some scattered clouds, he could no longer see them. But he now could hear them all too well. Massey had opened up on his radio and was frantically calling for fighter support.

Torpedo 3 had almost reached the outer screen—they were 14-18 miles from the carriers—when the first two Zeros hit. They came without warning, from above and to the left, and before CAP Wilhelm Esders knew what was happening, bullets tore through his cockpit, exploding a CO_2 bottle tucked between his feet.

Gas was everywhere—he couldn't see—he couldn't imagine

what had happened. For a moment he thought the plane was on fire. Then realizing it was the CO_2, he yanked back the canopy and gulped in the fresh air.

Massey nosed down, trying to reap as much advantage as he could from speed and low altitude. Esders was keeping alongside him, while Machinist Harry Corl flew the other wing. Together they made up the lead section of Torpedo 3. The rest of the planes were following, stacked down in sections of three.

They were over the screen now, beginning their approach. At ten miles, two more Zeros hit, then several more. Six to eight were constantly on them, making pass after pass, while the rear-seat men did their best to shoot back. They dropped down to 150 feet, and that was the limit; from here on, Torpedo 3 would just have to take it.

Massey picked out the lead carrier—the one farthest north— and the squadron split into two divisions of six. The first would take the starboard side, the other the port. As they bore in, the ship's guns opened up too. Generally the anti-aircraft fire was wild, but the Zeros were never in better form.

Someone shot away Corl's elevator controls, and his plane headed for the water. Seeing he was about to crash, he released his torpedo. Free of the weight, he discovered he could get his nose up again by using the tab control. He moved back into position, hoping he could at least help fight off the Zeros.

Then came the moment that overwhelmed all the rest. About a mile from the carrier, Lem Massey's plane was hit and caught fire. Still flying alongside, Esders watched the skipper climb out on the stub wing as the TBD, now engulfed in flames, headed down for the sea. Massey never had a chance.

Watching him go, it dawned on Esders that he was now the head of the squadron. Things were so critical it just wasn't possible to turn the lead over, as customary, to the next senior man. Although the junior pilot present, he must lead the attack the rest of the way.

As he took over, he glanced at the scene around him. It

was a weird and terrible sight: "Any direction I was able to look, I could see five, six, seven or more aircraft on fire, spinning down, or simply out of control and flying around crazily."

Seeing Esders begin his final run, Corl turned north to get clear of the fleet. He had done all he could; now even his guns were jammed. His rear-seat man Lloyd Fred Childers, though wounded in both legs, kept popping away with a .45 pistol.

Esders barreled in, as his own rear-seat man Mike Brazier came on the intercom. He had just been hit, Brazier explained, and would no longer be able to help. Nevertheless, he managed for quite a while to call out whenever the Zeros got on their tail.

At 600-800 yards Esders finally dropped his torpedo, turned sharply to the right, cleared the carrier by several hundred yards. Four other TBDs dropped too, one of them crashing just off the ship's bow. Esders never saw what happened to the rest, but whatever it was, they didn't escape. By the end of their attack, 10 of Lem Massey's 12 planes were gone; only Esders and Corl were left, and they still had to get home.

A thousand feet up, there was little that Jimmy Thach could do. He heard Massey's call for help, all right, but a horde of Zeros hurled themselves on Fighting 3 at the same time. "It was like the inside of a beehive," he later recalled, and it was all his men could do to stay alive.

"Skipper, there's a Zero on my tail, get him off," Thach's wing man Ram Dibb sang out at one point. Leading the Japanese around to the front, Dibb gave Thach a perfect target. He opened up, and the Zero reeled down toward the sea. But none of this helped Lem Massey below. There just weren't enough fighters to do the job. Torpedo 3 had to face Nagumo alone.

RAITA OGAWA, flying combat air patrol over the *Akagi*, felt these last two torpedo attacks were the most troublesome of the morning. The planes maneuvered better than the earlier bombers and it took longer to shoot them down. Also, they had a way of hanging around after delivering their attacks; this was annoying because it meant still more time had to be wasted chasing after them.

This new strike was a good example of Ogawa's problem. Coming in from the southeast around 10:10, there were only 12 TBDs, plus a few fighters, yet they caused no end of trouble. It took the air cover from all four carriers to handle them properly. Meanwhile there was nobody left to patrol up high.

By now the carrier formation was a shambles again. On the *Akagi* Captain Aoki could no longer even see the *Hiryu*— she was somewhere in the smoke to the north. The *Kaga* and *Soryu* were still around, but the distance had widened from the prescribed 1,300 to 4,500 or 6,000 yards. At 10:10 the Striking Force had been ordered to head east, but within a minute the *Akagi* was turning hard to the northwest, trying to keep her stern to the 12 TBDs. In the end they passed on north toward the *Hiryu*, but who could have guessed that? The formation ended up all the more jumbled.

Nor did it help to have an enemy submarine poking around. The destroyer *Arashi* gave the first warning when she saw some torpedo tracks coming her way around 9:10. She immediately countered with depth charges and stayed behind when the rest of the Striking Force turned northeast. The *Arashi* was still back there somewhere, hopefully sitting on the sub, but one never knew.

For all that, it had been a good morning. By 10:15 the latest batch of torpedo planes was going the way of the others. This would make eight attacks thrown back in three hours. Meanwhile all that work below deck was about to pay off— 93 planes had been rearmed or refueled, and at this very moment were being spotted on the flight decks. The First Carrier Striking Force had suffered enough indignities; the all-out attack on the American fleet would be launched, as scheduled, at 10:30.

At 10:20, even before the enemy torpedo attack had been completely throttled, Admiral Nagumo gave the order to launch when ready. Maybe a little ahead of schedule, but the *Akagi*'s planes were already in place, a flight of Zeros spotted first. The ship began turning into the wind. The other three carriers caught Nagumo's signal and did the same.

On the *Kaga* CWO Morinaga was standing with a group of pilots in the center of the flight deck, just aft of the second elevator. They were all slated to go on the coming strike, and while they waited to man their planes, they had orders from the bridge to stand by as extra lookouts. Now they were scanning the sky—mostly clear, but studded here and there with clouds.

No one can say who spotted them first. All the pilots were shouting at once. But there was no doubt what they saw, pouring down from the blue like tiny black beads falling loose from a string. With one voice, they yelled up to the bridge, "Enemy dive bombers!"

CHAPTER **8**

"Don't Let This Carrier Escape"

Tony Schneider's gas was almost gone . . . Bill Pittman's tank was getting low . . . and nearly everyone's nerves were on edge, but Wade McClusky flew stubbornly on. He was sure the Japanese were up this way, even though he saw nothing so far. Now it was 9:55, and the *Enterprise*'s dive bombers were nearing the northern end of their search pattern. If they found nothing within the next five minutes, McClusky would have to lead them back east—or they would never get home at all.

Suddenly, far below, he spied a lone warship going full speed toward the northeast. Anything kicking up that much wake must be on urgent business. He decided she might be some kind of liaison vessel between the occupation group and Nagumo's Striking Force. He altered his course to that of the ship; the rest of the dive bombers followed.

Actually, the ship was no courier; she was the destroyer *Arashi*, part of Nagumo's screen. Detached to deal with the American submarine, she had dropped a few depth charges and was now trying to catch up with the fleet. But if McClusky's reasoning was a little off, his hunch was 100% right—her course would take him straight to the carriers.

At 10:05, Ensign Pittman—flying wing with one eye on

his gas gauge—saw the skipper motion ahead. There, about 35 miles away and a little to port, he spotted the first wakes. Flying farther to the rear, Lieutenant Bill Roberts saw them too—at first just some "curved white slashes on a blue carpet," then suddenly ships everywhere—he never saw so many at the same time in his life.

For Ensign Schneider, they were an especially welcome sight. He was just about out of gas, and he assumed they were friendly. Certainly it seemed logical: the *Enterprise's* planes had been in the air three hours now; they were flying east; unable to find the enemy, Commander McClusky must be bringing them home.

At this point his engine gave a final gasp and quit. Starting a long glide down toward the fleet below, he was surprised to see a battleship there. The U.S. didn't have any around. Tony Schneider needed no more hints. He veered sharply south, now hoping to land as far away from these ships as possible.

Ensign John McCarthy was another who first thought the "old man" had brought them all back to the *Enterprise*. Now his rear-seat man E. E. Howell asked tentatively, "Do you think we're home?"

McCarthy took a closer look—the squirming wakes, the pagoda masts, the long yellow flight decks. "No," he told Howell, "that's not home."

Wade McClusky could see them pretty well now. They seemed to be in a sort of big circle—the four carriers rather loosely spaced in the center. Two of them were fairly close . . . another to the east . . . the fourth far off on the northern horizon. His binoculars were practically glued to his eyes, but they didn't explain what impressed him the most: nobody was shooting at him. No fighters; no antiaircraft. Yet most of the ships were frantically turning. Too far down to see, but they must be dodging some torpedo attack going on below. Meanwhile the sky up here was empty, the target wide open.

Not a moment to lose. McClusky now broke radio silence,

reporting his contact to the *Enterprise* and assigning targets to his two squadrons. Earl Gallaher's Scouting 6 was flying right up with him; Dick Best's Bombing 6 was a little below and behind.

Approaching from the southwest, McClusky picked the first two carriers in his line of advance. The nearer of these—the one on the left—he gave to Gallaher and himself. The other— farther off to the right—he gave to Dick Best.

Somehow Best never got the word. As the trailing squadron in the formation, he assumed that his group would take the nearer target—the usual practice. In fact, after radio silence was broken he opened up saying he planned to do this. But now it was McClusky's turn not to get a radio message. The two squadrons roared on toward the attack point—both planning to hit the same carrier.

Best was almost ready now. He carefully strung out the planes in his own division, checked the position of the rest of his squadron. All were in place—a division on either side of him. He opened his flaps, about to push over and lead the way down.

Then without warning a series of blurs streaked down from above. McClusky and Scouting 6 were diving by him. To Best, they were taking his target—but there was nothing he could do about it. He closed his flaps, signaled Bombing 6 to close up again—they'd have to go on to the next carrier, farther to the east.

Dick Best wasn't the only pilot surprised by McClusky's dive. The skipper's own wing man, Ensign Bill Pittman, was equally taken aback. Pittman had the squadron's camera, and since he was to take pictures, he assumed that McClusky would be the last to dive, allowing a better chance to photograph the bombing.

Not at all. McClusky wasn't about to follow anybody else down. At 10:22 he suddenly pushed over, leaving Pittman too astonished to do anything for a moment. As he hesitated, McClusky's other wing man, Dick Jaccard, took Pittman's place and also dived. But Jaccard must have been a little nervous himself. Instead of opening his diving flaps, he grabbed the wrong handle and let down his wheels.

Next, Pittman pushed over too. He remembered to switch on his camera, but that was all. He took pictures of nothing but sky and horizon.

Now Scouting 6 pushed over, Earl Gallaher leading the way. Then, unexpectedly, the second and third divisions of Bombing 6 too. Some of Best's pilots didn't see that he had moved on to the next carrier; they just dived where originally planned. Others followed Lieutenant Joe Penland, leader of the second division. He wasn't sure of what Best wanted; he saw a lot of near-misses on the carrier below; so he used his discretion and joined McClusky. In all, some 25 dive bombers were hurtling down.

For incredible seconds the carrier seemed oblivious of them. Earlier she had been turning, but now she was heading into the wind getting ready to launch. Wade McClusky was half-way down before anybody saw him. Then she fired a few antiaircraft bursts, but that was all.

At 1,800 feet he reached for the handle on his left, pulled the bomb release, and cleared out as fast as he could. One after another the 25 planes did the same, as the whole world seemed to erupt beneath them. A ball of fire, flying debris, a brief glimpse of a Zero blown to bits—each pilot came away with his own impression, the way it was when he dropped his particular bomb. By the time the next man reached the same point, another explosion had rearranged the scene completely. Nobody saw the whole thing; no two men even saw it the same way.

Wade McClusky, leading the group, had a picture of a clean hardwood deck, an untouched island on the starboard side, some planes tuning up toward the stern. Earl Gallaher, coming in fourth, saw fountains of water from two near-misses, the blinding flash of his own bomb landing among the parked planes. Dusty Kleiss, seventh to dive, found the after end of the ship a sea of flames, the painted red circle up forward still untouched—then his own bomb changed that.

And so it went until Ensign George Goldsmith, the 25th and last man down, had his turn too. By now the carrier was a blazing wreck, swinging hard to the right in a desperate effort to ward off further blows. Goldsmith kept her in his sights.

In the rear seat, Radioman James Patterson called off the altitude as they plunged down. During dive bombing practice they normally released at about 2,200 feet. This time 2,000 spun past the altimeter, and they were still going straight down. Then 1,500 and finally Goldsmith pulled the release. Patterson watched the results with amazement: "He had been the world's worst dive bomber pilot during the practice hops I'd flown with him previously, but that day Ensign Goldsmith earned every dime invested in him as he put our bomb right through the flight deck, just aft of amidships."

At 15,000 feet Dick Best turned right and headed for the next carrier farther east. Having missed McClusky's instructions, he felt the skipper had "pre-empted" his target, but far worse than that, most of Bombing 6 had joined the others. He only had the five planes of his own division left to make his attack. Very well, they would have to do.

"Don't let this carrier escape," he called over his radio as they approached the new target. Still farther east, he could see a third flattop, and well north of that a fourth one too. He had a fleeting impression that the third carrier was just coming under attack, but at the moment he was concentrating all his attention on the second one below.

Now they were right over her. Incredibly, McClusky's attack—well within sight—hadn't stirred her up at all. There was no antiaircraft, and she too was holding course, heading into the wind, getting ready to launch. Best again strung out his other planes, opened his flaps, and this time he really dived. . . .

He could hardly believe it. For months he had pictured

this moment, and here it was at last—the yellow flight deck, the big red circle, everything just the way he imagined. He always knew that this was a real war, that out there somewhere was a real enemy, that he would be sent on real missions to hunt and be hunted. Even so, it never seemed truly real until now—this moment—when he was actually doing it.

He coolly examined the Japanese flight deck through his sights, aiming the three-power telescope at a point just ahead of the bridge and in the center of the ship. At 3,000 feet a plane passed across the lens—it was a fighter taking off. Good: it still looked like business as usual down there.

Behind him streaked his other four planes, and it was not an easy job. All the pilots agreed that no one dived more suddenly or more steeply than Dick Best. But on they came, wondering whether the skipper would ever pull out. Apparently deciding that he never would, one of the planes released too soon, but the others hung on. If he could do it, they could. Best himself kept diving until he was good and ready; then at the last second he pulled his bomb release handle.

But even now he wasn't leaving. He hadn't trained all these years to miss the sight of his first bomb hit. He pulled back sharply, literally laid his plane on its side and tail, and sat there watching from his improvised front-row seat.

His bomb hit squarely abreast of the bridge. Two others seemed to land back toward the fantail. All three blew the carrier's planes into a blazing heap; their gas tanks began going off like a string of firecrackers.

It was a fantastic sight. Yet here again no two men saw it quite the same way. In the excitement of the moment the eye played all kinds of tricks, even with respect to the simplest details. Dick Best saw "very clearly and unmistakably" that the carrier's island was on the starboard side; his extremely capable No. 5 man, Bill Roberts, was equally sure it was to port.

Finally pulling away, Best was surprised to see a torpedo plane formation heading in on an opposite course. They were apparently some "tail-end Charlies" from the earlier TBD attack. Then he caught sight of that third carrier, farther to the east, that he had noticed just before diving. It was now taking a dreadful beating—any number of bomb bursts flaring through a wall of smoke. Somebody was doing a thorough job of gutting it.

COMMANDER Max Leslie banged on the side of his SBD, attracting the attention of Bill Gallagher in the rear seat. Gallagher looked down to where the skipper was pointing, and 15,000 feet below he spotted an aircraft carrier. The *Yorktown's* planes had now been approaching the Japanese fleet for 15 minutes, but this was Gallagher's first glimpse of the actual target Leslie had picked out for Bombing 3. She was the most easterly of three carriers he could see in the area.

Nothing ever looked bigger, especially the huge red circle painted on the deck up front. Until this moment Gallagher had been sitting facing forward—an informal arrangement the skipper often tolerated—but now he swung around to handle his gun.

Leslie was still trying to get Lem Massey on the radio to coordinate the attack. But he could no longer hear Torpedo 3 at all. There was just static and silence.

At 10:23 Gallagher, keeping an eye on the carrier, signaled that she was starting to launch planes. This was bad news, for until now the upper sky had been free of fighters. Leslie tried once again to reach Massey—still only silence. There was no more time to lose; he must attack alone.

It was just 10:25 when he patted his head—the standard signal for "follow me"—and pushed over from 14,500 feet. He picked up the target right away, and as he roared down there was no doubt in his mind: this was the best dive he had ever made. It seemed more ironic than ever that he had already dropped his bomb on the way out.

Well, he still had his guns. At 10,000 feet he opened fire

with his fixed mount, raking the carrier's bridge. Then at 4,000 feet his guns jammed. With his bomb already gone, he now had nothing at all to throw at the enemy. He kept diving anyhow.

Commander Max Leslie took his men down all the way. Only when completely satisfied that he could do no more, did he pull out and leave the squadron to deliver their bombs.

Lieutenant Lefty Holmberg, flying No. 2, now took over. Studying the carrier, he decided the red circle painted on her flight deck made a good aiming point, and he set his sights on it.

She was still holding course, but he began to see little lights sparkling around the periphery of her flight deck. They reminded him of candles on a birthday cake back home. Then shrapnel began rattling off his plane. No doubt about it: they were shooting at him and getting close.

At 2,500 feet he pressed the electrical bomb release button, then pulled the hand release just to make sure. As he flattened out from his dive, his rear-seat man G. A. LaPlant practically blew his earphones off, yelling with joy, shouting that it was a hit, urging him to see for himself. Holmberg made a shallow turn to the left, and did take a look. A huge column of orange, black and dirty gray smoke was billowing up from the center of the ship.

One after another, the members of Bombing 3 pushed over, dived, released, pulled out. And one after another they caught their own little vignettes of the scene below. So alike yet so different, depending on the exact instant when each man's eye stopped the action long enough to record his picture.

For Joseph Godfrey, rear-seat man in No. 5 plane, there was the Zero that belatedly turned up just as the squadron pushed over: "So close I felt I could have spit in the pilot's eye." For Lieutenant Dave Shumway there was the fighter plane blown over the carrier's side by the blast from Holmberg's bomb. For Ensign Charles Lane it was the pull-out after the dive—yanking on the stick with both hands and thinking he would never make it. For Ensign Philip Cobb there were the chunks of flight deck and planes thrown into the air. If he ever got back to the *Yorktown,* he knew this was one Japanese ship he wouldn't have to worry about for the rest of the battle.

The last four men to dive thought so too. The carrier was now a mass of flames, and it seemed a waste to drop any more bombs on her. So Ensigns Elder and Cooner picked out a nearby "cruiser" (actually a destroyer), while Lieutenant Wiseman and Ensign Butler went after a battleship. All had the satisfaction of seeing smoke and flames around the stern of their new targets.

Max Leslie was clearing out now. Going to the squadron rendezvous just over to the southeast, he circled for five or ten minutes waiting for other planes to show up. Only Ensign Alden Hanson appeared; the rest were probably going home on their own. But while he waited, Leslie watched with satisfaction as explosions continued to rock the carrier attacked by Bombing 3. Then he saw other huge explosions erupting from two ships some 10-12 miles to the west. They looked like carriers too and somebody was thoroughly wrecking them.

The dive bomber pilots from the *Enterprise* and the *Yorktown* would long argue who struck the first blow at Midway. Coming in from different directions—unaware that anyone else was there—each group told very much the same story. Each found Nagumo's carriers untouched. Each attacked in the same six-minute span. Pulling out, each suddenly noticed the other at work. And, it might be added, there were enough unprovable claims to remove any fears that the debate might end. No one would ever really know.

TAKAYOSHI MORINAGA could see it coming. The first three bombs were near-misses just off the *Kaga's* port bow, but there was no doubt about this fourth one. It was heading right at the flight deck . . . in fact, right at *him.*

He threw himself down on the deck, closed his eyes, held

his hands over his ears. It landed with a splintering crash by the after elevator. Raising his head, Morinaga looked around: only three of the large group standing with him were still alive.

Captain Jisaku Okada probably never even knew about it. At almost the same instant he was killed by another bomb landing just forward of the bridge. It happened to hit a fuel cart, temporarily parked there to service the planes back from Midway. The whole thing exploded in a ball of fire, drenching the bridge with flaming gasoline. Nobody up there escaped.

Standing a little aft in the air command post, Commander Amagai ducked the torrent of fire. He didn't know about the fuel cart and assumed the whole inferno came from an "awful new kind of Yankee bomb."

More hits were coming. As Petty Officer Yokochi tried to reach his plane; one blast stunned him, then another hurled him over the side of the ship like a ball. He came to seconds later, bobbing about in the water.

Commander Yamasaki, the *Kaga*'s chief maintenance officer, wasn't so lucky. As he raced for cover across the flight deck, a bomb seemed to land right on top of him. He simply disappeared in the flash—not a trace of him left. Watching from the air command post, Commander Amagai had a curiously philosophical reaction: "Those who vanish like the dew will surely be quite happy."

There was such an element of fate about it all, Amagai no longer felt frightened. With resignation he now looked unconcernedly at the falling bombs, even thought he could distinguish colors painted on them.

To some it seemed forever, but actually it was all over in a couple of minutes. As the last of those dark blue planes pulled out, the *Kaga* had been squarely hit by at least four bombs, and probably more, for in the chaos of exploding planes and ammunition nobody could really make a careful count.

On the *Akagi* Teiichi Makishima ground away with his movie camera. As the only newsreel man brought along, he had the run of the flagship, and now he was out on the air command post catching every dreadful detail of the *Kaga's* agony. The censors would have something to say about it later, but at the moment he was taking everything.

At first he thought the *Kaga* might somehow survive. The towering columns of water from those early near-misses looked hopeful. But then came the terrible moment when the whole front of her bridge turned yellow with flame, and he found himself muttering aloud, "She is beaten at last."

It was at this dramatic point that he ran out of film. Ducking into the chart room, he spent the next two or three minutes frantically threading a new cartridge. Then back on deck just in time to hear the *Akagi's* own lookout scream, "Dive bombers!"

Incredibly, they were all caught by surprise. Admiral Kusaka was watching the *Akagi's* first fighter take off for the coming attack on the U.S. fleet—that was still his chief concern. Captain Aoki was concentrating on the last of the American torpedo planes—a few were still hovering about. On the battleship *Kirishima*, some 5,000 yards away, they even saw the planes above the *Akagi*. The executive officer grabbed the radiophone, but by the time he got through it was too late.

Teiichi Makishima gamely swung his camera on the planes he saw hurtling down. He could make out three of them, getting bigger every second. Then he had enough—he was a landlubber cameraman, not a sailor—and he hit the deck.

Commander Fuchida watched a little longer. Suddenly he saw some black objects fall from the bombers' wings. Then he too had enough and scrambled behind a protective mattress.

A blinding flash—the whole ship shuddered—as a bomb ripped through the radio aerial and exploded only five yards off the port side forward. A mighty column of filthy black water rose twice as high as the bridge, cascaded down on the officers huddled there. For a brief, terrifying second *Nagumo's* navigation officer, Commander Sasabe, gazed at this water column and thought he saw his mother's face.

Right afterward—some say just before—a second bomb landed on the flight deck opposite the bridge. This time the shock wasn't so bad—but only because it cut so easily through the elevator amidships and exploded on the hangar deck below. There it set everything off—planes, gas tanks, bombs, torpedoes. Flames gushed up, spreading to the planes spotted on the flight deck.

Then a third bomb smashed the very stern of the ship, hurling the planes parked there into a jumbled heap. Worse, it jammed the ship's rudder so she could no longer steer.

That was all. Seconds later the planes were gone, and for a brief moment, anyhow, there was no sound but the crackling flames. Looking down at the blazing wreckage, Mitsuo Fuchida began to cry.

At about the same time Teiichi Makishima was taking his movies, Commander Hisashi Ohara stood on the navigation bridge of the *Soryu*, also watching the *Kaga* under attack. Bombs were hitting her, and he could see the fires breaking out. Then a sudden yell from the lookout on his own ship: "Enemy dive bombers—hole in the clouds!"

He looked up in time to see about a dozen planes screaming down on the *Soryu*. Next instant the first bomb hit the port side of the flight deck by the forward elevator . . . then another right in front of the bridge. The blast blew Ohara backward about five yards. It didn't particularly hurt—felt rather like being tossed in a steam bath. It wasn't until he returned to his post and everyone began throwing towels over his face that he realized how badly burned he must be.

By now a third bomb had landed aft, and the whole flight deck was blazing. There may have been other hits too, but it was hard to tell—planes and ammunition were exploding all over the ship. Within three minutes she was obviously gone, and some of the U.S. dive bombers shifted to the screening vessels. The destroyer *Isokaze* took a near miss off her stern.

It all happened so quickly many on the *Soryu* had no warning at all. Juzo Mori was down in the ready room with the other pilots from the Midway strike. They couldn't get anybody to hear their report, and now they were lounging in the big leather chairs, munching rice balls and griping about the mysterious ways of the bridge. Then the battle bugle blew, and a voice came over the loudspeaker saying the *Kaga* was under attack.

Some of the younger pilots rushed out to watch, but the debonair Mori preferred to take it easy. They'd call when they needed him. He was still relaxing with about a dozen others when, without warning, there was a frightful jar. The ship heeled violently to starboard, apparently in an emergency turn to port. Next instant the whole wall of the ready room split with a crash, and flames poured in.

The pilots made a mad dash for the single door. Mori happened to be last, but he remembered his Rugby—a game he enjoyed—and by the time they emerged, he was first.

Tatsuya Otawa, another of the pilots in the group, stumbled onto the flight deck to find it already a mass of flames. Everything was blowing up—planes, bombs, gas tanks. He had time for only the briefest glance. Then a roaring explosion blasted him over the side of the ship. Still perfectly conscious, he had the presence of mind to tuck his legs up under him and clasp his hands under his knees. He sailed into the water "cannonball-style."

On the *Hiryu* Lieutenants Tomonaga and Hashimoto had spent a busy hour getting ready for the coming strike against the U.S. fleet. Now everything seemed under control, and Hashimoto was catching a breather in the torpedo squadron ready room. A few minutes later Lieutenant Yasuhiro Shigematsu, leader of the *Hiryu's* fighters, came bursting in: "Hey, the *Akagi's* damaged; the *Kaga* and *Soryu* are burning—we're the only ship that hasn't been hit!"

Hashimoto could hardly believe it. He hurried to the flight deck and looked around. It was hard to see much: during the morning's maneuvering the *Hiryu* had somehow drawn steadily ahead of the other three carriers. Now they were perhaps 10,000 yards astern. But they weren't so far off that Lieutenant Hashimoto missed the towering smoke and three separate fires on the horizon.

The *Hiryu's* executive officer, Commander Kanoe, saw it all from the bridge. It was awful the way everything seemed to happen at once. As he watched those mounting columns of smoke, he was completely heartsick. He could only whisper to himself, "What will become of us?"

LEFTY HOLMBERG didn't care what happened now. Even if they never got back to the *Yorktown*, they had accomplished their mission. So when oil began to spatter all over his cockpit, it didn't make too much difference. He assumed the AA fire had cut his oil line, and he'd soon crash. Never mind. He still had gotten that hit. At worst, he felt like a football player who breaks his leg scoring the winning touchdown.

He waited for the engine to sputter and stop, but it kept running smoothly, the gauges all normal. Finally he realized there was nothing wrong with his engine after all; it was only hydraulic fluid from the system that worked his landing gear and flaps.

He flew on, safely dodging the Japanese destroyer screen. Soon he fell in with other planes from Bombing 3, and together they headed back for the *Yorktown*. The whole time he kept his eyes peeled for Zeros, but never saw a single one.

Others found them all too easily. Down low, working over the torpedo planes, the Zeros couldn't break up the dive-bombing attack, but they were in a perfect position to strike the bombers pulling out. Goaded by the three blazing carriers, they tried hard for revenge.

A stream of tracer bullets chopped the water around Wade McClusky's plane. Two Zeros began taking turns diving on him. They were so much faster, McClusky could think of only one thing to do. Every time one dived, he'd turn sharply toward it. This at least gave the Jap a tougher target and his own gunner Chochalousek a chance to try out the skills he had recently picked up at gunnery school.

Back and forth the three planes went for maybe five minutes. Then a Japanese burst caught McClusky's plane. The left side of the cockpit was shattered, and he felt as though his left shoulder had been hit with a sledge hammer. He was sure it was the end; he was a goner.

The gunfire died away. Did they get Chochalousek too? McClusky called out over the intercom, but there was no answer. His shoulder was killing him, but he managed to turn around. Chochalousek was still there—unharmed, facing aft, guns at the ready. He had finally picked off one Zero, and the other called it quits.

The SBD flew on, boasting numerous souvenirs of the duel. The plane had been hit 55 times, not counting a few extras contributed by Chochalousek. Noting that the twin barrels on his gun were about eight inches apart, he saw no reason why he couldn't shoot straight back on both sides of the rudder at the same time. Fortunately, there was enough of the rudder left to get them home.

Machinist's Mate F. D. Adkins, the rear-seat man in Ensign Pittman's plane, had a different kind of adventure with his twin gun mount. It broke loose from its rack during Pittman's dive, but Adkins managed to grab and hang on to it. Then, as they pulled out, a Zero attacked. Steadying the gun on the fuselage, Adkins opened fire and somehow shot down the fighter. No one ever knew how he did it: the gun weighed 175 pounds, and he was a very slight young man who couldn't even lift the gun when they later got back to the *Enterprise*.

And, of course, there were those who couldn't get clear at all. A Zero riddled Lieutenant Penland's tanks, forcing him down 30 uncomfortable miles from the Japanese. Others simply vanished—sometimes without a word, sometimes with a brief radio call to say they were going down. But for those who did get clear—who dodged the flaming guns of the carriers, who broke through the hail of fire from the screen, who escaped the last snarling Zero—there was a new lift to life as they headed safely home. Men like John Snowden, gunner in Dusty Kleiss's plane, felt a sudden glow of gratitude —"a good feeling that it was warm and sunny; that the airplane was apparently all in one piece and we had come through it alive."

For Stan Ring, leader of the *Hornet's* Air Group, there was only dark disappointment. His fruitless search to the south had yielded nothing; now he was heading back to the ship, all bombs still neatly tucked under the wings of his planes.

To make matters worse, most of Bombing 8 couldn't pick up the *Hornet's* homing signal and were groping around using up what little gas they had left. Fortunately Midway itself was only 60–70 miles away; so the skipper, Lieutenant Commander Ruff Johnson, decided to gas up there before flying on.

Even this was too late for three of the planes. Ensign Guillory's tank went dry 40 miles out . . . then Ensign Wood went down 10 miles out . . . and finally Ensign Auman in the lagoon itself. The remaining eleven planes came gingerly in, rightly suspecting that Midway's garrison was more than trigger-happy.

They jettisoned their bombs on the reef, hoping this would be interpreted as a friendly gesture—but it almost had the opposite effect. It was one of Colonel Shannon's favorite theories that the invasion force would begin operations by blasting a hole in the reef, and this certainly looked like it. A few scattered bursts of AA fire nicked three of the planes; then some sharp eyes detected the familiar dumpy silhouette of the SBD.

Lieutenant Stan Ruehlow, leading Fighting 8 back toward the *Hornet,* wasn't about to try Midway. It was an easy hop

—and he knew the squadron could never make it to the ship —
but that big column of smoke over the atoll just looked too
dangerous. It could mean almost anything—even that the invasion was on.

Far better to play it safe and get as close to the *Hornet* as
possible. His radio wasn't working, and the YE-ZB homing
device was on the blink, but if he got close enough, maybe
the ship could somehow catch his call.

So they all flew on. The minutes passed, the tanks drained
lower, and finally the first fighter fell. Then a second. Ruehlow
watched them go one after another—some singles, some pairs
—till finally there was only the skipper Pat Mitchell, Ensign
Dick Gray and himself left. Then Mitchell and Gray went too.

Now Ruehlow was all alone. In a few minutes he'd be down
anyway; so deciding there was strength in numbers, he pulled
around and slapped heavily into the sea near Mitchell and
Gray. By 11:00 A.M. all the planes of Fighting 8 were gone.

There was only one consolation. About half an hour earlier
Ruehlow had looked to the north and seen in the distance
what he had spent all morning searching for: the Japanese
fleet. As frustrating as it must have been to find them only
now—when Fighting 8's tanks were almost dry—it was "a
beautiful sight" to see those three carriers burning.

Five other American spectators had a much closer view.
Tony Schneider of Bombing 6 now knew all too well that he
had run out of gas over the Japanese, not the U.S. fleet. Gliding down as far away as he could, he watched the dive bombers strike. He was proud of the boys and chagrined at himself that he hadn't done a better job of managing his fuel. His
glide finally carried him to a dead-stick landing beyond the
sight of the Japanese. But he was close enough to see the
smoke and sometimes, he thought, hear the highly satisfying
sound of explosions in the distance.

Three other Americans were less fortunate. A pilot and
his gunner from Scouting 6 were fished out of the water by the
Japanese destroyer *Makigumo,* and a young ensign from Tor-

pedo 3 was picked up by the *Arashi*. Little is known about what followed, but it could not have been very pleasant. By now Nagumo's hopes and ships were shattered; chances are that the interrogation was less than polite. In any case, the men began to talk.

There was still one other American witness left. Peeping from beneath the black cushion that bobbed harmlessly amid the floating debris, Ensign George Gay of Torpedo 8 was very much alive and free.

Until the dive bombers came, he spent most of his time watching a nearby carrier with almost clinical interest. It was engaged in landing Zero fighters, and Gay carefully noted that the approaches were made from far and high (about 1,000–1,500 feet altitude) and coming in from straight astern. The landing intervals were longer than the American, but he was most impressed by the arresting gear.

His studies were somewhat interrupted when a screening cruiser passed within 500 yards of him. She didn't see him, and he continued his observations.

Then the dive bombers arrived. Gay watched these too with professional interest, and they never looked better. The SBDs seemed to dive faster and lower than he had ever seen them do in practice. He found himself cheering and hollering with every hit.

CAPTAIN Ryusaku Yanagimoto fought to get the *Soryu* under control. Three hits had knocked out the voice tubes, the bridge telephones, the engine room telegraph—there was no way to give orders at all.

Although badly burned, Commander Ohara took over the fire-fighting job. With the bridge communications out, he went down a deck to the air command post, hoping it might be easier to operate from here. No use—all the fire mains were out. He retreated down to the flight deck, where he finally fainted from his burns. At this point he either fell or was blown over the side of the ship. When he came to, he was in the water. A pharmacist's mate was swimming alongside him, slapping his face to keep him from fainting again and drowning.

By 10:40 both engines had stopped and the whole ship was in flames. The fire reached the torpedo storage room, and the blast almost tore the *Soryu* apart. At 10:45 a badly injured Captain Yanagimoto shouted orders to abandon ship.

When the order came, CPO Mori was with the rest of the pilots from the ready room, jammed into a small corner of the boat deck below the bridge. They were so tightly packed together they couldn't even raise their arms. As still more men crammed in, they began climbing on each other's shoulders to make more room. All the time the flames crept closer.

Somebody tried to lower a cutter; it stuck in the davits, one end dropping. Soon many of the men were jumping. Mori himself hung on; the distance down just looked too far. Finally he noticed that the long Pacific swell occasionally brought the sea within safer reach. Timing himself carefully, he leaped clear of the deck and grabbed the fall of an empty davit, hoping to lower himself into the water. But nothing was attached to the other end of the line; it simply shot through the pulley, and Mori plummeted straight down.

He bobbed to the surface and cleared the ship. Next instant a boat, loosened from somewhere, plunged into the water nearby. It landed upside down, but Mori helped some men right it, and he baled it out with his flying boot. They all climbed in and began paddling away. This proved a slow business, for they only had one oar.

CWO Otawa didn't even have that, as he treaded water some distance away. But he had something else, maybe better. In the pocket of his flight jacket he still carried his lucky talisman from the Narita Shrine near Tokyo.

He continued swimming—alone yet not alone. Every time the swell lifted him up, he could look "downhill" and see hundreds of heads dotting the water all around. In the distance he could see the *Soryu,* and farther off the burning *Kaga.*

The fire was now so hot on the *Kaga* that Commander Amagai could no longer hang on at the air command post. No one was around to give any orders, so on his own initiative he led a working party to a lower deck to try and organize the fire-fighting.

Huge explosions were ripping through the side of the ship, hurling out men and chunks of planes like projectiles. Amagai couldn't reach the hangar deck, where the fire was worst, but it looked like an inferno.

Indeed it was. Hearing shouts that the hangar deck was on fire, CWO Morinaga had rushed there right after the bombing, but the situation was already hopeless. None of the fire mains was working. In desperation Morinaga organized a bucket brigade, using the latrines alongside the deck. The results were as pitiful as might be expected. Then he tried throwing "combustibles" overboard—but on a carrier almost everything is combustible. The fires and explosions steadily spread, finally cornering him on a small open deck right under the bridge.

Above, everything was in flames. Below, he still had a chance if he could only get down to the next deck. The ladder was red-hot, but there was a cutter lashed to the side of the ship. The canvas lashing was taut, but he clutched at it and lowered himself by his fingers. Painfully he worked his way down the outside of the boat, finally swinging onto the deck below. He still wonders how he did it.

At last he was safe for a moment—better than that, with friends. Commander Amagai was here, along with many of the other pilots. The *Kaga's* air officer had given up any hope of stopping the fire; he was now mainly concerned with saving his pilots for some better day. He heard no orders to abandon ship, but what difference did it make? On his own initiative he told his men, "Jump into the sea."

Morinaga yanked off his summer flying suit, his flight boots,

even his *senim bari*. Stripped to his shorts, he leaped out as
far as he could. A few of the new conscripts said they didn't
know how to swim, but Amagai had them jump anyhow—it
was better than staying here. Only the assistant air officer
Lieutenant Ogawa didn't go. He was just too badly hurt by
one of the first bomb hits. He said good-bye to Amagai and
hobbled back toward the fire.

In the water Amagai pulled away from the ship, using a
stately breast stroke that was rather out of keeping with his
reputation as one of Nagumo's more dashing airmen. He was
none too soon. He looked back and could see the paint on the
Kaga's starboard side was starting to burn. Ahead in the distance, he noticed for the first time that the *Akagi* was on
fire too.

"Anybody who isn't working, get below!" Commander Masuda shouted above the general confusion on the *Akagi*'s
bridge. The fire was bad enough without a lot of bystanders
in the way. Commander Fuchida, still too weak from appendicitis to be of much use, went down to the ready room. So did
a thoroughly shaken Teiichi Makishima, who had stopped taking his newsreel shots.

But the ready room was no place to be. Already jammed
with burn cases, it quickly filled with smoke and heat, driving
both Fuchida and Makishima back to the air command post.
Clearly the fire was spreading fast.

No one knew it better than the *Akagi*'s damage control officer Commander Dobashi. He strung out his hoses, but the
power was out and the pumps didn't work. He tried flooding
the ammunition storage rooms, but the valves were too badly
damaged in the all-important after areas. In helpless rage he
buckled on his *samurai* sword; if he could do nothing else,
he'd at least go down in the ancient tradition.

On the bridge the *Akagi*'s navigator, Commander Miura,
found it impossible to steer the ship. The bomb that landed
by the fantail jammed her rudder 20° to port, and her speed
was falling off. She was just going around in circles. He rang

the telegraph to stop engines, but nothing happened. Since the voice tube and phones were all out, he finally sent a man below to find out what was wrong.

The machinery was all right, but it turned out that every man in the starboard engine room was dead—suffocated by fire sucked down through the exhaust system. The engines themselves were still running in eerie fashion, completely unattended.

Miura did the only thing he could do. With his rudder jammed and half the engineers gone, at 10:42 he shut off the boilers and stopped the ship.

As the *Akagi* lost headway, the flames roared forward. At 10:43 a Zero parked right below the bridge caught fire, and the blaze quickly spread to the bridge itself. Flames licked into the windows, and the heat was unbearable.

It was clear to Admiral Kusaka that the *Akagi* could no longer serve as flagship. She couldn't steer; the fires were spreading; the radio was out, and it was impossible to direct the battle by semaphores and signal flags from a burning bridge. He urged Admiral Nagumo to transfer to some other ship.

"It's not time yet," Nagumo muttered, standing transfixed near the compass.

Captain Aoki came over. Tears in his eyes, he begged, "Leave the *Akagi* to me; you must shift the flag."

Nagumo still refused.

It was too much for the pragmatic Kusaka. The *samurai* spirit was all very well, but a burning flagship was no place to run a fleet. "You are Commander in Chief of the First Carrier Striking Force as well as the *Akagi*," he scolded the Admiral. "It's your duty to carry on the battle. . . ."

A long silence; then with a barely perceptible nod, Nagumo agreed to go.

No time to lose. The destroyer *Nowaki* was hovering close by; they would go there. Kusaka had a signalman semaphore the decision and ordered her to send a boat. At the same time, he told the flag secretary Commander Nishibayashi to scout around, find the best way out of this furnace. Nishibayashi soon came running back: all the passages below were on fire.

The only escape was by window. At 10:46 they opened one on the leeward side, tossed out a couple of lines, and began to leave that way. Nagumo went first. An expert in judo, he landed lightly on the flight deck. Kusaka went next, using the other line. Plump and anything but agile, it was too much for him. He lost his grip and fell heavily to the deck, spraining both ankles.

At the moment, he didn't even notice it. Ammunition was exploding, bullets were flying about, and worst of all, he had lost his left shoe. It flew off as he landed, ending up on a part of the deck that was burning. Would it hurt more trying to retrieve it, or running after the others over a red-hot deck with one shoe off?

He hesitated interminable seconds while the rest of the staff—now waiting on the anchor deck—yelled at him to hurry up. In the end he dashed after them . . . half-running, half-hopping, burning his foot as expected.

The *Nowaki*'s launch was alongside, and they all piled in. But instead of going to the destroyer, they headed for the light cruiser *Nagara*. She had also come up, was bigger and much better equipped. But wherever they went, it couldn't remove the sting. As they shoved off from the blazing *Akagi*— every second wracked by some new explosion—Commander Chuichi Yoshioka felt as if he'd left his heart behind.

At 11:30 the *Nagara* dropped her Jacob's ladder, and Nagumo climbed aboard with his staff. They were met on the quarterdeck by Rear Admiral Susumu Kimura, who commanded Destroyer Squadron 10 and used the cruiser as his flagship.

"Kimura, do you think the *Nagara* could tow the *Akagi?*" were Nagumo's first words.

"It may be difficult," Kimura replied, choosing his words

tactfully, "in view of the actual circumstances of the *Akagi.*"

Kusaka went immediately to the bridge to break out a vice admiral's flag for Nagumo. It turned out there was none on board, so he took the flag Kimura flew as a rear admiral. It looked the same except for a red strip across the bottom. This was ripped off, and the remains hoisted to the yardarm. The effect was a bit tattered, but certainly no worse than the fleet.

ADMIRAL Isoroku Yamamoto was apparently feeling much better. Under the weather the day before, he had his usual breakfast this morning—boiled rice, *miso* soup, eggs and dried fish. His touch of vanity seemed to be thriving too. Most of the staff were dressed in fatigues or their regular blues (a few dandies wore British-type shorts), but the Commander in Chief—along with his chief of staff and Captain Takayanagi—was resplendent in starched whites. Yamamoto even wore his gloves.

Now he stood on the navigation bridge of the great *Yamato,* receiving reports, searching the seas, casually watching the 18 ships of the Main Body. It was just 7:00 A.M. and they were steaming along some 450 miles behind Nagumo's carriers.

So far there was not much excitement. Nagumo was still operating under radio silence, and on the *Yamato* they only knew what they could pick up by monitoring the planes. They learned that a PBY had found the carriers . . . that Tomonaga wanted a second strike . . . that the Midway-based planes were attacking. And at 7:28 they heard the *Tone's* No. 4 plane report that U.S. ships were already on the scene.

Considering that all their planning had been based on completely the opposite assumption, the Admiral and his staff adjusted to the new situation with surprising ease. Far from being alarmed, they were delighted. If the American fleet was already out, they'd polish it off that much sooner. And when the *Tone's* plane reported "what appears to be a carrier," they grew even more excited. Captain Kuroshima assured everyone that Nagumo had a reserve wave of torpedo planes with just this contingency in view.

"It all turned out just as we wanted," thought Commander Watanabe of the operations staff. Nothing that happened during the next two hours changed his opinion. By now, Nagumo had opened up his radio, and while he was in direct touch with Yamamoto only twice, the gist was completely reassuring: he had taken many blows; he had suffered no damage; he was hot after the enemy fleet.

Then, just before 10:30, an unexpected message came up from the radio room. Watanabe caught it over the voice tube —there was nothing formal about it—just something monitored over the air that the radio room thought the bridge should know right away. A hurried voice reported, "The *Akagi* is on fire!" Watanabe rushed to the battle command post and passed the word directly to Admiral Yamamoto. The Admiral asked Captain Kuroshima whether it might not be wise to confirm that the carriers had actually launched their torpedo strike at the U.S. fleet. If this hadn't been done, it could mean trouble.

No need to do that, said Kuroshima. Of course the attack had been launched. It was all in his plan.

More traffic was monitored—a fire on the *Kaga*, on the *Soryu* too. Still, Yamamoto's staff refused to get too worried. No reason to suppose the damage was serious . . . ships were bound to get hit in action . . . the *Hiryu* was going strong . . . the real battle was just beginning.

At 10:50 the *Yamato*'s communications officer hurried up to the bridge, handed a new message to Yamamoto's signal officer Commander Wada. He took a look, silently gave it to the chief of staff, Admiral Ugaki. He also looked and just as silently handed it to the Commander in Chief.

It was from Rear Admiral Hiroaki Abe on the *Tone*. Second in command of the Striking Force, he had automatically taken over while Nagumo was shifting his flag to the *Nagara*. Abe pulled no punches:

Fires are raging aboard the *Kaga, Soryu,* and *Akagi* resulting from attacks carried out by land-based and carrier-based attack planes. We plan to have the *Hiryu* engage the enemy carriers. In the meantime, we are temporarily retiring to the north, and assembling our forces. . . .

Yamamoto handed it back without a word. He seemed stunned. Searching his face for some kind of clue, Yeoman Noda felt it was utterly "frozen"—not even an eyebrow moved.

Aт тне same time that Admiral Abe radioed the Commander in Chief, he also sent a message to Admiral Yamaguchi on the *Hiryu,* now almost out of sight to the north. "Attack enemy carriers," he ordered.

Yamaguchi didn't need to be told. That was what he had wanted to do all morning. After taking one look at the billowing smoke far astern, he had already given the orders. He simply blinkered back to Abe: "All our planes are taking off now for the purpose of destroying the enemy carriers."

Men raced about the *Hiryu's* decks getting ready. If there was anyone in the crew who failed to appreciate the crisis, he soon got the word. The loudspeaker tersely described the damage to the other three carriers and announced it was "now up to the *Hiryu* to carry on the fight for the glory of greater Japan."

The air officer, Commander Kawaguchi, hammered out the plan of attack. Ideally, of course, both dive bombers and torpedo planes should go together on a coordinated strike. But it would take an hour to put torpedoes on the planes back from Midway, and the time had passed for games like that. The dive bombers were ready; they'd go at once. The torpedo planes would follow later. The all-important thing was to launch an attack—any kind of attack—as soon as possible.

Lieutenant Michio Kobayashi understood all this well. He would be leading the dive bombers, and he was a good choice.

A veteran of Pearl Harbor, he had been flying missions since the earliest days. Tall and taciturn, he had a kind of quiet drive that Kawaguchi could trust. Trouble was, he had only 18 dive bombers in his little force.

They were even worse off for fighter escort. They had used up too many trying to cover the carriers during the morning attacks. Now the best that Kawaguchi could do was scrape together six Zeros.

By 10:50 all was set. The dive bomber pilots poured out of the ready room as always, but then came an unusual step. Before manning their planes, they were assembled on the flight deck under the bridge, and Admiral Yamaguchi addressed them. He pointed out they all knew how "critical" the situation was—they were all that was left—hence everything depended on their efforts. But for this very reason, he stressed, they mustn't be reckless. It would be a temptation to do something foolhardy, but Japan's hopes depended on their coolness and skill.

The little group broke up, and the 18 men made for their planes as the motors began turning over. On impulse Commander Kawaguchi rushed up to his Academy classmate Lieutenant Takenori Kondo, leader of a bomber section. They shook hands as Kawaguchi urged his friend on. "I'll do my best," Kondo smiled. Then with a wave he was off.

At 10:54 the first Zeros roared off the deck, and by 10:58 the whole force was in the air. They wasted no time in climbing and circling; every minute counted as they quickly headed east.

Watching them go from the air command post, Commander Kawaguchi prayed for revenge.

CHAPTER 9

Dead in the Water

ONLY two hours had passed since Wade McClusky left with the *Enterprise*'s dive bombers, yet it seemed an eternity to Commander Leonard Dow. As Spruance's communications officer, "Ham" Dow would know the results of the strike as soon as anyone, yet he knew nothing—except that McClusky was long overdue. He should have reached the Japanese at 9:20; now it was 10:00, and still no word from him.

To make matters worse, radio reception was bad—lots of static and fading—and some fool in the Aleutians kept sending inconsequential messages, which CINCPAC dutifully relayed for the *Enterprise*'s information. Dow finally asked Pearl to stop. If he couldn't hear McClusky, at least he could be spared this useless stuff.

The tension seeped over the whole ship—in fact, the whole task force—affecting all ranks. Lieutenant Commander Bromfield Nichol, Spruance's operations officer, felt the "terrific anxiety" of a man who had been deeply involved in the planning. Lieutenant (j.g.) Wilmer Rawie, a young pilot not assigned to the strike, had the empty feeling that comes from not being with friends in trouble.

On the screening destroyer *Monaghan* a very green ensign named Robert Gillette stood nervous and fidgeting like the rest. Then he noticed the skipper, Lieutenant Commander Bill Burford, deeply engrossed in a book. Burford had a knack of being in the thick of things (he had rammed a midget sub at Pearl Harbor), and Gillette assumed he must now be doing some last-minute brushing up on tactics. Closer inspection revealed that the Commander, imperturbable as ever, was poring over a "girlie" joke book.

At 10:05 the long wait ended. Through the static-filled air came a message from McClusky indicating that he was at last in contact with the enemy. But beyond that, it was anybody's guess. More long minutes of static. At 10:08 a frantic Miles Browning shouted over the radio, "Attack immediately!" More static.

On the screening destroyer *Balch* Captain Edward P. Sauer was listening too. Reception varied so much from ship to ship that he never caught McClusky's contact report at all. His first clue that the Commander had found the enemy was an unmistakably American voice that suddenly burst over the circuit, "Wow! Look at that bastard burn!"

In the radio room of the cruiser *Astoria* a similar group was tuned in on Max Leslie and the dive bombers from the *Yorktown*. If Leslie sent a contact report, they never caught it, but they too got occasional hints that a lot was going on. Once through the static they heard an especially jubilant voice cry, "How we doin', Doc?"

More long minutes of waiting. Then, around 11:00, some specks in the western sky. But they turned out to be Jim Gray's Fighting 6—deeply disappointed men who never linked up with the SBDs and could shed no light on the attack.

Finally around 11:50 the *Enterprise*'s dive bombers began coming in. Not in proud formations, the way they went out, but in twos and threes . . . and sometimes alone. Wade McClusky led this straggling parade, and it had been a rough trip back for the air group's skipper. First, he was shot up by the Japs . . . next the ship was 60 miles from Point Option, where he was meant to find her . . . then he almost landed on the *Yorktown* by mistake. But now at last he was dropping down—with only five gallons of gas left.

At this point he was waved off by the landing signal officer Lieutenant (j.g.) Robin Lindsey. It seemed another plane was still in the landing area. But McClusky wasn't about to stay up any longer. He playfully thumbed his nose at Lindsey and came in anyhow.

Rushing to Flag Plot, he reported to Admiral Spruance: three carriers hit and burning; a fourth one hadn't been touched. He was still giving his account when the *Enterprise*'s executive officer Commander W. F. Boone suddenly broke in: "My God, Mac, you've been shot!" McClusky had forgotten to mention it, but blood was indeed trickling from his jacket sleeve to the deck. He was hustled off to sick bay with five different wounds in his left arm and shoulder.

In the confusion, his news of the fourth carrier was apparently overlooked. So was a similar report by Dick Best when he landed a few minutes later and checked in with Miles Browning.

On deck, anxious eyes carefully counted the planes from each squadron as they sputtered in. The task was anything but cheerful. Apart from the frightful losses of Torpedo 6, so many of the dive bombers were gone too—18 out of 32 altogether.

Most of them ran out of gas on the way back. Partly it was that long, relentless search for the enemy; partly the *Enterprise*'s miscalculation in estimating where she could be found again. At that, some of the pilots almost made it—Lieutenant Dickinson was picked up only ten miles from the ship. But others were gone for good. Lieutenant Charles Ware brilliantly guided his division through the attack and two melees with the Zeros . . . then vanished, choosing a course home that could lead only into the empty sea.

The *Hornet*'s fliers had an even rougher time. Stan Ring led Scouting 8 safely back after their wild-goose chase south; a plane from Bombing 8 came with them; then nothing. When

Clayton Fisher, the returnee from Bombing 8, went down to the squadron ready room, the unassigned pilots crowded around him in anguish: "Fisher, you're the only pilot in our squadron to get back; and nobody has come in from Fighting 8 and Torpedo 8!"

Ultimately three more SBDs from Bombing 8 did turn up, but that was it. The minutes dragged by with no sign of the rest. Thirty-nine planes had vanished. The only other arrival was a fighter from the *Yorktown,* badly mauled by Zeros. Returning from the strike, its wounded pilot picked the *Hornet* as the first U.S. carrier he saw. Thumping down heavily on the flight deck, his guns went off and raked the island structure, killing several men. A shaken crew went back to their vigil.

The shipboard members of Torpedo 8 refused to give up hope. The personnel officer, Lieutenant George Flinn, knew the planes could keep flying five hours and 20 minutes at the most, but long after that deadline he still searched the skies. Some miracle just might bring them home. Even when everyone else had given up, he kept chicken dinners ready for them all.

At least the wait was shorter on the *Yorktown.* Her planes had been launched an hour later, and except for the fighter that crash-landed on the *Hornet,* they had no trouble finding their way back. The ship was just where Commander Arnold said she would be. By 11:15 Max Leslie's dive bombers were overhead, but at the last minute it was decided not to land them until Fighting 3 returned—Jimmy Thach's men would be lower on gas.

So the bombers orbited, but their good news wouldn't keep any longer. One of them signaled by Aldis lamp that they had sunk an enemy carrier. Cheers rippled through Task Force 17, and scuttlebutt quickly took over. It was said that the Japanese fliers, having lost their ship, were landing at Midway and surrendering to the Navy.

Admiral Fletcher wasn't yet ready to celebrate. There were supposed to be four carriers out there, and he still knew of

DEAD IN THE WATER [193

only two. He had heard nothing from the PBYs for five hours, and so far it was impossible to get a clear picture from his own planes now circling above. Were there really two other carriers? If so, where were they?

He decided to have another look to the northwest. At 11:20 he sent off Lieutenant Wally Short with 10 of the 17 dive bombers he had been holding in reserve all morning.

Meanwhile, Jimmy Thach had returned, and after another interruption while the Combat Air Patrol was relieved and strengthened, the fighters began landing about 11:45. Once again the crew went through the agonizing business of counting. It was better than it might have been: four out of six came home.

Thach hurried to Flag Plot, reported to Admiral Fletcher: three carriers definitely out of action, the battle seemed to be "going our way." Well, that cleared up part of the mystery. Fletcher now knew there was at least a third carrier out there. What about a fourth? Thach couldn't say. He saw only the three that were burning. He didn't know whether there was still another one or not.

At this moment the *Yorktown*'s air-raid alarm began sounding: bogeys, lots of them, coming in from the west. Admiral Frank Jack Fletcher now knew definitely—beyond any doubt whatsoever—that there was indeed a fourth Japanese carrier around.

"Bogeys, 32 miles, closing," the *Yorktown*'s radar officer, Radio Electrician V. M. Bennett, reported at 11:52. They were also climbing, which ruled out friendly planes and the possibility of a torpedo attack. It all added up to enemy dive bombers, and since the *Yorktown* was first in their line of approach, she would clearly be the target.

The screening destroyers moved in close; the cruisers *Astoria* and *Portland* stood off to starboard, putting themselves between the carrier and the coming storm. The *Yorktown* herself turned southeast, showing her stern to the attackers. She cranked up her speed from 25 to 30.5 knots.

She was all buttoned up. Fuel lines were drained and filled

with carbon dioxide. A portable gasoline tank on the flight deck was pitched overboard. Repair parties were at their posts, doctors and medics at every dressing station. Her guns were manned, all pointing west.

And no carrier boasted more fire power. The *Yorktown*'s gunnery officer Lieutenant Commander Leonard Davis had a simple theory that if you put enough bullets in the direction of attacking aircraft, eventually some plane would run into one. Carrying out this idea, he even borrowed all the spare machine guns from the planes in the hangar and lashed them to the catwalk rails.

But the *Yorktown*'s first line of defense lay in her Combat Air Patrol—12 fighters orbiting restlessly above the ship. As soon as the alarm sounded, Lieutenant Commander Pederson moved into action, vectoring them out toward the approaching bogeys. Now they were converging on a point 10,000 feet up, some 15–20 miles to the west. Flying his F4F, Lieutenant (j.g.) Scott McCuskey peered ahead. There coming straight toward him was a group of 18 planes. He felt butterflies deep inside—like playing football, just before the opening whistle. . . .

LIEUTENANT Yasuhiro Shigematsu couldn't resist the temptation. His six Zeros were meant to escort the *Hiryu*'s dive bombers now winging toward the American fleet. But there, right below, was a group of U.S. planes heading home for their carriers. They looked like torpedo planes (actually they were SBDs), but whatever the type, they were perfect targets. He decided he could pick these off and get back on station before Lieutenant Kobayashi's bombers ever reached the enemy force.

The Zeros roared down on the SBDs, but they proved far more battle-wise than expected. Shigematsu got none of them, and they shot up two of his planes so badly they limped back home. Thoroughly mauled, he broke off and rejoined Kobayashi. The fighters were back in plenty of time, but there were now only four of them to protect the bombers.

The formation flew on. The *Chikuma*'s No. 4 and No. 5 search planes had been ordered to point the way, but Kobayashi now had some far better guides. The planes Shigematsu attacked were not the only Americans going home. The air was full of them, all heading back from the Japanese carriers. Kobayashi slipped behind one group and tagged along.

Just before noon, 30 miles ahead, he saw what he wanted. There, beyond a bank of clouds and surrounded by bristling cruisers and destroyers, steamed a great carrier. He opened up on his radio and ordered the rest of his 18 dive bombers, "Form up for attack."

Then it happened. From somewhere above—and with no warning whatsoever—a dozen U.S. fighters hurtled down on Kobayashi's little formation, ripping it apart, and dropping six planes almost simultaneously into the sea.

THE burning planes reminded Lieutenant John Greenbacker of falling leaves as he watched from the *Yorktown* on the horizon. The fighter-director radio crackled with the excited voices of pilots swarming in for the kill: "1202: all Scarlet planes, bandits 8 miles, 255° . . . 1204: planes still on course . . . 1204: OK, break 'em up, Scarlet 19; going to attack about 3 enemy bombers about 5 miles . . . 1205: TALLY-HO! Join up on me . . . Scarlet 19, get those bombers on my right wing. Let's go!"

Lieutenant Greenbacker felt sure that none of the Japanese would escape, but eight somehow broke through. On they came toward the *Yorktown*, fanned out in a wide arc, one behind the other. They were still out of antiaircraft range, and the wait seemed interminable as the men of Task Force 17 braced themselves for the blow.

"What the hell am I doing out here?" wondered Donat

Houle, a young seaman on the destroyer *Hughes,* and it was indeed a long way from home in New Hampshire. On the *Yorktown* herself Machinist's Mate Worth Hare waited silently in Repair 5, down on the third deck. It was dark, and he was deep inside the ship. A feeling of fear burned in his stomach. At the battle dressing stations, the medics lay down in their flashproof clothing, covered their faces with their arms. Out on deck the British observer, Commander Michael B. Laing produced a small black notebook and began jotting down impressions to send back to London.

Captain Buckmaster moved out on the navigation bridge. He was supposed to stay in the forward conning tower when the ship was in action, but he couldn't maneuver from there. So he kept his exec under cover instead, ready to take over if anything happened. Buckmaster himself stood out in the open, yelling instructions through the narrow slits in the side of the tower.

On the flag bridge Admiral Fletcher still worked at his charts. A staff officer entered and politely reported, "The attack is coming in, sir."

"Well," said Fletcher cheerfully, "I've got on my tin hat. I can't do anything else now."

In these last, suspenseful moments there were, oddly enough, a few men present who didn't have the faintest idea that the enemy was about to strike. Circling above the *Yorktown,* Max Leslie and his squadron of dive bombers had waited while the fighters landed; now they were about to come in themselves. Intent on their instruments, watching the carrier's movements, none of them noticed the air battle erupting to the northwest. Nor could they hope to know the tension and turmoil on the ships below.

Leslie led the way into the landing pattern. Lieutenant Lefty Holmberg followed close behind, concentrating on the job of getting his wheels and flaps down, his propeller in high rpm. He noticed that the skipper was in a nice position to get aboard; he was pleased to see that his own plane was just the right distance behind. Suddenly the landing signal officer gave Leslie a "wave-off." Strange—Leslie always made it the first try. Holmberg turned to land himself. He too was waved off. Puzzled, he passed close along the port side of the flight deck, trying to see why they didn't let him land.

He was just opposite the after gun gallery when the four 5-inchers opened up. Smoke, fire, blast scared him half out of the cockpit. Thoroughly frightened, he darted away from the ship and joined up with Leslie. The *Yorktown*'s radio crackled a belated warning: "Get clear—we are being attacked."

Gun bursts peppered the sky, but the Japanese planes kept coming. Soon they were easy to see, even without binoculars. A burst caught one; it flared up and fell; the other seven flew on. Now they were almost over the *Yorktown*.

Signalman William Martin watched them all the way. He was assigned to a searchlight mounted on the *Yorktown*'s smokestack; his job was to challenge approaching aircraft. He knew perfectly well who these were, but as a good signalman he flashed the challenge anyhow. He got his answer soon enough: the lead plane flipped over and began to dive. Unfazed, Martin opened the searchlight shutters wide, hoping to blind the pilot and spoil his aim.

No one would ever know whether it worked. At the same moment Commander Davis's whole arsenal of automatic guns opened up with a roar. No less than 28 different guns were firing from the starboard side alone. A rain of bullets and shells chopped the bomber in two. But even as it disintegrated, its bomb tumbled free and down toward the *Yorktown*. Captain Buckmaster caught a brief but vivid impression—it looked oddly like a small keg of nails coming down.

It exploded with a brilliant red-yellow flash, 60 feet high, as it landed on the flight deck aft of the island. Shrapnel swept the area, mowing down the men at the nearest 1.1 guns: 19 out of 20 at mount No. 3, 16 more at No. 4. Ripping through the deck, the blast also set fire to three planes in the hangar below—one of them armed with a 1,000-pound bomb. The hangar deck officer, Lieutenant A. C. Emerson, yanked open the sprinkler system; a curtain of water smothered the flames.

At the 1.1 mounts, a dazed Ensign John d'Arc Lorenz scrambled to his feet, miraculously unhurt. Rallying three other survivors, he somehow managed to get one of the guns going again. Their firing was a little uneven, but four men—two of them wounded—were doing the work of twenty.

Whatever they could do, it would help. The rest of the Japanese were diving now, and it was easy to see (as one man put it) that this was their "varsity." They were a far cry from the rather sloppy bunch the *Yorktown* met at Coral Sea—certainly sharper than most American pilots. While the Navy fliers normally released at 2,000 feet, these planes plunged below 1,000, then pulled out barely at mast top.

Leading Seaman George Weise watched one come right at him. Manning a machine gun on the side of the smokestack near Signalman Martin's searchlight, he fired at it all the way down. But it came on anyhow, dropping a bomb that slanted through the flight deck . . . through the hangar deck . . . through the second deck . . . finally exploding in the uptakes of the stack deep inside the ship.

Down in Emergency Boiler Control, Lieutenant (j.g.) Charles Cundiff never understood what premonition made him shout at this instant, "Hit the deck!" But he did, and as his men went flat, white-hot shrapnel ripped across his station from somewhere forward, passing on through the bulkhead aft. None of the men was even scratched.

But this bomb really hurt. Flames and smoke were everywhere—the boiler rooms . . . the exec's office . . . the photo lab . . . the personnel files . . . the laundry . . . the oil and water test laboratories . . . the officers' galley . . . the wardroom annex . . . the radar room . . . a whole cross-section of all the things that go into a modern warship. A roaring blast of heat swept up the smokestack, setting the paint on fire and jarring everything loose.

Signalman Martin was hurled from his searchlight platform. He had an odd feeling of floating lazily through the air, high enough to see the whole task force. He was sure he was dead and decided that dying wasn't so hard after all. He came to seconds later, hanging halfway over the rail two levels below his light. Incredibly, he was unhurt.

Seaman Weise wasn't as lucky. Legend says he was hurled so high he brushed the wing of the plunging Jap plane. Wherever he went, he ended up on the flight deck unconscious and with a fractured skull.

Heavy black smoke poured from the *Yorktown;* her speed fell off to barely six knots. Then another Japanese plane dived, this time from the starboard side forward. It was the first to come in that way, and almost made it unnoticed. There was a startled burst of antiaircraft fire, but the bomb was already on the way. It plunged through the forward elevator, exploding 50 feet down in the rag stowage space. The whole area flared up in a tough, persistent fire; but what really worried damage control was not the rag locker, but all the gasoline and 5-inch shells stored next to it.

As the bombers pulled out, skimming across the water, the destroyers and cruisers blazed away with everything they had. There was something intoxicating about seeing the enemy right there. Men noticed the most minute details—a yellow stripe on some rudder, two red bands around somebody's fuselage—and they fired away with abandon. On the destroyer *Hughes* Ensign John Chase's 20 mm. battery followed one plane right over the ship; only the gun stop kept them from shooting up their own bridge. Even so, the skipper, Lieutenant Commander Donald Ramsey, was startled enough to rush to the rail and shake his fist at them all.

The *Astoria* gunners were yelling like wild men, slamming in shells as fast as they could—they fired 204 5-inchers in ten minutes. Chaplain Matthew Bouterse found himself passing cans of 1.1 ammunition to the ready room aft. It was perhaps an odd thing for a chaplain to be doing, but he thought of Pearl Harbor and Chaplain Forgy's famous words, "Praise the Lord and pass the ammunition."

Pulling out of its dive, one Japanese plane turned right toward the *Astoria*, flying not much more than bridge height. The machine guns went to work, began chopping the plane to pieces . . . but still it kept coming. As it passed along the starboard side, the pilot turned—waved—and slanted down into the sea just astern. His mission completed, he apparently wanted a look at his enemy before he died.

Some 15–20 miles to the southeast the men on the *Enterprise, Hornet* and the rest of Task Force 16 strained to see how the battle was going. There were few clues—just the black puffs of antiaircraft fire in the distance, an occasional plane streaking into the sea. Then a heavy smudge of smoke appeared. It didn't drift away like gun bursts; it clung to the horizon, steady and black. Admiral Spruance judged right away that the *Yorktown* had been hit.

He detached cruisers *Pensacola* and *Vincennes*, the destroyers *Benham* and *Balch*, to go over and help. But for most of Task Force 16 there was only frustration. The *Yorktown* was getting it—just 15 or 20 miles away—and there was nothing they could do.

It was especially frustrating for the men flying air cover over the *Enterprise* and *Hornet*. Unlike the rest of the force, they *could* do something—and right away. When the dive bombers broke through the *Yorktown*'s fighter defenses, Lieutenant Roger Mehle requested permission to lead his 12 fighters to the rescue. He was told to stay where he was—his job was to protect the *Enterprise*. But he stretched his orbit (and his orders) anyhow, circling ever closer toward the *Yorktown*.

He finally got a go-ahead and raced over—just too late to intercept. The enemy planes were already in their dives.

Adding agony to agony, his guns jammed as he led his flight down on the end of the Japanese column. He disengaged and pulled away, turning the attack over to the next section leader.

In the end they never accomplished much, and the *Hornet* fighters even less. Still, there were some satisfactions. Ensigns Provost and Halford ganged up on one dive bomber just as he pulled out and started for home. Making a high side attack, they quickly sent him spinning into the sea.

Suddenly it was over. Men blinked, shook their heads, unable to believe the silence. The firing seemed to have gone on forever, yet it was just 12:16—11 minutes since the first ships opened up.

On the *Yorktown* Admiral Fletcher and his staff stood around on the flight deck, driven from Flag Plot by the fire in the island structure. For the moment Radio Electrician Bennett was about the only person working up there in all the fire and smoke. Normally a dapper little man, he now sat rumpled and grimy, wearing a gas mask, desperately trying to get his radar going again. Down in the galley an old chief spotted another chief—his good friend—lying dead on the deck. He broke down and cried like a child.

Commander Laing stood quietly on deck, as imperturbable as a Royal Navy officer should be. Later he missed his little black notebook—and it was never found. He finally decided it was blown out of his hands when one of the bombs landed. He shrugged off the loss, observing with a delicacy that was entirely unnecessary in the U.S. Navy: "Those Jap baskets came rather a long way to ruin my month's work."

The hard statistics, at least, required no notebook to be remembered. Only 7 of the 18 Japanese bombers managed to dive, but 3 of the 7 had scored clean hits—a remarkable performance for so few planes. And even the near-misses took their toll. One landed just astern, killing and wounding many men on the fantail. Another came in so close that it sent Admiral Fletcher diving for cover. He cut his head on something, went back to work, dripping blood on his charts. He finally got a medic to slap on a bandage, and the next time he thought about it was long afterward when, to his astonishment, he got a Purple Heart.

So much for the losses they took. They gave plenty too. The men in Task Force 17 would long argue over who shot down what, but on one thing most were agreed: none of the Japanese escaped. Of the seven that dived, the men said, there was not one who lived to tell the tale.

"ENEMY carrier is burning," radioed one of the *Hiryu* pilots at 12:45. His plane was now back at the rendezvous area, waiting to join up with any other dive bombers leaving the scene.

Spirits soared on the *Hiryu*. Lieutenant Hashimoto felt there was only one thing wrong with the message. It didn't come from Lieutenant Kobayashi . . . it didn't even come from a section leader like Lieutenant Kondo. It came, in fact, from a lowly petty officer (even now no one can remember his name) who flew the No. 3 plane in the second group. That meant all the senior pilots were killed; the toll must be very high.

He was right—but more escaped than any of the Americans believed. In the end five dive bombers and one fighter managed to scoot away from the blazing guns of Task Force 17. They escaped singly, in no particular order—just as their wits and luck happened to take them—but by 12:45 all six were heading back to the *Hiryu*.

Meanwhile preparations raced ahead for the torpedo strike. Commander Kawaguchi had been working on this ever since the dive bombers left. Now he was almost ready. It would be a patchwork affair: nine torpedo planes from the *Hiryu*, plus an orphan from the *Akagi*; four fighter escorts from the *Hiryu*, and one transferred from the burning *Kaga*.

Anything more would take longer, and Admiral Yamaguchi couldn't afford the time. Intelligence still said there was only one U.S. carrier, but he now doubted it. No single ship could have done all that to the *Akagi, Kaga* and *Soryu*. There must be a second one out there somewhere. Even so, that left it one to one; and the *Hiryu* would fight on these terms any day. One of the U.S. carriers, anyhow, was now burning—it would be out of action for a long, long time.

COMMANDER Clarence Aldrich seemed everywhere at once. As the *Yorktown*'s damage control officer he had his work cut out for him—three separate hits, four serious fires belowdecks. Somehow he managed to tackle them all.

There was not a moment to lose—especially with the burning rag locker up forward, next to all that gasoline and ammunition. Aldrich had the magazine flooded with sea water, the gas tank filled with CO_2. Other fire fighters smothered the flames in the island structure, while repair parties went to work on the holes in the flight deck. The big one aft—12 feet wide—called for extra ingenuity. Wooden beams were laid across . . . a quarter-inch steel plate put over them . . . then more steel plates tacked down on top of that. In 20 minutes the *Yorktown*'s flight deck was again open for business.

And all the time the work went on of clearing the dead, caring for the wounded. They were all kinds. There was George Weise, still unconscious from his fall, carried below to the main sick bay. There was the young boy, physically untouched but scared literally speechless. There was Boatswain's Mate Plyburn, raked across the stomach by a strafing machine gun. He had $500 in his pockets—saved for the day he planned to marry. Now he was dying and he knew it. He begged his friends to take the money and have a good time with it.

Far below, the engineers struggled to get the *Yorktown* going again. The bomb that exploded in the stack had wrecked two boilers and blown out the fires in the others. Heavy black smoke poured into the firerooms, choking the men at their posts.

Water Tender Charles Kliensmith, the short rough-tough sailor in charge of boiler No. 1, hung on anyhow. The hit had knocked down most of his boiler's interior brickwork, but otherwise did little perceptible damage. He and his men relit the fires.

None of the other boilers would relight at all. More smoke poured through the forced-draft intakes, smothering the fires. Kliensmith's gang kept working, although the place was now stifling, and the bare casing glowed red-hot. They knew they were the only source of power for the pumps and auxiliaries needed to keep the *Yorktown* alive.

But their boiler was not enough to run the ship, and the engine room was clamoring for steam to get the uninjured turbines running again. The boiler division officer Lieutenant Cundiff had been painfully burned, but something had to be done right away. Bandages and all, he crawled into the uptake-intake space, full of the pipes that normally draw the smoke up the stack and bring new air back down again.

A quick look around, and it was all too clear what had happened. The bomb had ruptured the uptake on Kliensmith's boiler, the intake on the others that could still give steam. Instead of continuing up the stack, Kliensmith's smoke was being drawn back down and into the other boiler rooms. Kliensmith was ordered to reduce his fires to the bare minimum necessary to keep the auxiliaries running, while repairs were made and the other boilers relit. In time they'd again build up enough steam to get the *Yorktown* moving.

Admiral Fletcher couldn't wait. He had a fleet to run, and a ship dead in the water was no place to do it. Besides, his radio was out, and smoke still billowed up, making flag hoists and the blinkers impractical. About 12:30 he decided to transfer to the *Astoria* and signaled her for one of her boats.

By 1:00 the *Astoria*'s No. 2 whaleboat was alongside. Knotted lines were dropped down from the *Yorktown*'s flight deck, and several staff officers lowered themselves hand over hand. Fletcher was about to go the same way, then thought better of it. After all, he was 56 years old. "Hell," he said to himself, "I can't do that sort of thing any more." So they rigged a line with a bowline in it and lowered the Admiral in style.

They shoved off at 1:13—Fletcher, part of his staff, several enlisted men, including the Admiral's yeoman Frank Boo. The trip took only 11 minutes, but that seemed plenty to Boo. The sea was calm—no enemy in sight—but he felt sure they'd be strafed if a new Japanese attack caught them there. A whaleboat just didn't go from one ship to another in mid-Pacific, unless it was important.

To make matters worse, countless 5-inch shell cases bobbed up and down in the water—all looking like submarine periscopes. The *Astoria*'s crew were especially sensitive about these, for they too felt like sitting ducks while they waited for their Admiral. When he finally climbed aboard at 1:24, everyone breathed more easily.

The *Yorktown*'s planes also had to transfer. Even with the flight deck repaired, they couldn't use it while the ship was standing still. Max Leslie's 17 dive bombers had been ordered to stay clear during the Japanese attack. Now they were told to land and refuel on the *Hornet* or *Enterprise*. They'd fly from there until the *Yorktown* got going again.

It was a relief to have someplace to go. For most of the SBDs it had been a nerve-racking noon hour—part of it spent in dodging bullets from both sides. As one Japanese pilot pulled out of his dive on the *Yorktown*, he made right for them with all guns blazing. A U.S. fighter appeared from nowhere and shot him down. But next minute it was a "friendly" pilot that attacked them. He veered away at the last second as somebody yelled over the radio, "You silly bastard! Can't you see these white stars?"

His confusion was understandable. Apart from the problem of split-second identification, everything was getting more and more mixed up: planes from one carrier plopping down on another . . . combat air patrols overlapping each other's sector . . . relays of fighters called in and taking off.

Radio traffic filled the air—a jumble of orders, questions and remarks tossed back and forth in airman's jargon. Tuned in on the *Enterprise*'s fighter-director circuit, an enemy eaves-dropper heard "Ham" Dow call in a three-plane section for refueling. This gave the Japanese an inspiration: why not clear the sky of every American fighter? Breaking in, he called in English, "All planes return to base, all planes return to base."

"That was a Jap!" Dow yelled. "Disregard that order to return to base—that was a Jap!"

The Japanese repeated his order.

"The bastards are using our frequency," Dow cried, and that was the mildest thing he said. This was the first time during the Pacific War that anybody had used radio decep-tion. Later it would be an old story on both sides, but right now it fitted perfectly the standard Western conception of the crafty Oriental. It was also fitting that Americans should see through the trick, and as Dow cursed away, the pilots listened with enjoyment and ever-increasing respect for the wide range of his vocabulary.

Max Leslie had a different kind of problem. Like the rest of his *Yorktown* dive bombers, he was about to shift over to the *Enterprise* or *Hornet*, when Bill Gallagher in the rear seat spotted something in the water maybe eight or ten miles away. They flew over to investigate, with Lefty Holmberg tagging along. It turned out to be a swamped U.S. torpedo plane; its crew were nearby in a rubber raft. Leslie alerted the destroyer *Hammann*, went back to the carrier to get a new bearing on Task Force 16. By the time he was squared away, he was nearly out of gas, and Holmberg was even lower. They'd probably never make the *Enterprise*; far better to play it safe and splash beside the *Astoria* directly below.

The men in Bombing 3 always considered Max Leslie the

most methodical pilot in the world, and according to squadron legend, he landed so close to the *Astoria* he simply walked the wing to the ship's ladder. It was almost that good. He came down about 50 yards off the cruiser, but as Bill Gallagher launched the rubber boat, he noticed that Leslie was still in the cockpit, apparently slumped over his instruments. Thinking the skipper was stunned by the landing, Gallagher scrambled alongside to lift him out. But there was nothing wrong. The methodical Leslie was just flicking every button on the instrument panel to an "off" position before abandoning his sinking SBD.

It wasn't as easy for CAP Esders, pilot of the swamped torpedo plane Leslie had spotted. Flying one of the two TBDs in Torpedo 3 to escape the Japanese, Esders started home with a leaking gas tank and his rear-seat man Mike Brazier desperately wounded. Then Machinist Corl joined up with the squadron's other surviving plane, and for a while the two flew together in the general direction of the U.S. fleet.

Esders asked Brazier if he could possibly change the coils on the radio so he could pick up the *Yorktown's* homing device. Brazier answered weakly that he was in very bad shape and didn't think he could.

"Very well," Esders replied, writing that hope off. But ten minutes later Brazier called and said he had managed to change the coils after all. By now Corl had drifted off (he later splashed safely near the *Enterprise*), but thanks to Brazier's supreme effort, Esders eventually caught the *Yorktown's* signal and came on in. Ten miles short of the carrier, he finally ran out of gas and glided down to a water landing.

It was only then that he saw how badly off Brazier really was. Both legs were terribly wounded, and he had been shot seven times in the back. Helped into their rubber raft, Brazier knew very well this was the end. Still, he conversed intelligently, saying he was sorry that he couldn't do more. He also said he was sorry that he would never see his family again. He finally drifted into a coma, as Wilhelm Esders did the only thing left to do: "I said a prayer to the Almighty, request-ing that He receive such brave and gallant men into the Kingdom, and that He bless those that he left behind."

LIEUTENANT Raita Ogawa aimlessly circled the blazing *Akagi*. Flying air cover, he was running out of gas with no place to land. The three carriers below were wrecks, and the *Hiryu* was now too far north to reach.

He looked at his gas gauge. He was down to five gallons. A few minutes more, and he'd be in the ocean. He headed for the cruiser *Chikuma*, hurrying north after the *Hiryu*. The other two planes in his section followed along; they were in the same fix.

Circling low, he signaled the *Chikuma* that he was about to come down by waggling his wings. It turned out that her business was too urgent; she semaphored back, "Can't pick you up." But she did hoist her wind-sock and turned briefly into the wind to make a smooth wake to land on.

At 11:50 Raita Ogawa splashed down, sustained by the thought that he was originally trained as a seaplane pilot. He made it easily, and so did the two pilots with him. They scrambled out of their sinking planes—three more swimmers in the ever-growing number that dotted the ocean.

Dozens of men struggled in the water alongside the burning *Soryu*. Some had been blown there by internal explosions; others jumped when trapped by the fire. Far above them Captain Yanagimoto suddenly appeared, limping onto the semaphore platform off the starboard side of the bridge. He yelled encouragement to the men below, and cried "Long live the Emperor!" About 30 men, swimming directly beneath the bridge, took up the cheer as Yanagimoto disappeared in the flames and smoke.

A crowd of survivors jammed the anchor deck forward, still free of the fire. Some were tossing lines to the men in the water, hauling them back on board to this small corner of safety. Among those brought back was Executive Officer

Ohara, faint from his burns. Now he lay on deck, little caring what happened. Dimly he heard the gunnery officer order a signalman to wigwag the *Akagi:* say the captain was dead, the exec unconscious, what should they do?

The *Akagi* never answered. She had too many troubles of her own. After Nagumo left, Captain Aoki and several of his officers stuck it out on the bridge as long as they could, but by 11:20 the heat was too much. They lowered themselves to the flight deck and went all the way forward on the windward side. Here they stood in a little group, uncertain what to do next.

They longed to smoke, but had only two cigarettes between them. In the end, they passed these back and forth, and it reminded Commander Miura of the popular song *"Senyu"* ("War Comrades"), which had a mawkish line about "sharing a cigarette in harmony." He quoted it, and it was good for a brief, grim laugh.

About 11:35 the torpedo and bomb storage rooms went up, and the fire surged forward. It soon forced Captain Aoki's group to retreat to the anchor deck, where they found a crowd of survivors already gathered. They were standing around together, when at 12:03 the engines unexpectedly started up and the *Akagi* began turning to starboard. It was hard to imagine what made this happen, and Ensign Akiyama was sent to try and find out. But no one would ever know what did it. The remaining engineers had all suffocated and were dead at their posts.

Captain Aoki still hoped to save his ship—he sent Nagumo an optimistic message around noon—but certainly the fire was spreading. By 1:38 the situation was bad enough to take a very grave step. He had the Emperor's portrait transferred to the destroyer *Nowaki*.

The same step had just been taken on the *Kaga*, where it had been a losing fight against the fires all morning. For a while the assistant damage control officer, Lieutenant Commander Yoshio Kunisada, felt he was making some progress on the hangar deck; but then the paint began to burn, spreading a thick, oily smoke that nearly suffocated his men. He had the portholes opened, but that was no answer. The draft only fanned the flames. The ports were slammed shut again, but soon Kunisada was back where he started—his men in more danger than ever.

There was nothing to do but leave. The exits were all blocked, so once again the portholes were opened, and about seven of the men, including Kunisada, squeezed through. They found themselves on a narrow bulge that ran along the side of the ship, perhaps 20 feet above the water. It had been built into the *Kaga* as a stabilizing device when she was originally laid down as a battleship; now it served as a ledge that just might spell safety. It was only a foot and a half wide and slanted down slightly, but they could stand up on it, bracing their backs against the side of the ship.

Still, they felt anything but safe. It was easy to slip off into the water, and stray shots were flying about as the antiaircraft guns on the destroyer screen occasionally opened up on some imaginary target. Soon there were about 20 men out there, all thoroughly frightened. On the way out Kunisada had grabbed a carton of cigarettes from the chief warrant officers' room, and now he handed the packs around, hoping to cheer the group up. He suggested a smoke might calm their nerves, and he made a great show of his own composure by lighting up in the most casual manner. Hardly anybody followed suit.

"Torpedo, right quarter!" somebody suddenly yelled, and there sure enough, was a white torpedo wake streaking toward the *Kaga* about 1,000 yards away. It passed just forward of the ship. A brief interval, then another white wake; this one passed just astern. Another interval, then a third wake . . . and Kunisada saw right away that this one would hit.

BILL BROCKMAN ordered Lieutenant Hogan to take her down. It was 2:05 P.M., and the U.S. submarine *Nautilus* had just fired her third torpedo at the shattered Japanese carrier

2,700 yards away. For Brockman and the 92 men on the *Nautilus* it was the climax of six hours and 55 minutes of infinitely careful stalking.

The hunt really began much earlier, on May 28, when the *Nautilus* took her place in the fan-shaped screen of submarines west of Midway. She was there, of course, in plenty of time; so she just loafed the first few days, while her crew got the feel of things. It was the first war cruise for them all, and for Brockman it was his first command. He was more than up to it. A big burly man, he had a great zest for combat.

On the morning of the 4th the *Nautilus* submerged at her station just before dawn. She was tuned in on the PBY circuit, and at 5:44 Lieutenant Chase's plain-English flash came through loud and clear: "Many planes heading Midway." The position was on the edge of the *Nautilus*'s sector; she started there right away.

At 7:10 Brockman—glued to the periscope—saw smoke and antiaircraft bursts beyond the horizon. He adjusted his course, and the *Nautilus* went to battle stations. At 7:55 he saw the tops of masts dead ahead. Soon he was in the enemy screen —strafed by Zeros, depth-bombed by a cruiser. He lay low for five minutes, then popped back to periscope depth for another look around.

He was right in the middle of the Japanese fleet. Ships were on all sides, moving by at high speed, circling violently to avoid him. Flag hoists were up; a battleship was firing her whole starboard broadside battery at him.

At 8:25 he fired two torpedoes at the battleship. Or rather, he thought he did, but almost immediately he discovered his No. 1 tube hadn't fired. The battleship dodged the other torpedo, a cruiser came racing over, and the *Nautilus* plopped down to 150 feet.

Now the depth bombing began in earnest. The charges this morning were the first anyone in the *Nautilus* had ever heard from inside a submarine, and the experience was anything but soothing. Mixed with the hammer blows and thunderclaps were occasional shrill whistles and an odd sound that reminded Radioman I. E. Wetmore of a boy dragging a stick along a picket fence.

To make matters worse, one of the *Nautilus*'s deck tube torpedoes was leaking air. A thin trail of bubbles rose to the surface, neatly marking the sub's position. More thunderclaps, then the explosions gradually died away.

Brockman began sneaking looks again. Around 9:00 he saw a carrier for the first time. She was dodging and firing her antiaircraft guns, but he had only a glimpse, for his old friend the cruiser saw the periscope and came charging back.

Down again. More depth bombing. Closer than ever before. The sonarman tracking the cruiser's movements kept up a running patter, like Graham McNamee calling a horse race. A mess attendant promised Brockman that if the *Nautilus* ever got out of this, he'd write a sermon every day. Then this attack, too, slowly died away.

At 10:29 Brockman was up again, poking around with his periscope. The ships had now vanished, except for some distant masts, but clouds of gray smoke poured up from the horizon. He headed for the scene, and by 11:45 could clearly make out a burning carrier about eight miles away.

The approach was a long, slow business. Even cranked up to two-thirds speed (the most Brockman dared with his batteries running down), the *Nautilus* only moved at four knots —about as fast as a man might walk. And it was a hot eight-mile "walk" too. To cut noise, all ventilating machinery was off. The sweat dripped into Lieutenant Dick Lynch's shoes, and his feet "sort of scrunched" as he moved about.

By 12:53 they were near enough to make out some details. Two "cruisers" were hovering near the carrier; her fires seemed to have died down; men could be seen working on the foredeck; it looked as if they might be planning to pass a towing hawser. On the *Nautilus* Brockman and his exec, Lieutenant Roy Benson, thumbed through their recognition books trying to identify her. There was always the dread of torpedoing a friendly carrier by mistake. No, this one was Japanese, all right; they believed it was the *Soryu*.

Brockman now faced a classic command decision: try for the undamaged escorts first, or go all-out for the damaged but "high-priority" carrier. He decided to make sure of the carrier.

At 1:59, he fired his first torpedo . . . then a second . . . then at 2:05 a third. Brockman—in fact all five officers in the conning tower—felt sure of hits. Fires were again breaking out all over the ship. Satisfied, he dived to 300 feet to sit out the new round of depth bombs that was sure to come.

"JUMP in the water!" Lieutenant Commander Kunisada shouted, as that third torpedo streaked toward the *Kaga*. But the men standing with him on the bulge wouldn't move. So he jumped himself, and called the others to join him. They finally did, and all frantically swam to get clear of the ship. Somebody called out that the torpedo was a hit, and Kunisada steeled himself for the concussion—but nothing happened.

Miraculously, it was a dud. Slamming into the *Kaga* at an oblique angle, the warhead broke off and sank. The buoyant air flask bobbed to the surface not far from Kunisada. Some of the *Kaga's* crew paddled over. One or two tried using it as a raft, but most were wild with rage. It was at least a symbol of their troubles, and they rained blows upon it with their fists. "*Konchkusho!*" they cursed, "*Konchkusho! Konchkusho!*"

Their best hope of revenge lay some miles to the north. The *Hiryu* was still very much in the fight. Her dive bombers had struck at noon; by 12:45 her ten torpedo planes were ready too. They would go in two five-plane sections—the first led by Lieutenant Tomonaga, the second by Lieutenant Hashimoto. Normally they flew together—Hashimoto as observer—but they were the only two Academy men left. They might get more mileage if each led a section.

The stocky, taciturn Tomonaga would lead the attack.

Hashimoto, still flying observer, would go with Petty Officer Toshio Takahashi. All this settled, they headed for the flight deck.

It was then they discovered Lieutenant Tomonaga's plane wasn't ready. The mechanics hadn't yet repaired the left-wing gas tank, damaged while they were bombing Midway. Tomonaga shrugged it off: "All right, don't worry. Leave the left tank as it is and fill up the other."

Hashimoto urged him to take a different plane. No, said Tomonaga, at this stage of the game they needed everything that would fly. To leave even one plane behind would seriously weaken the attack. As for swapping with someone else, he wouldn't think of it. Everything would work out; the enemy was near; he could get by on one tank.

This didn't fool anyone. One tank could never get him home again. But it was useless to argue; he had made up his mind. Tomonaga now went to the bridge with Hashimoto and Lieutenant Shigeru Mori, who would lead the fighters. Here they had a final briefing from Admiral Yamaguchi.

The Admiral had some astounding news. A special reconnaissance plane, sent out by the *Soryu* earlier in the morning, had just returned to report there were not one, or even two, but *three* U.S. carriers. In addition to the one just bombed, two others were lurking nearby. The *Soryu*'s pilot discovered them at 11:30, but his radio was out. Hurrying back, he found his own ship in flames and reached the *Hiryu* at 12:50. He had just made a message drop.

If any confirmation was needed, it came at 1:00. The captured *Yorktown* pilot was talking. Captain Ariga, commanding Destroyer Division 4, radioed the gist: the carriers involved were the *Yorktown*, *Enterprise* and *Hornet* . . . they had six cruisers and about ten destroyers with them . . . the *Yorktown* was operating independently with two cruisers and three destroyers.

This changed everything. Until now Admiral Yamaguchi assumed that, with one American carrier knocked out, the

Hiryu was at least fighting on even terms. But it was two to one against her. Worse, the *Hiryu* was down to her last planes. Go for the carriers that hadn't been hit, he stressed, go for the ones that hadn't been hit.

Again the pilots were assembled on the flight deck right under the bridge. Again Yamaguchi addressed them. They were the very last hope, he said, they must do their utmost for Japan. Then he noticed Tomonaga among the crowd and came down for a last good-bye. Like everyone else, he knew the Lieutenant was flying a plane that could never come back. Shaking Tomonaga's hand, he thanked him for all he'd done and said, "I'll gladly follow you."

The pilots were in their cockpits—the engines warming up—when fresh excitement rippled through the ship. The first planes were coming back from the dive-bombing attack on the U.S. carrier. They couldn't land until the torpedo strike took off, but Petty Officer Satsuo Tange swooped low over the flight deck, dropping a message in a weighted tube.

It was a new position for the U.S. force—more to the south than given at the briefing. Knowing that Hashimoto was usually Tomonaga's navigator—and forgetting they were in separate planes this time—Lieutenant Commander Kawaguchi rushed the information to Hashimoto. Before the mix-up could be straightened out, the planes began thundering off the *Hiryu*'s flight deck.

They left at 1:31—Tomonaga leading the way, Hashimoto trailing with the latest U.S. position in his pocket. As they turned and headed east, a silent Admiral Yamaguchi—alone with his thoughts—stood motionless, watching them go.

CHAPTER 10

Abandon Ship

Sᴵɢɴᴀʟᴍᴀɴ Peter Karetka let out a loud, long cheer. Stationed on the signal bridge of the destroyer *Hughes*, he was watching the motionless *Yorktown* when at 2:02 her yellow breakdown flag came down; up instead went a new hoist —"My speed 5."

On the *Yorktown* it meant that the battle of the boiler rooms had been won. Lieutenant Cundiff's diagnosis was correct. By cutting No. 1 down to a bare minimum, Lieutenant Commander Jack Delaney was able to get Nos. 4, 5 and 6 going again by 1:40, and 20 minutes later the ship was under way. With a little time Delaney thought he could work her up to 20 knots—enough to launch planes and get back into action.

Meanwhile there were other welcome developments. The cruisers *Pensacola* and *Vincennes,* the destroyers *Balch* and *Benham,* had appeared from the southeast—sent over by Spruance to beef up the screen. On the *Yorktown,* Commander Aldrich had the fires under control; by 1:50 it was safe enough to start refueling the fighters then on deck.

Solid evidence of recovery, but what gave the men their biggest lift was something less tangible. Captain Buckmaster— as good a psychologist as he was a sailor—chose this moment to break out a huge new American flag from the *Yorktown*'s foremast. No man who saw it will ever forget. To Ensign John

d'Arc Lorenz, who had just been through the carnage at the
1.1 guns, it was an incalculable inspiration: "I shall always remember seeing it flutter in the breeze and what it meant to
me at this critical time. It was new . . . bright colors, beautiful
in the sunlight. For the first time I realized what the flag
meant: all of us—a million faces—all our effort—a whisper of
encouragement."

They needed it at 2:10 when the radar first picked up a
new wave of bogeys to the northwest. "Stand by to repel air
attack," the TBS intership radio blared. The screen moved in
close, forming "disposition Victor" in a tight, protective circle.
The *Yorktown* strained to build up her speed; by 2:18 she was
making eight knots.

Then 10 knots . . . 12 knots . . . 15 knots by 2:28. But the
Balch radar reported the bogeys were now only 37 miles away.
Once again Worth Hare felt fear burning inside, and Signalman Donat Houle wondered what the hell he was doing out
here. On the *Benham* an Ivy League ensign nervously chat-
tered about debutantes he had known in better times.

Lieutenant Hashimoto knew they must be getting
close. It was 2:28—about an hour since they left the *Hiryu*—
the American ships should be coming into sight. He picked up
his seven-power binoculars and scanned the sea to his right.
That's where they would be according to the new position
handed him just before they left.

Two minutes later he saw them—tiny white wakes, 80° to
starboard, 30 miles away. A tight circle of ships, with a carrier
in the middle. And she looked in perfect shape. The last
message from the dive bombers said the carrier they hit
was "burning furiously"; so this must be a different one. No
burning ship could recover that fast.

Speeding up alongside Lieutenant Tomonaga, Hashimoto
pointed to the ships, then dropped back to his regular position.
Tomonaga swung sharply southeast, and at 2:32 ordered his
planes to form up for attack.

They broke into two groups, planning to hit from both sides. They would make their approach together; then Tomonaga would take the port side, Hashimoto the starboard. Like a pair of tongs, they would grab the carrier squarely between them. If she tried to turn from one group, the other would get her.

About ten miles out the U.S. fighters struck. Roaring down from above, they made a pass, got one of Tomonaga's section. Then Lieutenant Mori's six Zeros tore into the Americans, and a wild melee developed. But at last the torpedo planes slipped through, and they swept toward the carrier from her port side astern.

At 2:40 all the ships in the screen opened up. It was much worse than Hashimoto expected—machine guns, pompoms, 5-inchers, everything. He hunched low, feeling like a man leaving a warm house in the winter, stepping out into driving sleet. Shrapnel clattered on his wings—the way the hail used to do on a zinc roof back home.

The carrier veered hard to the right, and Hashimoto suddenly found himself on her port side, instead of her starboard as planned. It was even worse for Tomonaga. He was now left well astern. His formation broke up, with the planes trying singly to get into some sort of firing position. The cruisers and destroyers ripped into them.

For Hashimoto it was the wrong side, but he decided to make a run anyhow. He'd never get a better shot than this. He turned and headed for the carrier. The rest of his group moved into position. On they came, flying a loose V formation 150 feet above the water. The carrier's port side—ablaze with gunfire—lay directly ahead. At 800 yards Hashimoto released. . . .

CAPTAIN Buckmaster watched the streaks of white foam race toward the *Yorktown*—and yearned for just a little more steam. At Coral Sea he had dodged other Japanese torpedoes

—manipulating his 19,000 tons of steel with a grace that filled the crew with admiration—but then he had 30 knots to work with. Now he had only 19, and that was quite different. Still, he managed to dodge the first two streaks.

As the planes dropped, they veered away close alongside the ship. Watching from his searchlight platform, Signalman Martin wondered about the two flickering orange lights he could see in the rear cockpit. Suddenly he realized this was machine gun fire. He ducked behind a canvas wind screen and felt entirely different about the war. Bombs and torpedoes were impersonal, but this strafing was aimed at *him*. For the first time he felt really angry with the Japanese.

There were angry Japanese too. After dropping, one plane turned and flew along the *Yorktown's* port side not 50 yards from the ship. As it went by, the rear-seat man stood up in his cockpit and shook his fist in defiance. The plane disintegrated in a hail of fire—everybody claimed it. For Gunner's Mate Jefferson Vick it was "the only time I smiled during the battle."

At 2:44 another streak of white foam appeared in the water, this time heading directly for the port side, just forward of amidships. Standing on the port catwalk, Yeoman Joseph Adams watched it come right at him. He grabbed a door and braced himself.

The jolt was appalling. Like a cat shaking a rat, like shaking out a rug—the men searched their peacetime memories for something similar . . . and found nothing to compare. Paint flew off the deck and into their faces; the catwalk rolled up like fencing; fuel oil gushed out; a yellow haze settled over the port side.

For 30 seconds Captain Buckmaster felt they just might pull through. The ship was listing 6° to port, but she still had headway. In damage control, CWT George Vavrek talked over his headphones, telling the men in the forward generator room where to transfer oil to correct the list.

Then a second torpedo hit—killing the man Vavrek was

talking to . . . killing everybody in the generator room . . . knocking out all power, communications, even emergency lighting. The rudder jammed at 15° to port; a mushroom of gray-white smoke billowed up; the *Yorktown* stopped, listing 17° to port.

A sickening feeling came over Ensign Walter Beckham as he watched from the cruiser *Portland*. All antiaircraft guns were firing; 5-inch bursts blackened the sky; tracers criss-crossed in crazy patterns. Even the cruiser's 8-inch batteries were firing, in hopes that the splash would bring somebody down. The noise and clouds of smoke were bewildering, and there was something terrifying about those planes—the way they hung there in spite of all efforts to blot them out. Nothing worked, and they swept in "looking like some giant birds who were not to be foiled in their search for prey."

More planes kept coming. The *Astoria*'s gunners were again yelling like wild men. On the *Benham* a sailor named Lytells loaded 54 5-inch projectiles in a minute and 45 seconds—and each shell weighed 57 pounds. A 20 mm. crew on the *Russell* kept firing even after another destroyer fouled the range; skipper Roy Hartwig had to throw his tin hat at the gun to stop it. When the *Portland*'s 8-inchers let go, Marine Captain Donohoo—still recovering from the mumps—was knocked clear out of his bunk. Mumps or no, he rushed topside to his station. On the *Hughes* Signalman Houle no longer wondered what the hell he was doing here. He now stood on a corner of the bridge, blazing away with a Thompson .45 submachine gun.

Occasionally they got one. There was the plane that never had a chance to make a run at all. As it broke through the screen, a freak shot (probably from the *Pensacola*) struck its torpedo. A blinding flash, and it simply vanished. Another made its drop, pulled across the *Yorktown*'s bow, and headed straight for the *Vincennes*. Captain F. L. Riefkohl saw it just in time, put his rudder hard right. Riddled from gunfire, the plane crashed 50 yards off the cruiser's bow, catapulting the pilot out of his cockpit. Still another—crowded out of position during its run—circled wide to the left and tried again. Second time around, it also opened up on the destroyer *Balch,* which happened to be in its line of sight. The *Balch* replied with everything it had; the plane disintegrated into the sea.

The U.S. fighters were there too, braving their own fleet's fire in a desperate effort to ward off the blow. Planes from the *Enterprise* and *Hornet* pitched in, but the greatest contribution came from the *Yorktown* herself. Even as the alarm sounded, she began launching the ten fighters refueling on deck; she was still at it when the Japanese began their final runs. Eighth and last man off was Ensign Milton Tootle, Jr., who had been on carrier duty just six days. Making his first nontraining flight, Tootle took off, turned hard left, tangled with a Japanese plane, shot it down, got hit himself by "friendly" fire, baled out, took a swim and was picked up by the *Anderson*—all within 15 minutes.

While the battle raged above, the men deep inside the ships waited and listened and sweated it out. In the glow of red battle lights, the members of Repair II on the *Pensacola* crouched in the darkened mess hall. They could feel the ship lurch heavily as the torpedoes slammed into the *Yorktown*— but at the time no one knew what had happened. Wondering —and not being able to shoot back—often made it harder to be below decks than above.

In the engine room of the *Astoria* Lieutenant Commander John Hayes developed a sort of ascending scale, based on the sound of gunfire, that he felt kept him pretty well informed. The dull boom of the 5-inchers meant "Maybe they're not after us"; the surging rhythm of the 1.1 mounts meant "Here they come"; the steady, angry clatter of the 50-caliber machine guns meant "Hit the floor plates!" Now he heard it all at once.

Then silence. As quickly as the Japanese appeared, they were gone again. At 2:52 the *Portland* was the last ship to cease fire—just 12 minutes after she was the first to open up.

It was incredible that it all happened so quickly—and equally incredible that it all seemed so long. The men slumped by their guns in exhaustion. The elation of battle vanished; now there was utter weariness. Tears, too, as the gunners looked over at the *Yorktown*. She lay there, listing more than 20° now, wallowing in the gentle swell.

They had only one consolation. They had made the enemy pay a stiff price. Most were sure that none of the Japanese planes escaped.

"Head for the bow!" Lieutenant Hashimoto yelled as his torpedo sped on its way. Petty Officer Takahashi dropped even lower and skidded across the sea directly in front of the U.S. carrier. They drew little fire; Hashimoto thought the antiaircraft guns just couldn't get down that low.

"Did we get a hit?" Takahashi called. Hashimoto turned, but saw no sign of an explosion for a long, long time. Then suddenly a great geyser shot up so high he could see it clearly from the far side of the carrier. Without really meaning to, he let out a yelp of joy.

But his joy was interrupted. Looking around, he caught sight of CPO Nakane's plane and was horrified to see it still had its torpedo. Nakane was the "orphan" from the *Akagi*—maybe he was confused—but nothing excused this. "You fool," Hashimoto said to himself, "what did you come here for anyhow?"

He yanked back his canopy, attracted the attention of Nakane's rear-seat man, and pointed violently at the torpedo. The rear-seat man waved—yes, he understood—and jettisoned it into the sea. Hashimoto could only curse harder than ever.

Now he was back at the rendezvous point, waiting for Lieutenant Tomonaga's section to join up, but none of them ever appeared. Perhaps they were thrown off by the carrier's last-second maneuvering; perhaps Tomonaga took impossible risks. After all, he did know he could never get home on one gas tank. In any case, he and his five planes were gone.

But all five of Hashimoto's planes came through, and so did three of Lieutenant Mori's six fighters, and together they limped back toward the *Hiryu,* three of the torpedo planes too badly riddled ever to fly again. But they had done their job. Hashimoto was absolutely certain he got a different carrier from the one hit by the dive bombers. As he neared home, he radioed ahead the glad tidings: "Two certain torpedo hits on an *Enterprise* class carrier. Not the same one as reported bombed."

Watching the *Enterprise* and *Hornet* untouched on the horizon was too much for Seaman Ed Forbes. "When are those two over there going to get into the fight?" he asked aloud to anyone who would listen. It was small of him and he knew it, but he was scared. As a gunner on the *Anderson,* desperately trying to protect the *Yorktown,* all he wanted at the moment was another big target to attract the Japs' attention.

Certainly the *Yorktown* had taken her share. Five minutes after the attack the clinometer on the bridge showed she was listing 26°. Captain Buckmaster checked below over the sound-powered phone, but heard only bad news. Lieutenant Commander Delaney reported from the engine room that all fires were out—no hope for any power. The auxiliary generator snapped on, but with all circuits out, it made no difference. Lieutenant Commander Aldrich, down in central station, said that without power there was no way he could pump, counter-flood, shift fuel, or do anything else to correct the list. On the bridge, it looked as though the *Yorktown* might roll over.

Captain Buckmaster paced up and down in agony for several minutes. To no one in particular, he remarked aloud that he hated to give the order to abandon ship. The officers standing around gaped at him mutely. It was one of those moments that give true meaning to the loneliness of command.

Finally he said there was nothing else to do—they must abandon. The *Yorktown* seemed doomed, and as he later put it, "I didn't see any sense in drowning 2,000 men just to stick with the ship."

At 2:55 the order went out—by flag hoist to the screen, by word of mouth and sound-powered phone to the men below. From the engine room, the sick bay, the repair stations, the message center a stream of men stumbled through darkened passageways, up oil-slick ladders, working their way clumsily topside.

The list, the darkness, the oil all made it difficult. No abandon-ship drill was ever like this. In the confusion most of the men ignored or forgot the usual procedures. The rough log was left on the bridge. The code room personnel left the safe open, code books and secret message files lying around. The airmen were just as hurried: some 70 sets of air contact codes lay scattered about the squadron ready rooms.

Down in the sick bay the doctors and corpsmen worked with flashlights, trying to get some 50-60 wounded men to the flight deck. Nothing was tougher than carrying those stretchers up the swinging ladders, across the oil-smeared deck plates. In the operating room the senior medical officer Captain W. D. Davis and his chief surgeon Lieutenant Commander French continued treating a wounded sailor. No one even told them the ship was being abandoned.

Hundreds of men milled around the flight deck, not knowing quite what to do. Some waited patiently at their regular stations by the motor launches—forgetting there was no power to lower the boats. Others were throwing life rafts overboard —sometimes still bundled together. Some walked sadly up and down the slanting deck, heart-heavy at the thought of leaving the ship. Others laughed and joked, and if the laughter seemed a little forced—well, everybody understood that.

Not that there weren't sour notes. One commander—obviously in a state of shock, his face dirty and tear-streaked— found out that Radioman James Patterson was in the last SBD that landed before the attack. "You led them here!" he screamed, trying to hit Patterson.

Now it was after 3:00. The destroyers moved in reassuringly close, and the men finally began to go. Commander Ralph Arnold knew just how to do it; he had talked with survivors from the *Lexington*. He carried a knife, took some gloves, and he was especially careful to keep on his shoes: when picked up, he'd have something to wear.

Most of the crew were more like Machinist's Mate George Bateman. He carefully arranged a neat pile on the deck consisting of his shoes, shirt, gloves, hat and flashlight. Gradually, in fact, pairs of shoes lined the whole deck, all meticulously placed with the toes pointing out.

At first a trickle, soon a steady stream of men were pouring down the starboard side. Dozens of knotted ropes hung from the rails, and Lieutenant William Crenshaw felt this would be the perfect time to use the knowledge he gained at the Naval Academy on climbing and descending ropes. One should go down carefully hand over hand, the instructor said, but when Crenshaw tried it, he plummeted straight down into the sea. The difference between this rope and the one at Annapolis was oil—it was everywhere, making a good grip next to impossible.

Others had the same trouble. Worth Hare burned his hands sliding down. Seaman Melvin Frantz was making it all right; then the man above slipped, came down on Frantz's shoulders, and they both plunged into the sea. Boatswain C. E. Briggs lost his grip too, and felt it took forever to come to the surface. He forgot he had given his life jacket away and was wearing shoes, sweater, pistol, two clips of ammunition, plus all his regular clothing. The wonder was he ever came up at all.

Occasionally a man did it right. Yeoman William Lancaster put on a turtleneck sweater, tightened his life jacket, and carefully lowered himself down one of the lines. When he reached the end, he did not let go. To his own great surprise, he stopped, held on to the line, and instinctively stuck his foot down to test the temperature of the water.

Some added a dash all their own. Commander "Jug" Ray went down clenching his inevitable brier pipe. Chief Radioman Grew gave his famous waxed mustache a farewell twirl. A young fireman asked Radio Electrician Bennett's permission to dive from the flight deck—he had wanted to do it ever since coming on board. Permission granted.

For the swimmers there was now a new hazard. The oil from the ripped port side had worked around to starboard, making a thick film that gradually spread out from the ship. Men retched and vomited as they struggled toward the clear water farther off. Watching from the flight deck, it reminded Yeoman Adams of a large group of turtles or crawfish swimming in a half-dried pond of mud and muck.

The nonswimmers posed a special problem. The more knowledgeable men gave up their own life jackets to help, but few took as decisive action as Radioman Patterson. As he pushed away from the ship, a sailor grabbed his shoulder, saying he couldn't swim. Patterson gave the man a 30-second course in dogpaddling—not a word wasted—and the two moved off together.

Another special problem was the sailor trapped when the torpedo struck and curled up the port catwalk. The wire mesh pinned him against the side of the *Yorktown* in his own private prison. It was on the low side of the ship, leading to all sorts of unpleasant possibilities if she rolled over. His buddies worked on anyhow, trying to pry him out. They finally succeeded, but all the time he was there he kept begging his friends to leave him and save themselves.

Down in the operating room, Captain Davis and Lieutenant Commander French still worked over their wounded man, oblivious of everything else. Finally finished, Davis went out and called for a corpsman to move the patient. Nobody answered the call. He asked some sailor with a walkie-talkie where the corpsman was.

"Oh," explained the sailor, "they passed the word some time

ago for all hands to abandon ship." He added he was about to leave himself.

Davis and French carried their man to the flight deck; then Davis went down to check again. He looked around and called, but couldn't hear any one. Finally satisfied, he climbed back to the deck.

By now most of the swimmers, boats and rafts were all clear of the *Yorktown*. Looking around, Davis couldn't see any one else still aboard—just a vast, empty stretch of flight deck. He hung his gun on the lifeline and like so many before him, carefully placed his shoes at the edge of the deck. Then he inflated his life jacket and climbed down a rope ladder into the sea, feeling sure he was the last man off.

Captain Buckmaster watched him go, as did his executive officer Dixie Kiefer. Both men were standing on the starboard wing of the bridge—Buckmaster waiting to play out the old tradition that the captain be the last to leave his ship. Now it was Kiefer's turn to go. He swung over the side and started down a line toward the water. But he had burned his hands earlier and, like so many others, he lost his grip. Falling, he caromed off the ship's armor belt, breaking his ankle in the process. It took more than that to stop the ebullient Kiefer; he bobbed to the surface and swam for the rescue ships in the distance.

Buckmaster began a final tour of the *Yorktown* alone. First along the starboard catwalk all the way to the 5-inch gun platforms. Then back to the flight deck by No. 1 crane . . . down through Dressing Station No. 1 . . . forward through Flag Country and to the captain's cabin . . . across to the port side . . . down the ladder to the hangar deck.

Now it was really dark. There were a few emergency lamps in the island structure, but absolutely nothing down here— just yards and yards of empty blackness. He didn't even have a flashlight—someone had swiped that long ago.

He groped through a labyrinth of passageways and compartments, trying to walk with the list, keep his footing on the oil-slick deck. He banged into hatches, stumbled over bodies, slashed his leg on some jagged piece of steel. On he went—always searching for any sign of life, shouting from time to time into the darkness.

No answer, except great belching sounds of air bursting out of compartments as one more bulkhead gave way and the water rushed in. Or sometimes a clanking door or a grating of steel, as the ship rose and fell in the gentle swell.

He went as deep as he dared. Finding no one, he felt his way topside again and walked aft to the very stern. A brief pause for a last look at his ship; then Elliott Buckmaster swung over the taffrail, caught a line, and dropped to the sea.

"Well, there goes 20 years' sermon notes," sighed one of the *Yorktown's* chaplains as his raft moved clear of the ship. Captain Buckmaster also found a raft, loaded with wounded, and hung onto the ratlines. A launch came up, tossed over a line and began to pull. As the line jerked taut, a mess attendant lost his grip and drifted astern. He went under twice, yelling for help. A figure darted over and saved him. It was Buckmaster.

Dr. Davis had nothing to cling to. He was still swimming by himself, which perhaps made him all the more apprehensive when he glanced around and thought he saw the snout of a large fish. He turned the other way, but it followed him. Steeling his nerve, he made a grab—and came up with his own wallet.

Lieutenant Commander Hartwig could hardly believe his eyes. His destroyer *Russell* had been picking up scores of men —they came aboard in every conceivable way—but never anything like this. One of his launches was approaching the ship crowded to the gunwhales with perhaps three times its supposed capacity; it was towing a life raft so loaded with men it was invisible; and the raft in turn was towing a long manila line to which scores of men were clinging like bees. And as if all this wasn't enough, at the very end of the line was the

Yorktown's supply officer Commander Ralph Arnold, holding aloft his hat. Arnold, it later turned out, had just made commander; his wife had sent him a brand-new scrambled-eggs cap, and he wasn't about to ruin it in the oily water. At the moment Hartwig simply yelled down to him that no *Yorktown* sailor would ever have to tip his hat to get aboard the *Russell*.

Off to port Lieutenant Commander Harold Tiemroth on the *Balch* was putting into practice all the rescue plans he so carefully made after Coral Sea. His men tossed over the specially prepared cargo nets and were soon hauling in scores of oil-soaked men. His hand-picked rescue swimmers Seaman Lewis and Fireman Prideaux went after those too exhausted to reach the ship. Ensign Weber took the motor whaleboat on trip after trip, sometimes gathering in 50 men at a time.

It was much the same on all seven destroyers. The *Benham* alone picked up 721. By 4:46, when the *Balch* completed a final swing around the scene, the little flotilla had rescued a grand total of 2,270 men. But the real meaning of this lay not in statistics, but in the human beings themselves. There was the *Yorktown* cook who gave up his life jacket, swam a thousand yards to the *Benham*, then asked as he scrambled aboard, "Where's the galley? The cooks are going to need all the help they can get tonight." There was Commander Laing, Royal Navy; now dripping with oil, he reached the deck of the *Morris*, put on his British cap, saluted the colors and said, "God bless the King; God bless the U.S. Navy." There was the injured seaman—also on the *Morris*—who climbed aboard unassisted, saying, "Help some of those other poor guys that are really hurt." He had lost his own leg at the knee.

ON THE *Astoria* Admiral Fletcher had watched the Japanese torpedo planes wing in. He never felt more frustrated. They certainly knew how to find the *Yorktown*—but he was still in the dark about them. Where was that fourth carrier? Three hours had passed since he sent out Scouting 5 to search the northwest, but still no word at all.

Turning to Rear Admiral "Poco" Smith—his host on the *Astoria*—Fletcher told him to rush two cruiser seaplanes to Midway and tell the CO there, "For God's sake send a search and find out where this other carrier is."

If Fletcher sounded anguished, he had a right to be, but actually the answer was already on the way. Even before the first torpedo slammed into the *Yorktown*'s side, one of the scouting planes solved the riddle.

Lieutenant Sam Adams had gone out with the rest of Scouting 5, leading a two-plane section assigned to the most westerly sector. Like the others in the group, he found nothing but ocean for three long hours. By 2:30 he was heading back—nearly halfway home—when he suddenly saw those revealing white wakes.

He counted carefully. Ten of them down there. The two SBDs edged closer; Adams could now make out four destroyers, three cruisers, two battleships . . . and yes, there was the carrier. They were all heading north, 20 knots. He worked out the position, reported it by voice, told his rear-seat man Karrol to send it by dot-dash too.

"Just a minute, Mr. Adams. I have a Zero to take care of first."

Adams had been so absorbed in identifying ships that he missed the fighter completely. Somehow he and the other SBD dodged clear, and at 2:37 they turned for home.

The report reached the *Yorktown* just as the torpedo attack was breaking. There was a rush to relay it to Task Force 16 by TBS radio, but it didn't get off before the power failed. It was then blinkered to the *Astoria* to be relayed on, and Admiral Fletcher knew at last that his search for the fourth carrier was over.

Shortly after 3:00 Admiral Spruance had the message on the *Enterprise*, and his staff slapped together what strength they could: no torpedo planes, no fighters, bits and pieces from three different dive bombing squadrons. Bombing 6 and Scouting 6 had only 11 planes left between them, but Bombing 3 contributed 14 refugees from the *Yorktown,* and they made up for a lot. Lieutenant Earl Gallaher of Scouting 6 would lead the attack.

Down in the ready rooms the pilots restlessly waited. By now the excitement of the morning strike had worn off; most of the men were terribly tired, and they couldn't help looking at the empty chairs of those who failed to come back.

Then about 3:15 the teletype machines began clacking; the talkers moved into action; the rooms stirred to life. Out came the plotting boards; the men once again bent low, working away at their navigation.

"Pilots, man your planes." At 3:30 the *Enterprise* turned into the wind, and Gallaher led his mixed group off. One of them had engine trouble, returned almost right away. But the rest continued on, 24 planes heading into the afternoon sun.

Even as they left, a miracle was taking place on the *Hornet.* By 3:00 the crew had given up hope for her missing squadrons. Then, unexpectedly, planes were spotted coming in from the south. Japs? No, these were SBDs. Gloom turned to joy and relief as 11 lost planes from Bombing 8 began landing at 3:27. Lieutenant Commander Ruff Johnson had refueled his squadron at Midway and returned to the ship to get back in the fight.

They were gassed up and on their way out again by 4:03. Adding a few extra planes in shape to fly, the *Hornet* launched 16 dive bombers altogether. The *Enterprise* planes had half an hour's head start, but this didn't bother the green young ensigns who filled out the *Hornet's* group. Led by a reserve lieutenant named Edgar Stebbins, they'd get in on as much of the show as they could.

"TF 16 air groups are now striking the carrier which your search plane reported," Admiral Spruance radioed Admiral Fletcher as the dive bombers headed out. Then he added, "Have you any instructions for me?"

"None. Will conform to your movements." To Fletcher this was the only sensible thing to do. He was the over-all commander, but he trusted Spruance and Spruance's staff. They would do things the way he would himself. They had two carriers; he had none. So he bowed out, and from now on the battle was squarely in the hands of Raymond A. Spruance.

"IT's still possible to win this battle," thought Commander Kanoe, the *Hiryu*'s executive officer. "It's an even game at worst." Admiral Yamaguchi thought so too: with one U.S. carrier bombed out, a "second" torpedoed, it was again one-to-one. He quickly put Lieutenant Hashimoto—just back from the torpedo attack—in charge of a third strike at the U.S. force.

Trouble was, he had so little left. At best, only five dive bombers and four torpedo planes were in shape to go. No fighters were available—the six remaining Zeros had to protect the *Hiryu*. All the officer pilots were gone except Hashimoto and Lieutenant Shigematsu. Everybody was dead tired; Hashimoto, for instance, had been flying since dawn—this would be his third big mission of the day.

Still, it had to be done, and no time to lose. All would be lost if the Americans hit first. Yamaguchi decided the strike must leave right away—at 4:30—and once again the fliers lined up beneath the bridge. This time it was Captain Kaku who spoke. He told them he trusted them completely, but as he walked down the line, patting each man on the shoulder, he could see how exhausted they were.

He finally sent a mechanic running down to sick bay for some stay-awake pills. The man came back in a few minutes with a bottle cryptically marked "Aviation Tablet A." Commander Kawaguchi suggested they just might be sleeping tablets instead, and the very thought threw Captain Kaku into a rage. He turned on the mechanic, called him a fool and threatened the direst punishment. A quick phone call to sick bay straightened everything out—no mistake, these were indeed the stimulants. The storm blew over, but the incident suggested the pilots weren't the only ones whose nerves were frayed.

It was so clear, in fact, that everyone was exhausted, Admiral Yamaguchi decided to postpone the strike until 6:00 P.M. They'd lose 90 valuable minutes, but the gains should be worth it. The crew could get something to eat—no one had been given anything since breakfast. The change also meant they'd now hit the enemy at dusk; this gave the small handful of Japanese planes a much better chance against the U.S. defenses.

Down in the engine room the phone rang: send up a couple of men to bring back battle meals for the rest. Ensign Mandai watched them go—he could almost taste the rice balls coming. In the ready room, Lieutenant Hashimoto was too tired even to eat. He lay down on one of the brown leather sofas to catch a few minutes' rest. On the flight deck most of the mechanics took a break too, but a few kept working, tuning up the *Soryu*'s Type 13 experimental reconnaissance plane; it would go ahead of the rest to pinpoint the American position. In the air command post Lieutenant Commander Kawaguchi was just popping a rice ball into his mouth. . . .

It was exactly 5:03 when a startled lookout shouted the words all dreaded the most: "Enemy dive bombers directly overhead!"

CHAPTER 11

The Emperor's Portrait

THIS time they were easy to find. Around 4:45 Lieutenant Earl Gallaher sighted the telltale white wakes about 30 miles to the northwest. Several minutes later he could make out a carrier, half a dozen other ships, scurrying along on a westerly course. Gradually climbing to 19,000 feet, he circled around the Japanese fleet so as to attack from out of the sun. Far below, the ships steamed on, blissfully unaware.

At 4:58 all was ready. Neatly stacked down by divisions and sections, the dive bombers began a high-speed run-in. As they roared toward the target, Gallaher opened up on his radio: *Enterprise* planes would take the carrier, the *Yorktown* group the nearer battleship. Then a sharp, quick warning: Zeros, ahead and above.

They struck with that breath-taking rush the American pilots were getting to know so well. Some said there were 6, some 12; but they were everywhere at once and it was hard to tell. One pounced on Ensign F. T. Weber, lagging behind the rest of Bombing 6. Straggling was always fatal when Zeros were around, and this time was no exception.

Earl Gallaher almost collided with another as he pulled up out of the formation to start his dive. For a split second they squarely faced each other; then the Zero vanished as Gallaher

THE EMPEROR'S PORTRAIT [235

pushed over. Next instant he was screeching down, leading his makeshift squadron against the last of Nagumo's operating carriers.

Finally catching on, the ship twisted hard to port in a desperate evasion maneuver. It was too late for Gallaher to correct his dive; so he pulled up sharply just before release, hoping to lob his bomb at the vessel. The trick occasionally worked, but not this time. First Gallaher, then several other Scouting 6 pilots dropped near-misses just astern.

Seeing it happen, Lieutenant Dave Shumway made a fast decision. His *Yorktown* planes had been ordered to hit the battleship, but now he shifted to the carrier too. His first section swept past Dick Best's Bombing 6, just getting ready for their own pushover. Best dived on schedule anyhow, his little group from the *Enterprise* all mixed up with the *Yorktown* crowd. It was another of those moments that would have given fits to the instructor back at Pensacola.

The Zeros tore at the group all the way down. Their last flight deck was at stake, and they knew it. They performed amazing stunts. One fighter made a pass on Ensign Cobb, pulled out, then made another—all while Cobb was in the same dive. Another turned himself into a "falling leaf" to keep Lieutenant Harold Bottomley in his sights.

Lieutenant Wiseman crashed, then Ensign Johnny Butler. In the *Yorktown* wardroom Butler had always said how much he wanted to be a fighter pilot and tangle with the Zeros. He got his chance—but in an SBD. It wasn't nearly enough.

At first it looked as if the carrier might escape. Her sharp turn, the Zeros, a sudden dose of antiaircraft fire, all seemed to throw the dive bombers off. Ensign Hanson saw several misses ahead of him, then watched with dismay as his own bomb missed too. Disgusted, he looked back—and saw a sight that blotted out his disappointment. One, two, three bombs landed on the ship in quick succession.

They all claimed her. Scouting 6 probably got one hit . . . Bombing 3 certainly two . . . Bombing 6 another—but it was hard to tell. Toward the end everyone was diving at once, and in all that smoke the hits and misses looked pretty much alike. In any case, it was a thorough job. So much so that two of the last planes from Bombing 3 switched back to the battleship originally assigned. It seemed a waste to drop anything more on the carrier—her flight deck was a shambles.

GLASS showered down on Captain Kaku, navigator Cho, everyone else in the *Hiryu*'s wheelhouse. The first hit had landed squarely on the forward elevator platform, hurling it back against the island structure, breaking every window on the bridge. The blast blew Commander Kawaguchi clear off the air command post, down to the flight deck. Miraculously unhurt, he picked himself up just in time to be knocked down again by three more hits in the bridge area.

Down in the engineroom Ensign Mandai heard a bugle start sounding the antiaircraft alert over the loudspeaker system. It was still blowing when he felt a hard jolt, then two or three more. His heart sank. He could tell a miss because the shock always came from one side or the other; this time it came from directly above.

The lights went out, then came on again as the engineers switched over to emergency power. Other troubles weren't so easily solved. Smoke poured down through the air ducts; the two men sent up for food came scrambling back through an open hatch—smoke and flames swept in after them.

In the ready room Lieutenant Hashimoto lay dozing on his sofa when a sudden "hammer blow" slammed into his back. He awoke with a start, stumbled onto the blazing flight deck, blinked at the incredible sight of the elevator platform leaning against the front of the bridge.

Captain Kaku, of course, could see nothing. The engines were all right—the ship still raced along at 30 knots—but with his view completely blocked it was impossible to maneuver. Anyhow, they could keep moving and go to work on the fires. Commander Kanoe ordered the magazines flooded; damage control parties tackled the flames from the only fire main still working.

Commander Kawaguchi stood near the island structure, watching the men battle the blaze. There was very little left for an air officer to do—the forward third of the deck was one big crater. Then, as he stood there, several big geysers of water shot up perhaps 50 yards off the ship. He looked up in astonishment. As if they didn't have enough trouble already, B-17s were bombing them too.

It was a tough assignment for Major George Blakey, leading his six B-17s from Hawaii to Midway. They were coming to beef up the base's tiny force of heavy bombers—had been flying for over seven hours—and now, when almost in sight of Eastern Island, Midway was ordering them to attack the Japanese fleet before landing. Gas was low; the men were tired. It was a hard job under any circumstances, and even harder for men who had never been in combat before.

The flight leaders conferred by voice radio. Did they have enough gas? Midway said the Japs were 170 miles to the northwest—out and back meant perhaps 400 more miles of flying. They figured they could just about make it if they stuck to their present altitude of 3,600 feet. This was absurdly low (Colonel Sweeney's Midway group was operating at 20,000 feet), but it had to be this or nothing. Blakey radioed they were on their way.

Shortly after 6:00 Captain Narce Whitaker, leading one of the three-plane flights, spotted a column of smoke on the horizon ahead. Drawing near, he could make out a burning carrier, surrounded by a milling swarm of cruisers and destroyers. But in the compartmentalized way of war, even now there were those who didn't grasp the picture. Lieutenant Charles Crowell, a young officer in one of the B-17s, had no idea the Japanese were below. When the order came to prepare for the bomb run, he assumed the plane was lost and had to lighten its load.

At this point he learned. As the little squadron turned toward the carrier, all the ships in the screen opened up. Zeros swarmed around, and as one of the pilots put it, "With no place to land, these characters were really hopped up." A shell burst in the wing of one plane; shrapnel smashed through the nose of another, sending the bombardier sprawling. Yet the B-17s had a way of coming through. Shaking off the fighters, they thundered in, dropped their bombs, and burst clear on the other side still intact. One of them, unable to release on the carrier, dropped instead on an unsuspecting destroyer.

Untried, a year or so out of school, it was a weird experience for most of the men. A dozen disconnected impressions raced through their minds: the sudden fright . . . how busy they were . . . the overwhelming thirst when it was all over— and then not being able to swallow a drop of water.

For those lucky or unlucky enough to peer outside, the sight was breath-taking. Major Blakey was fascinated by the way the shells and small-arms fire whipped the sea like an angry storm. All of a sudden some splashes shot up far bigger than the rest. "My Lord," Blakey thought, "those are really big shells." It never occurred to him that still another group of B-17s, completely unknown to himself, was bombing the Japanese fleet from a point directly above.

But it was so. The Midway-based planes were back on the job. First, Colonel Sweeney arrived at 5:30 with a group of four. The carrier below looked finished; so he settled on a heavy cruiser. Then Carl Wuertele turned up with two more B-17s from Midway. The carrier was still burning, but he took it anyhow, while his wingman picked a battleship. They were the ones who were causing the commotion when Major Blakey appeared on the scene.

Meanwhile Stebbins had arrived with the *Hornet*'s dive bombers. He too decided the carrier was through and went instead for two ships in the screen . . . one of them the same target Sweeney was bombing.

Mass confusion, but by now it didn't matter. The strike was a picnic. Attacked from all sides—the Zeros finally used up—

the Japanese had little left to put up a fight. When the American fliers finally headed home, their estimates matched the rosy glow of the Pacific sunset. Bombing 8 claimed three hits on a battleship, two on a cruiser. The B-17s were just as confident—hits on the burning carrier, a battleship, a cruiser; a destroyer sunk; plus an assortment of lethal near misses.

CAPTAIN Michiso Tsutsumi, executive officer of the battleship *Haruna*, watched two dive bombers hurtle down toward the bridge. One of them looked as if it would never pull out—Tsutsumi could see the pilot's face clearly. Then at the last second it zoomed safely away, still so low that its trailing antenna caught that of the *Haruna*.

Somehow the bombs missed, landing with huge explosions just astern. For the next hour much of the fleet endured the same thing: 5:30, dive bombers on the *Tone* . . . 5:40, B-17s on the *Haruna* . . . 5:40, dive bombers on the *Chikuma* . . . 6:15, B-17s on the *Hiryu*. . . .

It seemed to go on forever. But finally at 6:32 some weary yeoman on the *Chikuma*'s bridge noted that the last of the attackers were retiring, and the fleet had a chance to take stock. Incredibly, none of the ships had been hit by these final blows. The near-miss off the *Haruna*'s stern bent a few plates and jammed the main battery range finder, but repairs would be easy. The only other damage came when one of those low-flying B-17s strafed the *Hiryu*'s shattered flight deck, knocking out an antiaircraft battery and killing several gunners.

One antiaircraft gun, more or less, made little difference to the *Hiryu* now. Captain Kaku knew his only hope was to get clear of the battle area. Once beyond range of the U.S. planes, maybe the ship could lick her wounds and somehow make it back to Japan. The phone still worked, and Kaku called his chief engineer, Commander Kunizo Aiso. He urged the chief to keep giving him 30 knots.

Aiso was optimistic. The master control room was in good shape, and the flash fire in Engine Room No. 4 was out. He couldn't get to the other three engine rooms—all hatches were blocked—but he could call them, and they said everything still was running. Their chief complaint seemed to be the fumes and smoke that steadily poured through the air ducts.

Soon they all noticed something else. Engine rooms were always hot, but now it was far hotter than usual . . . far hotter than it ought to be. In No. 4 Ensign Mandai looked up at the steel overhead and noticed that the white paint was starting to melt. It began dripping down on the engineers as they worked, burning them, causing little fires to flare up in the machinery. As the paint disappeared from the overhead, the bare steel began to glow. Finally it was bright red. Nobody mentioned it, but every man in the room knew they were now trapped beneath the fires raging above.

A few hundred yards off the burning carrier, the battleship *Kirishima* plowed along in the gathering dusk. She had been ordered to stand by for towing in case the *Hiryu* closed down her engines. As night fell, it became an increasingly unpleasant assignment. The fires on the *Hiryu* blazed up from time to time, offering a perfect beacon for enemy submarines. Finally the battleship's skipper Captain Iwabuchi radioed Nagumo, describing the situation, pointing out the danger to his ship.

At 6:37 Nagumo radioed back the welcome word to break off and rejoin the *Nagara*. The *Kirishima* turned northwest, and as she slowly drew off, her executive officer Captain Honda thoughtfully looked back at the *Hiryu*. She stood black against the evening sky, fires twinkling in every port. From a distance the little pinpoints of flame reminded him of lanterns—hundreds of them—strung to mark some happier occasion at home.

L ooking back at the *Yorktown*, listing heavily and silhouetted alone in the twilight, Commander Hartwig could barely stand the sight. For two years his destroyer *Russell* had been the carrier's guard ship. He felt almost a part of her. Now he was steaming away. With the survivors rescued, Admiral Fletcher had ordered the ships in the screen to head east and join up with Admiral Spruance. Orders were orders, but it wasn't easy to leave that sagging, lonely hulk. One thought, paraphrased from *Hamlet*, kept running through Hartwig's mind: "Alas, poor Yorick, I knew her well."

There were many others who felt, as they left the scene, that "it didn't seem right" to abandon the *Yorktown*. She was holding her own—the fires were contained, her list was no greater—and the *Portland* stood rigged to give her a tow. But there were other factors too, and Frank Jack Fletcher had to consider them all. It was getting dark . . . Japanese snoopers were about . . . Yamamoto's heavy ships were somewhere . . . enemy subs might turn up . . . a task force guarding a derelict carrier made an ideal target.

Once again war turned into a matter of "groping around." Fletcher weighed his chances, finally decided the odds were too dangerous. At 5:38 he issued his orders sending everybody east. For the next 35 minutes the *Yorktown* wallowed alone in the dusk; then at 6:13 new orders went out, detaching the destroyer *Hughes* to stand by her.

The rest of Task Force 17 continued on toward Spruance, who was just recovering his planes from the afternoon strike. Once again anxious faces turned skyward, counting the SBDs, searching for signs of damage or casualties. But this time there was much less tension than during the morning attack. The radio had seen to that. No one who listened could miss the note of jubilation as the pilots talked back and forth: "Hey, they're throwing everything at us except the kitchen sink . . . oops, here comes the kitchen sink."

Still, the Japanese had given some of them a bad time. Besides the three planes lost, several were badly damaged. Three Zeros teamed up on Lieutenant Shumway, wounding his gunner and smashing the right side of his plane. He managed to get it home, but it was certainly ready for the junk heap. Ensigns Cooner and Merrill had much the same experience.

Earl Gallaher, leading the *Enterprise* group, had a different kind of problem, but the way he felt, he would have traded it for Zeros. Pulling out from his dive, he started up an old back injury, and now the pain was killing him. He couldn't even reach down to drop his landing hook. Yet he couldn't come in without it, nor could he land in the water. With his back this way, he'd never get out of the cockpit.

He turned the lead over to his wing man and let everyone else land while he kept trying to get the hook down. There was no easy way, and in desperation he reached over anyhow. He got it, all right, but almost passed out from the pain. Finally set, he bounced down to a shaky landing at 6:34; the last of the *Enterprise* group was home.

Everything was falling apart on Admiral Nagumo's temporary flagship *Nagara*. The Admiral had drifted back to his destroyer days and talked vaguely of night torpedo attacks. His chief of staff Kusaka was in agony with his badly sprained ankles. He finally retired to a small cabin at the stern, where a medical officer tried to give him first aid. ("But you are a dentist," complained Kusaka. "I know," the man said cheerfully, "but a dentist is really a doctor.")

Most of the time Kusaka lay on a cot, but occasionally he was needed on the bridge. Then a sailor would carry him there piggyback. It was a ludicrous sight, somehow symbolizing the helpless plight of Nagumo's whole fleet.

Far to the rear, Admiral Yamamoto sensed the chaos. In the small operations room on the *Yamato*'s bridge, he worked with his staff on plans to save the day.

He had taken the first step at 12:20, 90 minutes after learning of the debacle. At that time he radioed a crisp set of instructions to the rest of the fleet. The transports were to retire temporarily. The submarines were to take position on a line to the west. Admiral Kakuta was to leave the Aleutians and hurry south with the light carriers *Ryujo* and *Junyo*. No need to give any orders to Admiral Kondo; he was already racing north with his battleships, the carrier *Zuiho*, in fact, everything he had. Yamamoto himself was churning east through a dense fog, bringing the mighty *Yamato*, two other battleships and the carrier *Hosho*.

With any luck these various units, including four small carriers, would converge on Nagumo within a day or so. Kondo was especially promising. Only 300 miles away, he should arrive by 3:00 next morning.

Built around the *Hiryu* and the hard-hitting Yamaguchi, this makeshift fleet could, Yamamoto hoped, still take care of the U.S. Navy. But there remained Midway, the original objective. With the greater part of the Imperial Combined Fleet now steaming into range, could the Americans turn the base into an "unsinkable carrier"? Captain Kuroshima, "the God of Operations," thought so. He persuaded Yamamoto that the base must be neutralized, even at the expense of some of the gathering strength. The Admiral agreed, and at 1:10 P.M. radioed Admiral Kondo, "The Invasion Force will assign a portion of its force to shell and destroy enemy air bases on AF. The occupation of AF and AO are temporarily postponed."

The Aleutian phase (AO) was soon revived, but Midway remained tabled, at least until Kondo could soften up the place. That should come soon enough. He was sending the cruisers *Kumano*, *Suzuya*, *Mikuma* and *Mogami* to do the job. They were the newest, fastest heavy cruisers in the Japanese Navy, perfect for the assignment. With Admiral Takeo Kurita commanding, they raced northeast at 32 knots.

A good start, but planning would be a lot easier if they knew a little more about conditions on Midway. Nagumo had yet to send a single message describing the morning raid. Of course, the man had his problems, but Combined Fleet really needed to know. At 4:55 a new message was fired off, needling Nagumo for some sort of progress report. It was never even acknowledged, perhaps because it arrived at a most inconvenient time: The U.S. dive bombers were just swooping down on the *Hiryu.*

Yamamoto remained unaware. He had heard nothing directly from Nagumo since 11:30 A.M.—almost six hours ago. He restlessly wandered to the front of the bridge, absent-mindedly raised his binoculars and peered east—as though that could possibly do any good.

The ax fell at 5:30.

"*Hiryu* burning as a result of bomb hits," Nagumo radioed. Yamamoto sank down heavily on a chair in the center of the battle command post. He said nothing. Lost in his own private thoughts, for minutes he sat motionless as a rock.

On the *Nagara* Admiral Nagumo continued to tinker with the idea of a night surface engagement. His scheme at the moment was to retire west, then reverse course in the dark and catch the Americans by surprise. Studying Nagumo's expression, Commander Yoshioka thought the old sea dog looked cheerful for the first time since morning.

Then at 6:30 the *Chikuma* blinkered a message which blasted every hope: "The No. 2 plane of this ship sighted 4 enemy carriers, 6 cruisers, and 15 destroyers in position 30 miles east of the burning and listing enemy carrier at 5:13. This enemy force was westward bound. . . ."

That changed everything. Previously Nagumo had assumed the Americans were badly hurt too. Now it appeared he had knocked out only one carrier, that four others were steaming straight for him. An old-fashioned sea battle was one thing, but neither Nagumo nor his staff had any appetite for this sort of aerial avalanche.

Nor did they doubt the news. Stunned by the unexpected American assault, they were now ready to believe anything. Nobody even bothered to double-check. Had they done so, they might have been far more skeptical. The information was based on two supposedly separate sightings by the *Chikuma's* plane—but the second "sighting" was clearly the pilot trying to correct and amplify his original flash.

But Nagumo's officers were no longer in a mood to analyze contact reports. Their only reaction was to run for it. At 7:05 the remnants of the Striking Force turned tail and fled northwest.

Admiral Yamamoto sensed there might be a morale problem. He had been shocked himself by these stunning blows, but resiliency was one of the Admiral's fighting qualities. Soon he was ready to jump into the fight, but he wasn't so sure about his unit commanders. Maybe they needed something to buck them up until he could get there and take over himself. At 7:15 he radioed all commands:

1. The enemy fleet, which has practically been destroyed, is retiring to the east.

2. Combined Fleet units in the vicinity are preparing to pursue the remnants and at the same time, to occupy AF.

3. The Main Body is scheduled to reach 32° 08′ N, 175° 45′ E at 0300 on the 5th. Course 90°; speed 20.

4. The First Carrier Striking Force, Invasion Force (less Cruiser Division 7) and Submarine Force will immediately contact and destroy the enemy.

Admiral Nagumo must have found it bitterly ironical: at the same moment he received another message reporting that the *Soryu* had gone down.

All afternoon she had smoldered away, racked by occasional explosions, while the stand-by destroyers circled helplessly about. Toward sunset the fires died down enough to send Chief Petty Officer Abe aboard in an attempt to rescue Captain Yanagimoto. Abe was a Navy wrestling champion, and his orders were to bring Yanagimoto off by force. But the Captain refused to budge, and Abe couldn't bring himself to lay hands on his skipper. He returned from the carrier in tears and alone.

The *Soryu* wallowed lower in the water. On the *Makigumo*, standing by, somebody began singing the Japanese national anthem "*Kimigayo*." Others took it up. As the strains pealed out over the water, the *Soryu*'s stern dipped under, her bow rose high—paused for a second—and at 7:13 she was gone.

Twelve minutes later it was the *Kaga*'s turn. She had been drifting all afternoon, while a small bucket brigade remained aboard fighting the flames. It was a hopeless battle, and around sunset the destroyer *Hagikaze* sent a cutter over to get the men off. They merely sent it back for a hand pump. The cutter went over again, this time with a written order for the men to return. They now obeyed, but it was hard. As one old warrant officer climbed aboard the *Hagikaze*, he kept looking back at his burning ship. Tears streamed down his cheeks, even running down his beautifully trimmed mustache. Shortly afterward two mighty explosions ripped the dusk, and at 7:25 the *Kaga* too was gone.

At this same moment a few miles away, Captain Aoki of the *Akagi* summoned all hands to the anchor deck. Hope was gone for saving the carrier, and now Aoki praised the men's courage, bade them farewell, and ordered all to abandon ship. The destroyers *Nowaki* and *Arashi* moved near, and at 8:00 a flotilla of small boats began transferring the survivors.

A message was sent to Admiral Nagumo, asking permission to scuttle her. Nagumo never answered, but Yamamoto did. The Commander in Chief monitored the request and at 10:25 radioed a brief order not to sink the ship. Partly it was Yamamoto's fighting spirit, but partly it was sentiment too. The *Akagi* was a great favorite of his—in younger days he had served on her for years—now he was determined to tow her back if he could.

The *Akagi*'s navigator Commander Miura got Yamamoto's message on the *Nowaki*, where he was directing the rescue operations. He quickly took a launch over to the *Akagi*, found Captain Aoki waiting to go down with his command (some say tied to the anchor). Miura was a great talker, and he used all his art now. Instead of mournful pleading—which might have been expected—he scolded Aoki, told him he was making a nuisance of himself, above all pointed to Yamamoto's order not to scuttle the ship. It would be far more useful, Miura observed, to come over to the *Nowaki*, and help save her.

Aoki remained utterly dispirited (he would for the rest of his life), but he nodded and dropped down into the *Nowaki's* launch. The party shoved off, leaving behind the black, silent *Akagi*—now truly abandoned—lying helpless in the moonlit sea.

A few scattered swimmers remained—combat air patrol pilots who had run out of gas, occasional crewmen from the three carriers. All afternoon and into the evening destroyers scurried about, picking them up: Raita Ogawa, the Zero pilot from the *Akagi,* treading water in his life jacket . . . Tatsuya Otawa from the *Soryu,* hugging a piece of timber . . . Takayoshi Morinaga of the *Kaga,* clinging to a floating hammock . . . a handful of others. At first there was a good deal of shouting to attract attention, but as evening drew near the cries grew thinner. At last all was silent; the darkened destroyers ended their search and rushed northwest to rejoin the fleet.

Ensign George Gay was all alone under the mid-Pacific stars. He had been anything but that during most of the afternoon. Once a patrolling destroyer came so close he could see white-clad sailors moving about the decks. ("If there had been anybody on board that I knew I could have recognized them.") Gay tried to make himself smaller than ever as he hid in the water under his black cushion.

His burned leg hurt dreadfully . . . his hand was bleeding . . . he began to think of sharks. Then he had a comforting thought. He had heard somewhere that sharks didn't like explosions—well, there'd been plenty of those. In the distance he could still see ships, but he didn't look very often. The salt water hurt his eyes so much he could hardly see anything. He finally kept them shut most of the time, opening them only occasionally for a quick glance around the horizon. He noticed that the Japanese were gradually moving out of the area.

As darkness fell—"maybe a little earlier than was wise"—

he broke out his yellow life raft, inflated it and scrambled in. His eyes felt better now, and at last he could rest. He lay back exhausted—sometimes dozing, sometimes watching the glow of searchlights far to the north, where the Japanese still struggled to salvage something from their wreck.

COMMANDER Yoshida eased his destroyer *Kazagumo* alongside the blazing *Hiryu*. His men worked fast in the night, unloading fire-fighting equipment and a rather grim supper of hardtack and water for the carrier's crew. The destroyer *Yugumo* headed over too, bringing extra fire hose picked up from the *Chikuma*. Two other destroyers hovered nearby, ready to help if needed.

The *Hiryu* herself lay dead in the water. She had finally lost power around nine o'clock. The phones still worked, though faintly, and down in Engine Room No. 4 Commander Aiso eventually got a call from the bridge. Someone up there wanted to know whether the engineers could get out. Aiso glanced up at the red hot steel overhead and said no. A long pause . . . then the bridge asked if the men had any last messages.

This infuriated Aiso. He knew the situation was bad, but surely not hopeless. The *Hiryu* seemed in no danger of sinking, and once the fires were out, he felt they could somehow get her back to Japan. With the passion of a man trapped far below, he urged the bridge not to give up. He never knew whether they heard. The phone faded and went dead.

Whatever the actual situation at the time of this exchange, it became all too clear at 11:58. At this moment something touched off a great blast. The fires—which had begun to die down—flared up again, spreading everywhere out of control.

This new crisis posed an important decision for Ensign Sandanori Kawakami. He was a young paymaster on the *Hiryu*, but tonight he had a far greater responsibility. He was also custodian of the Emperor's portrait. Normally it hung in the captain's cabin, but at Midway certain precautions had been taken. When general quarters sounded, Kawakami placed it in a special wooden box, and a petty officer carried it by rucksack down to the chronometer room below the armored deck. Here it should be safe. But that was as far as planning went. No one dreamed it might have to leave the ship.

Now Kawakami had to act on his own. He couldn't raise the bridge, and there was no time to lose. The petty officer again buckled on his rucksack, and guarding their treasure, the two men fought their way forward through the flames. They broke out onto the anchor deck, where Kawakami tenderly transferred the portrait to the destroyer *Kazagumo*.

None too soon. The *Hiryu* was listing 15°—shipping water constantly—and there was serious question how long she could last. At 2:30 A.M. on June 5 Captain Kaku finally turned to Admiral Yamaguchi and said, "We're going to have to abandon ship, sir."

Yamaguchi nodded, sent a message to Admiral Nagumo reporting that he was ordering off the *Hiryu's* crew. Then he directed Kaku to summon all hands to the port quarter of the flight deck. Some 800 survivors reported, crowding around their two leaders in the flickering glare of the flames.

The Captain spoke first. "This war is yet to be fought," Kaku declared, and he urged them to carry on the struggle. They must live and serve as the nucleus of an ever stronger navy.

Now it was Yamaguchi's turn. He told the men how much he admired their bravery—how proud he was of their achievements in the battles they had fought together. As for this time, "I am fully and solely responsible for the loss of the *Hiryu* and *Soryu*. I shall remain on board to the end. I command all of you to leave the ship and continue your loyal service to His Majesty, the Emperor."

With that, they all faced toward Tokyo, and Yamaguchi led them in three cheers for the Emperor. Then they solemnly lowered the national ensign, followed by the Admiral's own flag. As the Rising Sun fluttered down from the yardarm, a flourish of bugles rang out in the night. They were playing the national anthem, *"Kimigayo."*

As the men began leaving, Captain Kaku turned to Admiral Yamaguchi: "I am going to share the fate of the ship, sir."

The Admiral understood. He repeated that he too planned to stay till the end. Then they drifted off into a colloquy that meant little outside Japan. "Let us enjoy the beauty of the moon," Yamaguchi remarked.

"How bright it shines," Kaku agreed. "It must be in its twenty-first day. . . ."

Oddly enough, this sort of talk was not unusual between two close Japanese friends. By itself, it had no connotation of death. Rather, it was a traditional, almost ceremonial way of saying that they shared much in common.

But tonight that certainly included going down with the *Hiryu;* and overhearing their talk, the executive officer Commander Kanoe felt that the principal officers should also remain. He put the matter to them, and all agreed. Captain Kaku couldn't have been less sympathetic. He said he alone would stay and flatly ordered them, "All of you—leave the ship."

Then Admiral Yamaguchi's senior staff officer, Commander Seiroku Ito, proposed the same thing on behalf of the Admiral's staff. Yamaguchi too rejected the idea.

From time to time, other officers also came up—there were countless details to attend to. "There's a lot of money in the ship's safe," the chief paymaster reported. "What shall I do with it?"

That one was easy. "Leave the money as it is," Captain Kaku ordered, "we'll need it to cross the River Styx."

Yamaguchi joined in the joke: "That's right. And we'll need money for a square meal in hell."

Now it was time for parting. Ito confirmed the Admiral's decision to stay, then asked if he had any last messages. Yamaguchi said yes, he had two. The first was for Admiral

Nagumo: "I have no words to apologize for what has happened. I only wish for a stronger Japanese Navy—and revenge." The second was for Captain Toshio Abe, commanding Destroyer Division 10 on the nearby flagship *Kazagumo*. This one was crisp and to the point: "Scuttle the *Hiryu* with your torpedoes."

Finally, a farewell toast. Someone noticed a cask sent over earlier by the *Kazagumo*. Taking the lid, they filled it with water and silently passed it from one to another. That was all, except as Commander Ito left, Yamaguchi handed him his cap as a keepsake for his family.

It was 4:30—the first light of dawn glowed in the east—when the transfer of the *Hiryu*'s crew was complete. Commander Kanoe was last off, and as the cutter carried him away he could see Yamaguchi and Kaku waving from the bridge.

At 5:10 Captain Abe carried out his final orders. The destroyer *Makigumo* turned toward the *Hiryu* and fired two torpedoes. One missed; the other exploded with a roar. Losing no more time, Abe turned his destroyers northwest and hurried off after the fleeing Admiral Nagumo.

It had been a bad night for Nagumo too. It took more than a hearty message from the Commander in Chief to steady his nerves. At 9:30 he radioed Yamamoto the grim news about all those American carriers steaming toward him. He added that he himself was now retiring northwest at 18 knots. No answer, so at 10:50 he sent the report again, in slightly modified form.

This time he got an answer in five minutes. Yamamoto removed him from command, replacing him with the aggressive Admiral Kondo, rushing up from the south with his battleships and cruisers. As Chief of Staff Ugaki put it, Nagumo seemed to have "no stomach" for the work.

Nagumo took it without comment. Not so his staff. In the excitement of battle—even while going down to defeat—there hadn't been much time to think. Now there was plenty. During the evening the senior staff officer Captain Oishi visited Admiral Kusaka. "Sir, we staff officers have all decided to commit suicide to fulfill our own responsibility for what has happened. Would you please inform Admiral Nagumo?"

The pragmatic Kusaka saw it differently. Summoning the whole staff, he scolded, "How can you do such a thing? You go into raptures over any piece of good news; then say you're going to commit suicide the first time anything goes wrong. It's absurd!"

He went immediately to Nagumo and reported the incident. It turned out the Admiral was toying with the same idea himself. "What you say is certainly reasonable," he remarked, "but things are different when it's a question of the chief."

"Not at all," Kusaka said. And then once again he launched into his lecture: it was nothing but weakness to commit hara-kiri right now. The thing to do was to come back and avenge the defeat.

Nagumo finally agreed, and the First Carrier Striking Force —now bereft of all four of its carriers—raced on through the night, ever farther away from the scene of the day's disaster.

CHAPTER 12

Winners and Losers

MIDWAY couldn't believe it was over. The morning raid was just a softener. The Japanese would be back.

Anticipating a heavy surface bombardment by sunset, Captain Simard dispersed his PBYs, evacuated all nonessential staff, warned the PT boats to be ready for a night attack. Colonel Sweeney sent seven of his B-17s back to Hickam; he didn't want them caught on the ground. On Eastern Island an old Marine took the bank roll he won at craps and hurled it into the surf—he'd rather lose it this way than let the Japs get it.

Actually, by early afternoon the only seaborne "invaders" still heading for Midway were two men in a rubber boat about 10 miles out. Ensign Thomas Wood and his gunner belonged to Bombing 8, the *Hornet* squadron that came in to refuel, but their own tank went dry just short of the base. Ditching, they launched their boat and began paddling toward the smoke they saw in the distance.

It was dark by the time they reached the Midway reef. Once across they still had a five-mile paddle to solid ground, but at least they'd be in the calm waters of the lagoon. All they had to do was get across the reef.

But that was just the trouble. There was only one easy place

254] INCREDIBLE VICTORY

to cross, and guarding it was a huge bull sea lion. He refused to budge and ignored all shouts and threats. Finally Wood sloshed up to him and delivered several solid kicks in the rear. Thus persuaded, the sea lion flopped into the water, but he didn't give up that easily. As the two men rested on the coral after getting their boat across, he swam around the reef, barking at them and generally showing displeasure.

Ultimately they reached shore safely, to find Midway scared and discouraged. The remaining Marine dive bombers had staged an evening attack but couldn't locate the Japanese. They finally returned minus their new skipper Major Norris —apparently a victim of vertigo. Meanwhile the B-17s were coming in from their afternoon strike . . . some of them with hair-raising stories of Zeros. These might be orphans (actually the case) or just possibly from a fifth carrier somewhere. Then there were all those ships to the west and southwest—latest reports said they were still advancing.

Around 9:54 a Marine at Battery B saw a submarine cautiously surface about two miles off Eastern Island. Midway held its fire, not knowing what to expect. Colonel Shannon didn't want to give away his gun positions yet. By the light of a half-hidden moon, the men watched the sub silently glide along the shore, working its way west and south. Then at 10:21 it slipped out of sight in the dark.

The suspense grew. On Sand Island Ensign Leon Grabowsky cleaned up his M-1 and .45 for the landings he felt sure to come. On Eastern Island Lieutenant Jim Muri and his B-26 crew loaded themselves with all the weapons they could scavenge. Then they bedded down in the sand by their plane, restlessly watching a cloud-swept sky flecked by occasional stars.

PEARL HARBOR couldn't believe it was over either. Workers still manned the rooftop guns in the Navy Yard. At Hickam Captain D. E. Ridings, skipper of the 73d Bombardment Squadron, got a hurry call at 10:00 P.M.: Collect all the B-17s available and get over to Midway. He was off before dawn. On Ford Island the pilots of Detached Torpedo 8 manned their planes at 4:00 A.M.—ready for anything.

It was much the same on the West Coast. All radio stations went off the air at 9:00 P.M. on orders from the Fourth Fighter Command. The Seattle waterfront was closed to all but "official and legitimate" traffic. California's Attorney General Earl Warren warned that the state stood "in imminent danger" of attack.

At sea the destroyer *Hughes* stood lonely guard on the deserted *Yorktown*. As Commander Ramsey saw the situation, he could expect the Japs to send one or two surface ships to finish her off during the night. He could also expect submarines, and perhaps an air attack after dawn. He had orders to sink the carrier to prevent capture or if serious fires developed—in any case, sink her before he got sunk.

All through the night he steamed an unpredictable course around the hulk. In the dark the *Yorktown* was an eerie sight. There were what appeared to be flickering lights, and members of the crew thought they could even hear voices and strange noises when the destroyer was close. Ramsey considered boarding to check—then thought better of it. That would mean stopping, lowering a boat, using lights. He would be just inviting trouble on a night like this. So the *Hughes* continued her nervous vigil.

It was a restless, worried night on Task Force 16 too. The pilots were too tired to think, but in the *Hornet* wardroom nobody could overlook those 29 empty chairs. On the *Enterprise* Ensign Charles Lane, an orphan from the *Yorktown*, was assigned the room of a Torpedo 6 pilot who didn't come back. Walking in, the first things Lane saw were the man's family pictures and a Bible lying on his desk. It was almost too much to bear.

Down in the enlisted men's quarters Radioman Snowden of Scouting 6 stared at the empty bunks all around. He felt overwhelmingly depressed. He wasn't questioning why they were there, or the reason for war. He just had a feeling of deep, personal emptiness at the thought of losing so many good friends. . . .

Topside, the officers on watch searched the night. But not for the Japanese. After recovering the *Hiryu* strike, Task Force 16 swung east at 7:09 and was now heading away from the enemy.

Many of Halsey's old staff were dismayed. He would never have done it that way, they said. It seemed such a perfect opportunity to polish off the rest of Nagumo's fleet. The Japs' air power was obviously gone—every pilot swore to that. This, then, was the time for all-out pursuit. Perhaps a night torpedo attack; or the dive bombers could deliver the *coup de grâce* at dawn. That was all it would take. Why couldn't Spruance see it?

Spruance could. It was a great temptation, but there were other factors too. He was all Nimitz had, and at this point no one knew what the Japanese might do. Yamamoto still had his great collection of battleships and cruisers, maybe even another carrier somewhere out there. Certainly the enemy had strength enough to blast him out of the ocean . . . enough still to take Midway if the cards fell right. As he later wrote in his report to Nimitz:

I did not feel justified in risking a night encounter with possibly superior enemy forces, but on the other hand, I did not want to be too far away from Midway next morning. I wished to be in a position from which either to follow up retreating enemy forces, or to break up a landing attack on Midway. . . .

So east it was. Fifteen knots due east until midnight . . . then north for 45 minutes . . . then back south . . . then west again. In this way Spruance cautiously kept his distance. He didn't want to be trapped; those big Jap battleships and cruisers might be steaming toward him right now.

THE heavy ships of Admiral Kondo's Invasion Force raced northeast in the dark. At 11:40 the Admiral radioed his plans: he expected to be in position at 3:00 A.M . . . then he would search east, hoping to trap the Americans into a night engagement.

At midnight he was back on the air, handing out specific assignments. Briefly, his force would form a line and sweep northeast at 24 knots, combing the sea for the U.S. fleet. It would be a "comb" with plenty of "teeth"—21 ships spaced less than four miles apart. These would be his cruisers and destroyers. Behind them would come his battleships *Kongo* and *Hiei*, ready to rush where needed. It all added up to a line about 75 miles long—certainly enough to turn up something.

Yamamoto couldn't have asked for more. Trouble was, he finally realized the time had passed for this sort of show. Five hours earlier, yes; but by now he knew all four of Nagumo's carriers were lost, and Kondo couldn't even get in position until 3 A.M. That left little more than an hour to find the Americans and fight his night engagement. Once daylight came, those U.S. carrier planes would be at his throat.

Nor could Admiral Kurita's four sleek cruisers—previously sent to shell Midway—do any good. They had been ordered to open fire at 2 A.M., but here was another miscalculation. They couldn't arrive until nearly dawn. Then they too would be wide open to air attack.

The staff babbled with alternatives. All were hopelessly hare-brained, and the chief of staff Admiral Ugaki plainly showed his contempt. Yamamoto didn't even deign to comment. Finally somebody asked a little hysterically, "But how can we apologize to His Majesty for this defeat?"

"Leave that to me," Yamamoto broke in coldly. "I am the only one who must apologize to His Majesty."

At 12:15 A.M. on the 5th the Commander in Chief suspended the plans for a night engagement, ordered Kondo, Nagumo and Kurita to rendezvous with himself instead. He would be at a given point some 350 miles northwest of Midway at 9:00 A.M. Five minutes later he followed this up with another message, specifically for Kurita, canceling the 2:00 A.M.

bombardment of the base, and again ordering him to rendez-vous.

In the confusion Yamamoto forgot that he had also ordered the submarine *I-168* to shell Midway. Commander Tanabe had been poking around the atoll for several days now, in perfect position to help out. Under the plan, he was to open the show and keep firing until Kurita took over at 2:00. All very well, but when the cruisers were called off, nothing went out to Tanabe. Now he lay on the surface, antenna up, listening in vain for any further instructions. Around 1:20 he quietly glided into firing position.

A FLASH to the south—a sharp crack in the night—punctured the uneasy silence on Midway. A shell screamed overhead and landed in the lagoon. Then another. At Jim Muri's B-26, the crew jumped up with a start, grabbed their BARs and dived for a slit trench. It was the same everywhere —men racing for rifles and shelter. Most of the aviators had done plenty of bombing, but they had never heard a shell before. The sound was anything but pleasant.

At 1:23 Battery C began firing star shells . . . 1:24, search-light No. 102 picked up the sub, bearing 110° . . . 1:25, Batteries B, D and E thundered into action.

For three minutes the duel continued. The Marine guns belted out 42 rounds; the sub rather casually lobbed eight shells into the lagoon. Then at 1:28 it submerged as unexpectedly as it had opened fire. On Sand Island a sailor sighed with relief and swore he'd take back everything he had ever said about the Marines.

ADMIRAL Kurita's four big cruisers were less than 80 miles from Midway when he got the message to cancel the bombardment and rendezvous with Yamamoto instead. In many ways it was a relief. The whole business looked more and more like suicide. Yet some were still eager; a squad of volunteers stood ready to sneak ashore and blow up installations.

But now they were heading back, steaming northwest at 28 knots in the dim moonlight. The flagship *Kumano* led, then the *Suzuya*, the *Mikuma*, and finally the *Mogami*. A pair of destroyers—the *Arashio* and *Asashio*—panted along in the rear.

It was 2:15 when the *Kumano* spotted a surfaced submarine just off her starboard bow. Using her low-powered directional signal lamp, she flashed "Red! Red!"—meaning a 45° emergency turn to port. On the bridge of the *Mogami* the navigator, Lieutenant Commander Masaki Yamauchi, elbowed the officer on duty aside, took over this tricky maneuver himself. As he turned, he thought he saw too much distance between himself and the *Mikuma*, next up the line. He adjusted course a little to starboard. Suddenly, to his horror, he saw he wasn't looking at the *Mikuma* at all, but at the *Suzuya*, two ships up the line. The *Mikuma* lay in between, directly ahead.

"Port the helm . . . hard a-port . . . Full astern!" The commands came in quick succession, but it was all too late. With a shower of sparks the *Mogami*'s bow ground into the *Mikuma*'s port quarter. The two ships shuddered, then drifted apart. The *Mikuma* got off lightly—only a ruptured fuel tank —but the *Mogami* lost 40 feet of her bow. Everything back to the first turret was bent to port at right angles. Painfully she inched up to 12 knots again.

That wasn't enough for Admiral Kurita. He had an appointment with Yamamoto. He detached the *Mikuma* and both destroyers to provide escort, then hurried on northwest with the *Kumano* and *Suzuya*.

To Admiral Yamamoto, steaming east toward the rendezvous point, the collision must have seemed a relatively minor matter. Nothing could compare with the step he took at 2:55 A.M. For it was then that he finally faced the inevitable and radioed all commands, "Occupation of AF is canceled." He had reached the end of the line as far as invading Midway was concerned. When Commander Watanabe sought to query him, he simply answered, "*Sashi sugi*"—roughly meaning, "The price is too high."

Before sunrise he made another decision almost as hard. At 4:50 he again faced the facts and ordered the hulk of his beloved *Akagi* scuttled. After this night he was ready for anything—even the fiasco of having two of his finest cruisers lumber together in this clumsy fashion.

LIEUTENANT COMMANDER John W. Murphy, skipper of the submarine *Tambor,* adjusted his periscope and carefully studied the two cruisers he had been shadowing. It was 5:00 A.M. now, and he could see them much better. One of them had lost about 40 feet of her bow.

Murphy had been playing hide-and-seek with these ships, along with several others, for nearly three hours. He was part of Admiral English's submarine screen, and he was patrolling on the surface when he first saw them at 2:15 A.M. They were 89 miles from Midway and heading away from the base.

But that was all he could tell. They might be Japs—or U.S. ships chasing Nagumo. He ordered right rudder and began following a parallel course. The minutes ticked by, and still he couldn't figure them out. At 3:00 he finally sent a contact report anyhow, calling them simply "many unidentified ships."

Daylight solved his problem. He could see only two of them now, but at 4:12 he definitely made out the truncated stacks of Japanese warships. Next moment he thought he was spotted and made an emergency dive. He lay low for 25 minutes, then popped up for a look with his periscope. By now he could see they were *Mogami*-type cruisers, and he radioed this news too. It was at this point he noticed that one had a damaged bow. And that was about all he saw, for they were steaming west, moving faster than he could follow.

MIDWAY was ready to believe the worst. The *Tambor's* contact report didn't say which way the "many unidentified ships" were going, but "89 miles" was mighty close. It seemed all too likely that the invasion was still on. At 4:30 A.M. Brooke Allen led eight B-17s to counter the threat. But the early morning weather was so thick they saw nothing. By 6:00 they were aimlessly circling Kure.

It was a PBY that produced the first hot information. At 6:30 it reported "two battleships streaming oil," heading west about 125 miles west of Midway. Clearly they were retiring; a surge of relief swept the base.

The first Marine dive bombers roared off in pursuit at 7:00. VMSB-241 was now down to 12 planes; Captain Marshall Tyler was the squadron's third skipper in two days; but the men were as aggressive as ever.

Forty-five minutes out they picked up the oil slick—a broad inviting avenue leading straight west. Twenty minutes later they were there. Dead ahead, already tossing up antiaircraft shells, were two big warships—one of them trailing the oil, the other with a smashed bow. A couple of destroyers hovered nearby.

The Marines began attacking at 8:08. First Tyler dived with the six remaining SBDs, but no hits were scored. Then Captain Fleming arrived with the Vindicators, slanting down in a glide-bombing run. No hits here either, but on the way in, Fleming's plane began to burn. Somehow he kept his lead, made his run, dropped his bomb. Then—a blazing comet— he plunged into the after turret of his target.

"VERY brave," thought Captain Akira Soji of the *Mogami*, watching the U.S. bomber crash into the *Mikuma's* turret. His own ship took a handful of near-misses, one about 10 yards away. Splinters riddled the bridge and stack, but no serious damage.

The *Mikuma* fared worse. The crash dive started a fire that soon spread to the intake of the starboard engine room. Flames were sucked down, and the fumes suffocated the engineers.

The two cruisers continued plodding westward at 12 knots. But the *Mikuma* was no longer just keeping the *Mogami* company. Thanks to that American flier, she now couldn't do any better herself.

Admiral Spruance, too, had his eye on these Japanese cruisers. The *Tambor*'s first report reached him a little after 4:00, relayed from CINCPAC. Like nearly everyone else, he felt the invasion might be still on. At 4:20 he turned southwest and raced toward Midway at 25 knots.

By 9:30 it was clear that his fears were groundless. Spruance now eased off to the west, in good position either to attack these damaged ships or go after what was left of Nagumo. Important information was coming from that direction too. At 8:00 a PBY had reported a burning carrier trailing two battleships, three cruisers and four destroyers. For some reason the message didn't reach Task Force 16 till late in the morning, but once Spruance had it he made his choice. The carrier was 275 miles away, the contact was cold, but it was still the "prime target." At 11:15 he turned northwest and began a long stern chase. If a carrier was up there at 8:00 A.M., he'd take a chance on it now.

Commander Aiso decided it was high time to leave the *Hiryu*'s engine room. He felt it was about 8:00 A.M.— hours since his last contact with the bridge. Meanwhile the fires had died down, a torpedo had slammed into the ship, and now Ensign Mandai—up on the next deck battling a blaze in some rice sacks—was yelling down to get out: the *Hiryu* was beginning to sink.

Aiso led some 50 men up through a hatch, where they

joined Mandai and his fire-fighting party. They found themselves on the port side of the ship, in a long steel corridor
that led nowhere. The one exit was sealed, and the only other
opening was a tiny pinhole in the inboard wall of the corridor
—apparently a flaw in the weld. Here they could peek out
onto the hangar deck, empty and strangely flooded with
sunshine.

Aiso decided that their only hope was to break through
the wall by the peephole. Here the steel was very thin, and
the daylight spelled escape. They found a hammer and chisel
and went to work. Gradually they punched through a hole
about a yard wide—just big enough for one man at a time.

Squeezing through, they emerged on the deserted hangar
deck. The forward end was wide open—the result of the
hit that blasted the forward elevator—hence the sunlight
streaming through. The men now worked their way up to the
flight deck and found that deserted too. Looking up at the
mast, they saw even the flag was gone. The halyard flapped
loosely in the morning breeze. To Ensign Mandai it said
more eloquently than words that the ship had been abandoned.

Mandai idly looked into the hole where the forward elevator had been. Sea water was swirling onto the hangar deck
—covering the spot they just left. He alerted Commander Aiso,
who called the men together. Aiso told them the situation
looked hopeless and he simply wanted to thank them for
doing their duty so well.

Most of the men slumped down on the flight deck—that
was as good a place as any to await the end. Mandai dozed
off—then was awakened by a kick in the ribs. To his amazement several other survivors had now appeared from the
quarterdeck—an aircraft mechanic, four or five firemen. They
had escaped from below a good deal earlier, and they brought
exciting news.

It seemed that when they first reached deck a destroyer
was just leaving. They frantically signaled her, and she blinkered back. Nobody understood code, but it might mean help

later. Even more exciting: around 6:30 a Japanese plane flew over—a plane *with wheels*. It could only have come from the carrier *Hosho* . . . which must mean Yamamoto was near. Suddenly it was worth trying to stay alive.

Aiso led all hands aft and down to the boat deck. Here he found two launches, plus a 30-foot cutter already lying in the water just astern. Perhaps they could float around in these until help came. But the *Hiryu* was now sinking fast by the bow, and he soon realized they could never get the launches off before she went down. He hastily divided the men into two groups, told them to jump from the stern and make for the cutter.

Ensign Mandai leaped as far out as he could, grabbed at a dangling line. It was attached to nothing, and he plummeted into the sea. Popping up, he turned and looked back at the *Hiryu*. There, high above him, were the carrier's great bronze propellers, dripping and gleaming in the sun. He swam for dear life . . . heard a great detonation . . . turned again and saw only the empty sea.

When the men looked at their watches afterward (one of them a Mickey Mouse watch), they found that all had stopped between 9:07 and 9:15—thus fixing the time when the *Hiryu* finally sank. But right now their only concern was to get to the cutter still floating nearby. Thirty-nine of them made it, including Commander Aiso and Ensign Mandai. Aiso took charge, announced that they would wait right here till help came. The plane with the wheels would alert the fleet; Admiral Yamamoto himself was on the way.

Actually, Yamamoto had no intention of coming. He was, in fact, shocked by the report from the plane with the wheels. It looked as though somebody had botched the job of scuttling the *Hiryu*, and what could be worse than to have her fall into American hands? He radioed Admiral Nagumo to make sure she was sunk.

Meanwhile another derelict was occupying Yamamoto's attention. At 6:52—just a few minutes before the report on the

Hiryu—an intriguing message came in from the *Chikuma's* No. 4 plane, off to the east scouting the U.S. fleet: "Sight an enemy *Yorktown* class carrier listing to starboard [*sic*] and drifting in position bearing 111°, distance 240 miles from my take-off point. One destroyer is in the vicinity."

The *I-168*, still patrolling off Midway, was immediately ordered to leave station and destroy this target. Commander Tanabe pulled out his charts and began his calculations. He figured that the carrier was only 150 miles away—no trouble reaching her. The real trick was the approach. He wanted to come in from the west at dawn. Then the carrier would be nicely silhouetted while he remained hidden in the dark. He carefully plotted the course and speed that would do just that, then turned the *I-168* away from Midway and headed north-northeast.

No ONE on the destroyer *Hughes* actually saw the Japanese search plane. It was just a blip on the radar, picked up at 6:26 A.M. as the ship continued her lonely job of guarding the *Yorktown.* Commander Ramsey ordered the crew to stand by to repel air attack, but no one ever came. The blip just hovered there, 20 miles to the west, for about ten minutes. Then it gradually faded away.

The incident made the men all the more nervous when at 7:41 machine-gun bullets began cutting the water off the port side of the *Yorktown.* At first Signalman Peter Karetka was sure some Jap had sneaked in for a strafing run, but when no plane appeared, he knew it couldn't be that. Commander Ramsey thought it might be a gun going off, overheated by a smoldering fire somewhere.

More splashes, and the men suddenly realized it could only be somebody still alive on the *Yorktown,* trying to attract attention. The *Hughes* stood in close. There, sure enough, was a man waving from the port side of the hangar deck. Ramsey lowered his motor whaleboat, and the boarding party soon found Seaman Norman Pichette, now slumped unconscious beside his gun. He had a bad stomach wound and was wrapped in a sheet. They were all back on the *Hughes* by 8:35, and moments later the ship's doctor was cutting away the sheet. This seemed to rouse Pichette, who came to long enough to mumble there was still another man alive, lying in the *Yorktown*'s sick bay.

Again the whaleboat chugged over. This time it returned with Seaman George Weise, who had fractured his skull when blown off the smokestack. Weise never knew how he got to sick bay; he just remembered dimly hearing the alarm and the call to abandon ship. It was dark; the *Yorktown* was listing heavily; the ladder topside hung loose at a crazy angle. In the blur of shapes and shadows trying to get the wounded out, he recalled someone coming over to help him. Then he heard, or thought he heard, a voice say, "Leave him and let's go—he's done for anyway."

The last thing he remembered was sitting up in his bunk and swearing a blue streak . . . but by then everyone was gone. For hours he lay helpless in the dark, semiconscious and never able to move. Finally he became vaguely aware that Pichette was in the room too, also left behind in some fashion. Pichette was very badly off, but at least he could move. In the end it was he who found the strength to get up, wrap himself in his sheet, and stagger up three decks for help.

Were there any others? The men in the motor whaleboat thought so. They reported strange tapping sounds from deep inside the carrier, suggesting men trapped below. Ramsey sent the boat back again—this time with orders to explore everywhere. They found important code materials but no human beings. The tapping, it turned out, was just the sound of creaking steel as the *Yorktown* wallowed in the swell. No one else was alive on the ship.

But someone was very much alive in the water. While the whaleboat was off exploring the *Yorktown,* the men on the *Hughes* were amazed to see a man in a yellow rubber raft paddling furiously toward them. He turned out to be Ensign Harry Gibbs of Fighting 3. Gibbs had been shot down defending the *Yorktown* the day before. He spent a long night in his raft, then sighted the carrier at sunrise. He paddled six miles to get back to his ship.

Around 10:00 the mine sweeper *Vireo* turned up, and Ramsey arranged for a tow. A line was rigged, and by early afternoon they were under way, heading east at about two knots. The *Yorktown* yawed dreadfully. She seemed unwilling to leave the scene of battle. At times, in fact, she appeared to be pulling the *Vireo* backward.

Other destroyers began turning up—the *Gwin*, the *Monaghan*. With more muscle on hand, a jettisoning party went over to the *Yorktown*, began dropping loose gear overboard to help straighten her up. During the afternoon Ramsey also sent a message to CINCPAC, urging the organization of a salvage party. The carrier was holding her own; he was sure she could be saved.

Admiral Fletcher and Captain Buckmaster needed no prodding from CINCPAC. They were working hard on their own to save the *Yorktown*. But it wasn't a simple matter. By the morning of the 5th, Task Force 17 was 150 miles east of the carrier, and over 2,000 survivors were scattered among six different destroyers. It would take time to cull out the specialists needed for a proper salvage party and then get them back to the scene.

One by one the destroyers came alongside the *Astoria*, and the men needed were transferred by breeches buoy to the cruiser. Here they were organized, briefed, and transferred again to the destroyer *Hammann*, which would take them back. They were mostly engineers and technicians, but there was no lack of volunteers among the cooks and yeomen. Everybody wanted to go. Finally guards had to be placed at the highlines to keep useless personnel from sneaking over in their determination to get back to the "Old Lady."

Midafternoon, and the *Hammann* started off. On board

were Captain Buckmaster and a crack salvage team which, with the addition of a few from the *Hughes,* totaled 29 officers and 141 men. Escorted by the destroyers *Balch* and *Benham,* they reached the *Yorktown* shortly after 2:00 A.M. on the 6th.

Far to the west Spruance continued his pursuit of the Japanese fleet, but it had been a discouraging day for Task Force 16. The trail was cold, the chase long, and when the strike was finally launched at 3:00 P.M., the distance was still 230 miles. On the hopeful side, the attack packed a powerful punch: 32 dive bombers from the *Enterprise,* 26 from the *Hornet.*

Two hours passed, but they saw nothing below. Three hours —still nothing. Gas was low . . . it was getting dark . . . the fliers were tired and hungry. Over the radio a voice kept saying, "Let's go home."

Finally at 6:20 someone spotted the wake of a single ship hurrying westward in the gathering darkness. Not much of a target, but it was this or nothing. With Dave Shumway leading the way, the 58 dive bombers poured down on their lone quarry.

It should have been an unequal fight, but it wasn't. The ship, which turned out to be a destroyer, twisted and squirmed with fantastic skill. Fifty-eight bombs rained down—but not one hit. Worse than that, a blast of antiaircraft fire caught Lieutenant Sam Adams's plane. He plunged into the sea.

As the rest headed home, the big trouble began. It was really dark now, and the pilots knew little about night carrier landings. On the *Enterprise* Captain George Murray turned on his deck lights to help. Robin Lindsey, the landing signal officer, switched from paddles to illuminated wands. He nursed down plane after plane, until it seemed the parade would never end. Finally he turned to his signalman and asked how many more. "I'll be damned if I know," answered the sailor, "we've got more than we're supposed to have already."

It turned out that five of the *Hornet's* planes had come in too. Completely green, their pilots were happy to land on the first carrier they saw. In return, one *Enterprise* plane came down on the *Hornet.*

Lieutenant Ruff Johnson, leading Bombing 8, couldn't find any carrier at all. His homing signal was out; his tanks were all but drained. He called his rear-seat man McCoy and asked if he could swim. McCoy answered "negative," so the skipper told him to get out his survival book and learn quickly. Then at the last minute they sighted the task force, and Johnson asked the *Hornet* to blink her side lights.

Marc Mitscher did better than that. These were dangerous waters—enemy subs might be lurking—but fliers were sacred to Mitscher, and he didn't hesitate a minute. Two searchlight beams shot into the sky. Johnson landed without even enough gas to taxi down the flight deck. As he rolled to a stop his chief mechanic leaped on his wing with joy: "Captain, you S.O.B., are we glad to see you—oh, I beg your pardon."

It was also a fruitless day for the B-17s. During the morning Colonel Allen's eight bombers finally located the two damaged ships west of Midway. Arriving at 8:30, they dropped a total of 39 bombs from 20,000 feet, but even the communiqué writers found little to cheer about. The fliers themselves, one of them later recalled, considered the attack "a terrible disappointment."

Undeterred, the B-17s went out again in the afternoon. First Colonel Allen's group, then a separate bunch under Captain Ridings took off after the same "burning carrier" Spruance was chasing. They had no better luck than the Admiral. Like the Navy planes, they searched in vain far to the northwest. And also like the Navy planes, they finally settled for that lone destroyer. Attacking at various levels from 9,000 to 16,000 feet, they aimed 79 more bombs at the target. The Jap skipper proved as elusive as ever.

COMMANDER Motomi Katsumi was one of the best in the business; he maneuvered the destroyer *Tanikaze* with enviable skill as the American bombs rained down from above. For Katsumi it was the climax of a wasted day. Early in the morning Nagumo had sent him to check the reports that the *Hiryu* was still afloat. He found nothing and was returning to rejoin the fleet when he was hit by both dive bombers and B-17s.

All those bombs on one destroyer. Yet Katsumi managed to dodge everything. The only damage came from a fragment of a near-miss that slashed through his No. 3 turret; it set off an explosion that killed all six men inside. The *Tanikaze* continued on, linking up with the fleet shortly after sunset.

It turned out that the other ships too had spent some anxious moments. Around 2:30 P.M. radio intelligence had warned of enemy aircraft high overhead. A false alarm, but no less nerve-racking. Then at 5:25 the *Nagara* detected some heavy bombers heading west. These planes were real indeed, but friendly clouds intervened, and the fleet was never discovered.

It was a curious scene the Americans missed. Most of Yamamoto's great armada had now rendezvoused 350 miles northwest of Midway, and dozens of ships lay motionless on the gray sea as a stream of cutters shuttled back and forth, transferring survivors from the stand-by destroyers to the battleships *Haruna, Kirishima, Mutsu* and *Nagato.*

All through the afternoon and into the evening the fleet lay licking its wounds. During the night Yamamoto steamed still farther west out of carrier range. Early on the 6th Admiral Kurita joined up with the cruisers *Kumano* and *Suzuya.* That meant every major element in the fleet was now safe, except for the damaged *Mogami* and *Mikuma,* left behind with a couple of destroyers. They would have to fend for themselves.

ALL through the night of June 5, and the predawn hours of the 6th, Admiral Spruance steamed west at a conservative 15 knots. Having failed to overtake the ships to the northwest, he didn't want to overrun the cripples to the southwest.

At 5:10 A.M. the *Enterprise* sent 18 scouts on a 200-mile

sweep to the west, and around 6:45 two separate contacts were made. The *Hornet* launched the first strike—26 dive bombers, 8 fighters—and by 9:30 they could see the Japs ahead. There were two big cruisers and two destroyers trying to screen them. At 9:50 Stan Ring called, "Attack when ready," and Gus Widhelm replied with his favorite battle cry: "Widhelm is ready; prepare the Japs!"

Down they screeched, getting hits on both cruisers and a destroyer. But the Japanese fought back hard, and heavy antiaircraft fire knocked down one of the SBDs. The *Hornet* group headed home for more bombs.

Now it was the *Enterprise's* turn. At 10:45 she launched 31 dive bombers, 12 fighters and 3 torpedo planes, all led by Lieutenant Wally Short. They found the cruisers easily, but wasted half an hour searching for a nonexistent battleship 40 miles farther on. By 12:30 they were more than willing to settle for what they had. Cocky from past triumphs, hungry for a kill, and free at last of the deadly Zeros, they tore into the Japanese with fierce elation. Their radios told the story:

> This is Wally pushing over on the rear ship now.
> Close up on me.
> Hey, any of you fellows got any bombs? There is a
>   *Mogi* class cruiser in the rear.
> Oh baby, did we put that God-damn can on fire.
>   Looks like that battleship blew up too. . . .
> Get the sons-of-bitches again. OK, that's fine.
> Hit em again—give em hell.
> They will never get that fire out.
> Put all of them smack on the bottom.
> That one blew up too. Good hit. Good hit.
> Boy that's swell. Boy, oh boy. You son of a gun,
>   You're going up . . . wish I had a camera along.
> Tojo, you son-of-a-bitch, you'll not get your
>   laundry this week.

And if all this wasn't enough, the *Hornet* planes were back with a second load at 2:45 P.M. By now both cruisers were a shambles, and one of them was being abandoned. A destroyer stood alongside, taking men off, when the bombers began to dive. As she tried to pull clear, Lieutenant Clayton Fisher plastered her too.

The *Hornet*'s eight fighters came next. There was no anti-aircraft fire now, so they swooped low, ripping into one of the cruisers with their machine guns. As Lieutenant J. F. Sutherland whipped by, he noticed a mass of people huddled on the stern, shaking their fists in futile rage. His reaction was one of sudden sympathy for their helplessness, and he flew back to the *Hornet* contemplating how quickly a hated enemy could become a pitied human being.

One final touch. In the late afternoon the *Enterprise* launched two camera planes to record the day's handiwork. Reaching the scene, Lieutenant Cleo Dobson, leading the flight, found the abandoned cruiser still burning and dead in the water. Men were swimming all around her. He dropped to 100 feet and took his time. His crystal-clear pictures froze the ship in all her agony—her amidships torn and smoldering, a sailor climbing down a rope ladder, another in a small raft by the stern.

Off to the west he sighted the other cruiser and the two destroyers crawling away as fast as possible. In a magnificent golden sunset he headed back to the *Enterprise* thinking of the small difference that separates the winners from losers. That night he confided in his diary, "I keep thinking to myself how I would hate to be in the place of those fellows in the water. I offered a prayer to God that I be spared their fate."

Fireman Kenichi Ishikawa could make out several hundred other men swimming in the water; so he was all the luckier to reach this raft. Scrambling aboard, he lay exhausted and looked back at the sinking *Mikuma*. She was going fast now—though not as fast as the setting sun. It was dusk when she finally rolled over on her port side and disappeared into the Pacific.

Even so, she lived up to her reputation as one of Japan's toughest big cruisers. The very first attack knocked out her bridge, fatally wounding Captain Sakiyama, yet the exec Commander Takagi took over and fought on. The second attack finished her—five hits and then her torpedo supply exploded.

Takagi ordered abandon ship. As the men poured over the side, Lieutenant Nasao Koyama drew his sword and committed hara-kiri on the forward turret. The destroyer *Arashio* moved in and was picking up survivors when the third attack came in. Scores were killed when a bomb landed squarely on the destroyer's stern.

It was almost as bad on the *Mogami*. She took five hits altogether, the last exploding amidships, where it permanently sealed a number of men in the engine room. A near miss also honeycombed her port side—someone later counted 800 holes. About 90 men were lost altogether. But Captain Soji and his leading officers came through, and Lieutenant Saruwatari did a superb job at damage control. By sunset the fires were out and the bulkheads holding. Escorted by the two damaged destroyers, she limped away toward Truk and safety.

SAFETY for the *Yorktown* meant Pearl Harbor, and by the dawn of June 6 the chances seemed better than ever of getting her there. Sunrise found the battered carrier still holding her own in a calm and dazzling sea.

Captain Buckmaster led the salvage party aboard. With a small burial party he first climbed to the sharply canted flight deck, where many of the dead still lay at their posts. Chief Pharmacist's Mate James Wilson turned to give some instructions, but the Captain silenced him with a wave of the hand. Uncovering, he addressed himself in prayer, gave thanks for the victory, and recited verbatim the beautiful but seldom-used service for Burial of the Dead at Sea.

This moment of reverie soon gave way to the clatter of

hammers and the sputter of acetylene torches. Working parties started cutting away loose gear to lighten the ship. Others pitched two stranded planes, all live bombs and torpedoes into the sea. Lieutenant Greenbacker began collecting the classified papers strewn about.

The *Hammann* nudged up to the starboard side to provide power, portable pumps and fire hoses. Down below, men attacked the blaze still smoldering in the rag locker and began the important work of counterflooding. A high moment came when the first 5-inch gun on the port side was cut loose and dropped overboard. Free of the weight, the whole ship shook . . . and seemed to straighten up a little in relief.

By 1:00 P.M. they had worked 2° off the *Yorktown's* list. It was time for a break, and the *Hammann* sent over fruit and sandwiches. Some distance out, the other five destroyers slowly circled the carrier. They were listening for submarines, but it was hard to tell. Echo-ranging conditions were poor due to what destroyer men call a "thermal barrier." Yet this was often the case on calm days, and there was no hint of real trouble. It was just 1:30, and on the *Yorktown* the men were about to go back to work. . . .

COMMANDER Tanabe raised his periscope for a last look. The carrier was now about 1,300 yards away. She was still under tow, but barely moving. The destroyer was still alongside. The others were still circling slowly—no sign they suspected. The hydrophone man said he couldn't even hear the enemy's sound detection system working. Tanabe made a mild joke about the Americans all being out to lunch.

The *I-168* had worked hard for this perfect chance. Nearly eight hours had passed since the lookout's cry of a "black object" on the horizon. It was, of course, the crippled U.S. carrier, just where Tanabe expected to find her at dawn.

It was only 5:30, and for the first 10 or 20 minutes he stayed on the surface. Approaching from the west, he was still sheltered by darkness. Then it got too light for that, and he submerged, poking up his periscope every 15 minutes.

By 7:00 the *I-168* was about six miles off, and Tanabe had a much better picture of the situation. For the first time he could see the destroyers guarding the carrier. To make detection harder, he now cut his speed to three knots and raised his periscope only once or twice an hour.

Ever so carefully, he stole closer. To get a sure kill, he decided to fire his four torpedoes with a spread of only 2°, instead of the usual 6°. This meant a bigger punch amidships, but it also required getting as near as possible.

He dived still lower, hoping to get through the destroyer screen. Next time he looked he was safely through, but now he was too close. The carrier loomed like a mountain only 700 yards away. He needed that much for the torpedo to run true. Slowly he curled in a wide circle to starboard, coming around to try again. This time everything was perfect. . . .

"Hey, look, porpoises!" CPO Joseph Kisela heard somebody call, pointing off the starboard side of the *Yorktown*. A couple of men stared out to sea. "Porpoises, hell!" a sailor snorted.

A machine gun on the bridge began firing. This was the prearranged signal in case of danger. There was a wild scramble topside. Coming up from the engine room, Lieutenant Cundiff looked to starboard and saw four white torpedo streaks heading straight for the ship. An avid photographer, he gasped. "What a once-in-a-lifetime shot, and no camera!"

Lieutenant Greenbacker, about to transfer some files to the *Hammann*, fled "downhill" to the port side of the quarterdeck. Then the thought occurred that torpedoes might be coming from that side too. He worked his way back "uphill" to the center of the ship—as close to neutral ground as he could get. Here he waited for the torpedoes to hit, and that seemed to take forever.

One missed . . . one struck the *Hammann* . . . the other two passed under the destroyer and crashed into the *Yorktown* amidships. Once again there was that teeth-rattling jar that came only from torpedoes. It whipped the tripod mast, shearing off most of the rivets at the base. It knocked down the ship's bell, shattering it completely. It bowled over the damage control officer, Commander Aldrich, breaking his left arm. It hurled Commander Davis, cutting loose the 5-inchers, right into the sea. It almost made Commander Ray bite off the stem of his pipe.

Seeing it was about to happen, Chief Electrician W. E. Wright made a wild leap to the deck of the *Hammann*. But this was no solution, for she was hit at almost the same instant. Wright was blown high in the air, landing in the water.

Commander Arnold True was desperately trying to back the *Hammann* clear when the torpedoes hit. To the end his gunners were firing at the streaks, hoping to explode the warheads. The crash hurled True across the bridge and into a chart desk, breaking two ribs and knocking out his wind. He couldn't speak for several minutes.

Few words were needed. The *Hammann's* fate was clearly sealed. The concussion from the two hits on the *Yorktown* stove in her plates, and the direct hit snapped her almost in two. She looked like a toy ship that had been dropped from a great height—upright but broken.

Within two minutes the foredeck was awash, and the executive officer Lieutenant Ralph Elden ordered abandon ship. As the bow went under, most of the crew swam off. Chief Torpedoman Berlyn Kimbrell, however, remained on the rising stern, trying to put the depth charges on "safe" and handing out life jackets. When Boilermaker Raymond Fitzgibbon went over the side, Kimbrell shook hands with him and gave him the Churchill "Victory" sign.

Then she was gone, but the worst was yet to come. The depth charges—though presumably set on "safe"—went off anyhow. (There are a dozen theories.) An immense explosion erupted under the water, right where everyone was swimming. The concussion was fantastic: one sailor's metal cigarette lighter was mashed absolutely flat in his pocket. The effect on a man's body could be far worse than that.

The destroyers *Benham* and *Balch* left the screen, rescuing the lucky ones who escaped, plus several from the *Yorktown* too. One man swam up to the *Benham* and climbed aboard unassisted. It was the same ship's cook they had saved on the 4th, who wanted only to help in the galley. This time he simply said, "I know where the galley is, I'll go get to work."

Long after everyone else was picked up, the *Balch* spotted a lone swimmer among the debris. He was desperately trying to hold the faces of two other men out of the water. It was the *Hammann's* skipper Commander True. Barely conscious himself, he had struggled alone for nearly three hours to keep two of his dying men alive.

On the *Yorktown* it was time to leave again. The two new hits on the starboard side had the effect of straightening her up, but that was deceiving. She was definitely lower in the water. The *Vireo* pulled along the starboard side, and the salvage party swung down the lines to safety.

When everyone else seemed to be off, Captain Buckmaster came down hand over hand. Then at the last minute Commander Delaney and one of his engineers appeared from a final inspection below and also left the ship. Deprived of the privilege of being the last to leave, Buckmaster was enormously upset. He even wanted to swing back up the line and touch the *Yorktown* again, but the *Vireo* cast off before he could make it.

While the rescue work went on, the *Gwin, Hughes* and *Monaghan* charged here and there looking for the submarine. The three destroyers dropped numerous depth charges, but for five hours there was no evidence of success. Then at 6:45 the *Hughes* suddenly saw smoke on the horizon. A check with the glasses showed a sub on the surface about 13 miles away. Its diesels were smoking, and it was racing west, trying to get clear of the area.

The *Hughes* and *Monaghan* set off in pursuit, and at 7:05 they opened fire. Bracketed by shell explosions, the submarine soon disappeared into the sea. On the *Monaghan* Fireman Edward Creighton was sure they got her. That night he wrote in his diary, "We had a 15 or 20 minute gun battle, and she finally went down. There were no survivors."

COMMANDER Tanabe had one last trick up his sleeve. He dived into his own smoke and went right under the destroyers that were chasing him. They throbbed by overhead, and the crisis was passed.

He breathed easily for the first time since torpedoing the carrier. Except for a brief moment of exhilaration—the *banzais,* the touching gift of cider from all hands—the whole afternoon had been hell. Lieutenant Tomita counted 61 depth bombs altogether. The *I-168* finally had to break surface at 6:30, but happily the American destroyers were now far astern. They gave chase soon enough, but Tanabe stayed up as long as he dared, gulping in air and recharging his batteries. He also took the occasion to radio Yamamoto the good news about the carrier.

On the *Yamato* the Admiral now had bigger game in mind. All morning his radio had crackled with the troubles of the *Mogami* and *Mikuma.* Apparently the U.S. force was moving steadily west, farther and farther from home. Perhaps he could trap it yet. Around noon he sent Admiral Kondo south with the carrier *Zuiho,* six cruisers and eight destroyers. They were to join up with the *Mogami* and *Mikuma* and lure the Americans into a night battle.

At 3:50 P.M. Yamamoto broadened this plan into an all-out effort. The *Yamato* was also ordered south with the Main Body and what was left of Nagumo's fleet. Land bombers were ordered up from the Marshalls and put on Wake. These plus his own scattering of planes would give him real air power again. His heavy ships would do the rest. All that remained was for the Americans to walk into the trap.

Admiral Spruance had a feeling ("an intuition perhaps") that he had pushed his luck far enough to the west. He was over 400 miles from Midway, and he was determined to keep out of the range of Japanese planes based on Wake. Besides, he was low on fuel, short on destroyers, and had lost a lot of good pilots. From his long walks on the flight deck, he also sensed how weary the others were.

Shortly after 7:00 P.M.—as soon as the two planes returned from photographing the dying *Mikuma*—Task Force 16 turned and headed back east. Astern lay the remnants of Japanese hopes; ahead lay good things like oil, sleep and ultimately home.

For Midway, too, it was over. A final flight of B-17s on the afternoon of the 6th reported sinking an enemy "cruiser" in 15 seconds; but this turned out to be the U.S. submarine *Grayling*, crash-diving to escape the bombs. During the evening Major General Clarence L. Tinker—just in from Hawaii—led four Liberators in a long-range attempt to neutralize Wake, but the effort was in vain. The bombers never found the target, and Tinker himself was lost.

By dawn on the 7th, all was quiet again on Midway.

"My God, she's going right on over, isn't she?" Boatswain Forest Lunsford gasped to Ensign J. T. Andrews, as they stood on the *Benham* watching the *Yorktown* in the first light of day, June 7. For the men in the destroyer screen, the sight of the carrier at dawn ended any hope they still had of saving her.

Some time during the night the *Yorktown* had heeled back

heavily to port, and by 4:30 her flight deck slanted into the water. Great bubbles were foaming up, and loud cracking noises came from somewhere inside her. From the halyards her last signal hoist hung straight down—"My speed, 15." Captain Buckmaster's American flag was still flying, but it almost touched the sea.

At 4:43 she lay on her port side, revealing a huge hole in her starboard bilge—the result of yesterday's submarine attack. The end was near, and at 4:54 all ships half-masted their colors; all hands uncovered and came to attention. Two patrolling PBYs appeared overhead and dipped their wings in salute.

At 5:01, well down at the stern, the *Yorktown* slowly sank from sight. There were the usual noises, the veil of smoke and steam, but to most of the men she went quietly and with enormous dignity—"like the great lady she was," as one of them put it.

On the *Hughes* Signalman Karetka fought to hold back his tears. He was very young and wanted to appear grown up. Then he saw that even the old-timers were crying, so he didn't feel too badly when he wept too.

CHAPTER **13**

Home Again

O NLY the litter of battle was left: the empty shell
cases . . . the oil slicks . . . mattresses . . . the black rubber
rafts of the Japanese, the yellow of the Americans. And occasionally—not too often, but sometimes—a bedraggled, sun-
burned figure, hoping and waiting.

Right from the start Captain Simard had his PT boats and
PBYs looking for survivors. By noon on June 4 *PT 20* had
already picked up three of the Marine pilots. On the 5th
Lieutenant "Pappy" Cole put his PBY down on the open sea
and scooped up Ensign Gay, none the worse for his day with
Nagumo. On the 6th Lieutenant Norman Brady brought back
some of his own kind: four survivors from the only PBY
caught by the Japanese. They had been shot down, strafed,
and spent 58 hours bailing out a leaky raft. Brady spotted
them some 400 miles west of Midway.

But a man in the ocean is hard to see, and sometimes those
adrift thought help would never come. It wasn't so bad at
first for Pat Mitchell, Stan Ruehlow and Dick Gray. When
Fighting 8 ran out of gas, they managed to land close to
each other. Mitchell didn't salvage his raft, but the other two
did, and they tied them together about 12 feet apart. For
food they had pemmican, malted milk tablets and a canteen of

water. Planes were flying all around, and they felt sure they'd soon be picked up. They settled back and waited that night and all the next day.

It was the second night when the shark came. He nudged the raft where Gray was sleeping—that brought a yell—then headed for the one shared by Ruehlow and Mitchell. His dorsal fin knifed through the bottom, dumping them both into the water. Ruehlow, in fact, came down on the shark's back, slashing his hand on the fin. He set a new swimming record getting to Gray's raft, while Mitchell scrambled back into the one just attacked. It was now half-swamped, and he lay sprawled across it, his legs dangling in the water. Ruehlow wrote him off as a goner, but for some reason the shark swam off.

In the morning they patched the raft with a tube of cement and managed to get it reasonably seaworthy again. Then they went back to their waiting. June 6 . . . June 7, and still no rescue. Occasionally planes flew overhead, and once they saw a destroyer in the distance, beautifully silhouetted against a line squall. As always, they flashed their hand mirror, but again no one spotted them. To keep their spirits up, they played "Ghosts." Ruehlow's favorite word "syzygy" served him as well in mid-Pacific as it ever did at home.

June 8 started like the other days. Then a PBY appeared, and this time it came directly overhead. They waved wildly, and their hearts almost stopped when it seemed to fly by. But at the last minute it circled back, and the pilot, Lieutenant Frank Fisler, brought it down to a beautiful landing. He taxied over, and three more fliers were saved.

And so it went. In ten days the PBYs picked up 27 airmen altogether, and on June 9 the submarine *Trout* added to the collection a pair of Japanese from the *Mikuma.* Fireman Ken-ichi Ishikawa and Chief Radioman Katsuichi Yoshida were all that were left of the 19 originally on their raft.

There remained the men in the *Hiryu's* cutter. Commander Aiso had long since given up waiting for Admiral Yamamoto.

When the great battleships failed to appear, he decided to head for Wake instead. He had no maps, charts or compass—only the sun and the stars—but with six good oars and a blanket for a sail, they could get there just the same. To sustain and encourage them, they also had a little food and 48 bottles of beer.

Day after day they saw nothing but ocean. Mostly it was calm, but they had three storms—wild, violent affairs in which four men had to hold an oar at right angles to keep the boat from rolling over. Then it would be calm again, brilliant and blazing hot. During the nights they wrangled over food; Aiso was far from generous with the rations. During the day the men talked of home, good times and milk shakes. Ensign Mandai promised to treat all hands after they got back to their home port, Sasebo. The milk shakes at Sasebo Naval Base were the best in the world, something worth living for.

The tenth day, June 14, a man died of exhaustion. They said a prayer for him and gently lowered him over the side. Eventually four men went the same way.

On the twelfth day they sighted a big patrol plane, and another on the thirteenth. They were overjoyed, certain that these planes were Japanese. Next afternoon one flew very close. It circled, and to their dismay they saw painted on the side a large white star.

Finally on the fifteenth day a ship appeared. She was a four-stack U.S. warship, and as she drew near, the men in the cutter debated whether to surrender or not. They finally talked themselves into it. Maybe, they agreed, they could capture the ship. Fantasy, perhaps, but it made the decision easier. The vessel, which was the seaplane tender *Ballard*, came alongside. A sailor tossed them a line, and their war was over.

Speaking to interrogators later, they said politely but firmly that they did not wish to return to Japan under the circum-stances; that they did not wish Tokyo to be informed of their capture; and that they preferred to have it believed that they sank with the *Hiryu*.

IT WAS hard to imagine anything worse than going home this way. Admiral Yamamoto had finally given up the game early on June 7, then promptly took to his bed. Chief Steward Omi brought a tray of rice gruel, but the Admiral really wasn't hungry.

On the 9th there was an interruption—one of those moments everybody dreaded but had to face. Admiral Kusaka was coming over to the *Yamato* to make a report. About 11:00 A.M. a launch bobbed alongside, and a crane hoisted a bamboo stretcher aboard.

Kusaka was still in his battle-stained uniform, limping badly from his injuries. Accompanied by Captain Oishi and Commander Genda, he hobbled to the bridge, where he faced Yamamoto and his staff. To Yeoman Noda, quietly watching in the background, Kusaka looked like a suitor who had just lost his best girl.

Yamamoto was most considerate. He patted Kusaka on the shoulder and thanked him for his efforts. He urged that everything possible be done to restore the men's morale; he arranged for cakes, pocket money and even fresh underwear to be sent to the survivors.

Kusaka then asked for a word in private. In a small room just off the bridge he told Yamamoto how personally crushed Nagumo's staff felt—there was all this talk of suicide—and he begged the Commander in Chief to reorganize the carrier fleet and give them all another chance. Yamamoto's eyes filled with tears; he answered simply, "I understand."

This ordeal over, the fleet continued its gloomy retreat. The operations room on the *Yamato* was like a wake. The air officer, Commander Sasaki, sat in a daze at the back of the flag bridge. He was said to be drinking far too much *sake*.

On the *Nagara* Admiral Nagumo turned morose again. Word was passed to keep an eye on him, see he didn't do anything foolish. Admiral Kusaka dreamed of revenge; Commander Sasabe felt utterly drained of energy; the staff surgeon brooded over all the valuables he could have saved but left behind. Listening in the background, Commander Genda grunted to himself, "It's no use talking about might-have-beens now."

He could have added a few: if only the *Tone*'s No. 4 plane had gotten off on time, they would have discovered the U.S. fleet before rearming for that second attack on Midway . . . if only the enemy dive bombers had attacked a few minutes later, Nagumo's own strike would have been launched . . . if only they had attacked the American carriers right away, as Yamaguchi wanted, instead of holding back until all the planes were ready. . . .

There were deeper weaknesses too. In the last analysis the whole Midway plan depended too much on the U.S. fleet reacting exactly the way the Japanese expected. It frittered away Yamamoto's great strength all over the Pacific, instead of concentrating his ships where needed. And finally it reeked of overconfidence—of a dangerous contempt for the enemy—that the Japanese perhaps best described as "victory disease." It would have been so easy to have had a better submarine cordon, a stronger air search, an extra carrier on the scene.

But these post-mortems lay in the future. Right now the problem was how to handle this stunning defeat. As Yamamoto turned homeward, he radioed a full summary to Admiral Nagano, Chief of Naval General Staff. Nagano contacted Army General Staff, and a small top-drawer meeting convened on Monday, June 8. It was here that they broke the news to Prime Minister Tojo. He had only three comments to make: no one was to criticize the Navy; materials would be made available at once to replace the losses; and finally, the facts of this disaster must not go beyond the doors of the room.

June 10, a blare of trumpets and the now familiar strains of the "Navy March" told Tokyo radio listeners to get ready for another great naval victory. And great it was: two American carriers sunk . . . 120 planes downed . . . landings in the Aleutians . . . heavy damage to American installations at Midway. Japanese losses amounted to a carrier sunk, another carrier and a cruiser damaged, 35 planes down.

Next day Masanori Ito, Japan's leading military commentator, examined the victory. "The brilliant war results obtained are beyond all imagination," he declared. In another analysis Captain Hideo Hiraide, chief of the naval press section at Imperial Headquarters, ventured an interesting thought: the enormous success in the Aleutians was made possible by the diversion at Midway.

"You may not go back to Tokyo. If you dare to return, you'll be arrested by the military police," newsreel man Teiichi Makishima was told after the *Nagara* reached Kure on June 14. For weeks he languished in what he called a "stragglers' camp"; then he was packed off to sea again. The carrier crews were isolated at Saheki or Kanoya Air Base, and Yeoman Noda wasn't allowed ashore at all when the *Yamato* returned to Hashirajima. He couldn't even get a day to see his girl in Kure.

It was hardest on the wounded. Commander Ohara spent ten weeks in the hospital recovering from his burns on the *Soryu,* but during the entire time he was never allowed a visitor, or even to see the other patients. When Commander Fuchida was carried ashore, he was handled like a victim of some medieval plague. He was landed at night, carried to the hospital on a covered stretcher, and whisked inside through the back door.

THE ambulances waited in the afternoon sunshine, lined up in neat rows at Pearl Harbor. Admiral Nimitz was there too, standing on the pier with some of his staff. The destroyer *Benham* was coming in—the first ship back that had been in the battle, arriving on June 9 with most of the *Hammann*'s injured.

As she glided toward her berth, the other ships dipped their flags in salute. The men on the *Benham* felt self-conscious but infinitely proud of the shrapnel holes in her hull, the antenna loose and hanging.

As the ship tied up, Admiral Nimitz came aboard. He greeted the skipper, Lieutenant Commander Joseph Worthington, then turned to the men standing on the deck. He shook hands with them individually, thanking them for what they had done. The work of unloading the injured began—50 stretchers transferred to the ambulances and off to the Navy Hospital.

The *Enterprise* and the rest of Task Force 16 filed in on June 13, flying their largest flags from the main. Navy Yard workers, ships' crews, everybody who could make it lined the piers and decks. It was a quiet crowd—no bands, no cheering —and one man on the *Pensacola* wondered whether something was "wrong." He needn't have worried. Pearl Harbor's appreciation was too deep to express.

A little later there was a smaller welcome in Admiral Nimitz's office. Captain Simard was on his way home from Midway— reassigned to new responsibilities—and had dropped by to pay his respects. Nimitz thanked him and congratulated him on the spot promotion sent out on the eve of battle. Pointing to Simard's new silver eagles, the Admiral observed, "I sent you the flowers before the funeral."

Some time during this period—the exact date is uncertain— another visitor turned up at CINCPAC with a special mission to perform. It was the Army's General Emmons, who solemnly presented the Admiral with a magnum of champagne, decorated with ribbons of Navy blue and gold. He just wanted to say, the General announced, that he had been wrong and the Navy right in the crucial planning before the battle. Now he wanted all to know it.

Someone thought of Joe Rochefort down in the basement where all that solid-gold intelligence came from, and Nimitz sent a message to get him. As usual, Rochefort was deep in his files and scratchwork, puttering about in his smoking jacket and carpet slippers. By the time he straightened up, it was like his last appointment with the Admiral: he was again half an hour late. But today the Admiral didn't bawl him out. Before the assembled staff, Nimitz declared that the victory was due to the great work done by Rochefort's Combat Intelligence Unit. Rochefort said something about just doing what they were paid to do—he was never much at this sort of fancy exchange.

The initial glow would wear off. The Army and Navy pilots soon fought a pitched battle at the Royal Hawaiian Hotel over who deserved the most credit. Men from the *Enterprise* and *Yorktown* wrangled over the first day's honors. The intelligence outfits went back to their Byzantine infighting. The high-level and dive-bombing enthusiasts sniped at each other. (It only became clear after the war that the B-17s dropped 322 bombs, yet failed to score a hit.)

The second-guessers were soon at it too. Strategists argued, perhaps correctly, that the submarines were badly deployed . . . that the scouting was poor . . . that communications were slow and overly complicated . . . that there wasn't enough coordination between the Task Forces . . . that the *Yorktown* might have been saved . . . that Task Force 16 was too slow in following up the first day's success.

In ticking off the things that weren't done, it was easy to forget the big thing that *was* done. Against overwhelming odds, with the most meager resources, and often at fearful self-sacrifice, a few determined men reversed the course of the war in the Pacific. Japan would never again take the offensive. Yet the margin was thin—so narrow that almost any man there could say with pride that he personally helped turn the tide at Midway. It was indeed, as General Marshall said in Washington, "the closest squeak and the greatest victory."

None knew this narrow margin better than Commander Brockman, skipper of the submarine *Nautilus*, as he approached Midway on June 5. He had been called in to patrol offshore, and at this point he had no idea how the battle turned out . . . whether Midway was still in U.S. hands or not. The place looked the same, but it always did—the swooping birds, the pale blue lagoon, the white surf pounding on dazzling sand. His periscope swept the atoll, and then at last he knew. There, high above the Sand Island command post, still flew the American flag.

The Riddles of Midway

As THE Japanese bombs rained down on Midway a Marine sergeant named Anderson was hit on the bridge of his nose by a flying can of beans, nuts or tomato juice—depending on who tells the story. Anderson has never been located, and the incident remains one of the minor riddles of Midway.

There are many more. The excitement and confusion of battle always breed conflicts on numbers, distances, hits and misses, the time things happened. Added to these, Midway has a built-in problem of its own: it was fought back and forth over the international date line. The log of one PBY showed that it took off on June 3, made an attack June 5 and landed June 4. To complicate matters further, the Japanese always used Tokyo time. In this account, local time is followed during the preparations, but once the fleets are at sea, everything has been translated into Midway time.

Beyond these minor problems, two major riddles remain. They will never be solved for certain. Like the skill and courage of the men who unconsciously propounded them, they are now a living part of the incredible victory at Midway. . . .

The Riddle of the Dive Bombing Attack

At 10:22 A.M. on Thursday the 4th of June 1942, the crack Japanese carriers *Akagi, Kaga* and *Soryu* were heading proudly for the battle that was to finish the U.S. Pacific Fleet. By 10:28 all three were blazing wrecks. The job was done by three squadrons of American dive bombers—two from the *Enterprise*, one from the *Yorktown*. Each attacked a different carrier, but to this day the debate has continued over who got which ship.

If the squadron action reports are taken at face value, everybody hit the *Akagi* or the *Kaga*. Nobody claims the *Soryu*—she presumably got back to Japan. Yet if the specific recollections of the three attack leaders are accepted, nobody got the *Akagi*. Each is convinced his target had its island on the starboard side—yet the *Akagi*'s island was to port.

It's the very similarity of impressions and experiences that makes the problem so baffling. Approaching at nearly right angles (the *Enterprise* planes from the southwest, the *Yorktown*'s from the southeast), both groups sighted the Japanese force a few minutes after 10:00. In both cases the enemy carriers appeared as yet untouched. Both groups selected as targets what appeared to be the larger carriers in the formation. Pulling out, both leaders had the same experience: each saw the other attacking for the first time.

The problem is compounded by a common misconception as to what the Japanese carriers looked like. The pilots' recognition cards were absurdly outdated, assuming those used by one *Enterprise* squadron are a fair example. The *Akagi* was depicted as of 1936, before she was given a full-length flight deck, and there was no silhouette at all of the *Soryu*. It's ironic that the writer sitting in the Yale Law School had better information through *Jane's Fighting Ships* than the fliers who depended on these silhouettes that morning.

Also, the *Soryu* was much bigger than she was thought to be. Even today it's generally assumed she was around 10,000 tons, and more than one pilot has indignantly protested, "You can't tell me I got the small one." Actually she was about 18,000 tons and roughly comparable to the *Enterprise* and *Yorktown*.

Despite all this, there do remain clues that suggest what really happened. First is the Japanese formation at the time of the attack. During the southeasterly approach to Midway the carriers steamed in a box: the *Akagi* leading the *Kaga* on the southwesterly side, the *Hiryu* leading the *Soryu* on the northeasterly side. (See Fig. 1, page 298.)

Then at 9:17 an important turn took place as Nagumo swung northeast to meet the new threat of the U.S. carriers. In making this change in course, the Japanese did not turn in formation, as is often supposed; rather, the individual ships turned in their tracks. Both Admiral Kusaka, Nagumo's chief of staff, and Commander Sasabe, his staff officer for navigation, have been interviewed at length on this, and both are firm that this is the way it was done. The result left the carriers still in box formation, with their position changed relative to each other but remaining the same in terms of the compass. That is, the *Akagi* and *Kaga* were still to the southwest, the *Hiryu* and *Soryu* still to the northeast. (See Fig. 2, page 298.)

About 10:00 Nagumo made a further change in course, still more to the northeast, and again each ship individually turned in its tracks. But by now the situation was complicated by American torpedo plane attacks. The box was loose, and the distances between the ships much greater. Judging from the accounts of Japanese survivors, the *Akagi* and the *Kaga* were still fairly close together, but the *Soryu* had pulled ahead, and the *Hiryu* even more so. (She was now almost on their horizon.) But the basic situation remained the same: the *Akagi* and *Kaga* lay to the southwest, the *Hiryu* and *Soryu* to the northeast.

Another clue to bear in mind lies in the position of the three carriers when they finally sank. They did not move much after the bombing. The *Akagi*'s engines worked erratically from time to time, but the *Kaga* and *Soryu* soon went dead in the water and finally sank toward evening within a few minutes of each other. Their relative position when they sank strongly suggests their relative position when hit: the *Kaga* lay to the southwest, the *Soryu* to the northeast. (See Fig. 3, page 299.)

The next clue lies in the position of the ships as seen by the approaching U.S. dive bombers. Both the *Enterprise* and *Yorktown* pilots seem agreed that the three carriers lay in a rough row, running from southwest to northeast, or as the leader of Bombing 3 saw it, more from west to east. In either case, the two *Enterprise* squadrons took the two westerly carriers, while the *Yorktown* squadron took the easterly one.

Moving to the actual bombing, another clue emerges. Of the two attacking units from the *Enterprise*, Dick Best and the 1st Division of Bombing 6 certainly dived after Wade McClusky's mixed group. This happened when McClusky dived on the carrier Best planned to take. Best made a quick shift to the next one up the line but inevitably lost several minutes in the process.

This becomes important when considered in terms of what was happening below. Japanese accounts differ on many things about this attack, but there's marked agreement that the *Kaga* was hit first. Seven witnesses on six different ships are sure of this. Assuming it is so, it means that whatever else occurred, Dick Best did not hit the *Kaga*.

What then did happen? It's a rash man who sets himself up as final arbiter on those six fantastic minutes, but based on the known facts, and other more murky clues, here are the probabilities. . . .

1. **Dick Best and the 1st Division of Bombing 6 attacked the AKAGI.** He approached from the southwest, and that's where the *Akagi* was. The *Soryu,* on the other hand, was to the north and east. He attacked with five planes, which comes closest to the Japanese estimate that the *Akagi* was bombed by three planes. Certainly it's hard to square this estimate with McClusky's 25 or Max Leslie's 13 from the *Yorktown.* (Leslie had 17, but four dived on other ships.) Conversely, Best's five don't fit the 12-13 bombers that the Japanese say attacked the *Soryu.*

Other reasons: Best spotted a Zero taking off as he dived, and the *Akagi* launched one just before the first hit. Best saw a group of TBDs coming in as he was pulling out, and the *Akagi* reported torpedo planes at just this time. Best's men recall damage concentrated on planes parked aft on the flight deck—just where the *Akagi* was hardest hit. In contrast, the *Soryu* was hit hardest up forward.

The time also fits. Best recalls a third carrier (in addition to McClusky's) just coming under attack farther east as he was pushing over. This would make his carrier the last one hit. Japanese sources indicate the *Akagi* was bombed at 10:26 —i.e., the last of the three.

Against all this are two major stumbling blocks. Best and at least one other pilot in his group are certain his bomb was a hit, while most Japanese sources say that the first bomb dropped on the *Akagi* was a near-miss, just off the bridge. But the Japanese evidence is not conclusive: the near-miss and the first hit came so close together it was hard to tell. Also, one of the planes following Best down released its bomb before he did—and that might have been the near-miss.

The other hitch concerns the location of the *Akagi*'s island structure. Best has always felt the island on his target was on the starboard side, yet the *Akagi*'s island was to port. On the other hand, one of Best's pilots, Bill Roberts, is certain that the target's island was indeed to port; he says he especially noticed this because it was the opposite of U.S. practice. If so, the target would have to be the *Akagi*, since both the *Kaga* and *Soryu* had the usual starboard-side islands.

2. Wade McClusky and the rest of the ENTERPRISE planes attacked the KAGA. As the other carrier to the southwest, she too was a logical target for the *Enterprise* planes approaching from that direction. Again, the *Soryu* was to the north and east—farthest off in the line of advance. McClusky dived with 25 planes, and that seems to fit with the deluge that poured down on the *Kaga*. Her air officer says she was attacked by 30 planes; Nagumo's antiaircraft records indicate

18; his battle report says nine; but all agree she took at least four hits and five near-misses. Leslie's planes from the *Yorktown* were also capable of delivering this kind of punishment, but they were approaching from the southeast, while the *Kaga* was the most westerly of the three carriers.

The pattern laid down by McClusky's group also fits the *Kaga's* experience. The first three bombs dropped were near-misses; so were the first three that fell on the *Kaga*. The fourth bomb, according to the Scouting 6 action report, hit the center of the flight deck about 200 feet from the stern. This roughly corresponds to the best information on the *Kaga*. Later bombs hit up forward; the same was true with the *Kaga*. There's some evidence, although inconclusive, that McClusky's target had only a few planes on the flight deck; this would match the recollection of the only *Kaga* survivor to comment on this point.

The time also fits. Radio traffic monitored on the *Enterprise* indicates McClusky pushed over between 10:21 and 10:23. Nagumo's battle report says the *Kaga* was dive-bombed at 10:22.

3. Max Leslie and Bombing 3 attacked the SORYU. This is more than a matter of elimination. It's backed by positive evidence. Approaching on a northwest course, Leslie took the first carrier he came to—the most easterly or northeasterly of the three attacked. The *Soryu* was to the north and east of the *Akagi* and *Kaga*.

Also: Leslie's target had many planes on the flight deck; the same was true of the *Soryu*. Leslie dived with 13 planes; some 12-13 attacked the *Soryu*. Leslie's last four planes shifted to other nearby targets; the *Soryu's* screening destroyer *Isokaze* was bombed at this time. None of the other squadrons attacked the screening ships, and the only screening destroyer bombed was assigned to the *Soryu*.

The pattern of hits likewise suggests the *Soryu*, although there is nothing conclusive here. In his action report, the acting squadron commander, Dave Shumway, says the first bomb landed in the midst of planes spotted on the flight deck, but most accounts—including Shumway's in a later Navy interview—say it landed amidships forward. According to most Japanese sources, this is also where the first hit landed on the *Soryu*. In any event, Bombing 3's recollections tend to rule out the *Kaga*. There's emphatic agreement that the squadron's first bomb was a hit, while Japanese sources indicate that the first three bombs on the *Kaga* were near-misses.

Finally, the time of Bombing 3's attack fits the *Soryu* best. Leslie's action report says the *Yorktown* planes pushed over at about 10:25. He also recalls glancing at his instrument panel clock in pulling out, and that it said between 10:25 and 10:26. Nagumo's battle report says that the *Soryu* was first hit at 10:25.

The Riddle of the Submarine Attack

After three and a half hours of the most patient stalking, the U.S. submarine *Nautilus* fired three torpedoes at a stationary burning Japanese carrier in the early afternoon of June 4. The *Nautilus*'s skipper, Lieutenant Commander Bill Brockman, was sure the torpedoes hit: the fire on the carrier, which appeared to be under control, suddenly erupted anew. All five officers in the sub's conning tower had a chance to view the results of the attack.

From the recognition materials available, they identified the carrier as the *Soryu*, and the Navy has always credited the *Nautilus* with delivering the *coup de grâce* that finally sent her to the bottom. Yet most Japanese sources maintain that the *Kaga* was the only carrier attacked by a submarine, and that the torpedo that struck her was a dud. It would appear these sources are right:

1. The carrier's position fits the *Kaga* far better than the *Soryu*. The *Nautilus*'s action report says the target she attacked lay in latitude 30° 13′ N, longitude 179° 17′ W. According to

Nagumo's battle report, the *Kaga* sank in 30° 20′ N, 179° 17′ W, while the *Soryu* sank in 30° 42′ N, 178° 37′ W.

2. The *Nautilus* approached from the south, and the *Kaga* sank farthest to the south of the three wrecked carriers. She should have been the first one the *Nautilus* encountered. In contrast, the *Soryu* sank farthest to the north.

3. The *Nautilus* action report says she fired her torpedoes between 1:59 and 2:05 P.M. Nagumo's action chart indicates a submarine attacked the *Kaga* at 2:10 P.M. No Japanese records mention any other carriers receiving an attack; no U.S. records mention any other submarine delivering an attack.

4. Survivors from the *Kaga* remember a submarine attack, but none is recalled by those from the *Soryu*. Her executive officer, Commander Ohara, is quoted as saying there was one in a U.S. Strategic Bombing Survey interrogation right after the war, but he has since maintained that this was not so.

5. Only one other Japanese has been quoted as saying the *Soryu* was attacked by submarine. This is Rear Admiral Komura, captain of the screening cruiser *Chikuma*. In another USSBS interrogation he recalled the torpedoing, said he attacked the sub and sent a boat over to help the *Soryu*. But in a recent interview he denied ever seeing the *Soryu* attacked —he merely recalled a sub warning while he was trying to help the carrier. Moreover, Nagumo's radio log shows that Komura sent his boat over at 11:12 A.M.—after the dive bombing—and by the time the *Nautilus* attacked her target, he had rejoined the *Hiryu* far to the north.

6. The *Nautilus* fired three torpedoes at the starboard side of the carrier she was attacking. According to Lieutenant Commander Kunisada, damage control officer of the *Kaga*, the sub attacking her also fired three torpedoes at the starboard side. He saw them all. The first passed across the bow, the second just astern, the third hit amidships but was a dud.

Nothing is certain, but in view of all this it would seem that the *Nautilus* mistook the *Kaga* for the *Soryu*. They looked fairly similar, and certainly the opportunities for study were fleeting and difficult. Mistakes were easy—it's interesting to note that the *Nautilus* also identified two stand-by destroyers as cruisers. As for the "hits," it's suggested they were one or two more of the internal explosions that occasionally racked the *Kaga* throughout the afternoon until she finally sank at dusk. Duds, incidentally, were no novelty to attacking American submarines in these early days of the war.

None of this should detract from the *Nautilus*'s glory, or the magnificent work of her crew. She remains the only U.S. submarine to have struck a blow at Midway.

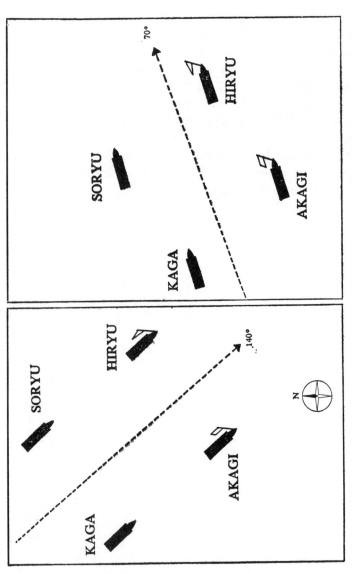

1. The Japanese carriers approach Midway, early June 4. *Akagi* and *Hiryu* lead the box formation. Course 140°. Distance between ships roughly 1,300 yards. The screening battleships, cruisers and destroyers (not shown) are deployed in a rough circle around the

2. Nagumo changes course at 9:17 A.M. Carriers turn individually, not in formation. New course 70°, later adjusted to 30°. Distance between ships still 1,300 yards, but lengthens as U.S. torpedo attacks begin. Screen still in rough circle around the carriers.

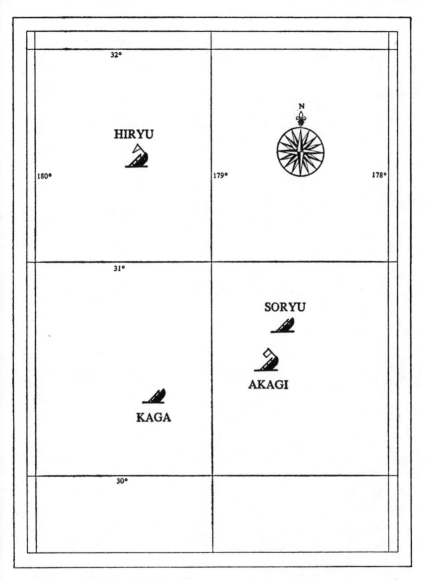

3. Positions of the Japanese carriers when they finally sank, according to Nagumo's battle report. *Akagi:* 30°30'N, 178°40'W; *Kaga:* 30°20'N, 179°17'W; *Soryu:* 30°42'N, 178°37'W. The *Hiryu,* which escaped the first U.S. carrier strike, was caught later and finally sank at 31°27'N, 179°23'W.

Acknowledgments

"After 24 years, I can still feel like weeping with pride, admiration, and humility when I recall the courage those men displayed," writes Daniel Grace, then a Marine Pfc stationed on Midway. He was referring to the American fliers, but judging from the correspondence, it could have been almost anyone speaking of almost anyone else at the Battle of Midway.

Perhaps because it was such a close thing . . . perhaps because the sacrifices were so great . . . perhaps because the war was so young and the warriors so impressionable—whatever the reason, the men of Midway have a generosity all their own. They show it in viewing each other, in sharing their triumphs, in understanding the other man's problem when something went wrong. They are deeply reflective about this battle and what it meant to them.

Happily their spirit has overflowed on this book. Some 350 American participants have contributed their recollections, and there has seemed no limit to their willingness to help. "Deacon" Arnold takes the evening off to explain how he made all those booby traps; Doug Rollow borrows time from a hectic business trip to talk about VMSB-241. Don Kundinger writes 16 pages on flying with the B-17s; John Greenbacker tops him with 19 on the *Yorktown*. Admiral Fletcher patiently discusses the uncertainties of war; Admiral Spruance even throws in one of his famous walks.

A number of these participants have generously made available various letters, notes and journals written at the time. I'm especially grateful to Aaron Bagley, Burdick H. Brittin, Eugene Card, Edward Creighton, Cleo Dobson, Alden W. Hanson, and Joseph Love in this connection. Likewise Mrs. John C. Waldron has kindly given me permission to quote from the touching letter sent her by her gallant husband just before the battle.

Gradually some of these contributors came to be regarded as "specialists" on particular areas, and I'm afraid I imposed upon them unmercifully: Howard Ady on the PBYs . . . Ham Dow on communications . . . Eddie Layton on CINCPAC . . . Bob McGlashan on anything to do with the Marines . . . Joe Rochefort on radio intelligence . . . Bob Russell on the screening destroyers . . . Dick Best and Max Leslie on air operations in general, vintage 1942. Jasper Holmes was a gold mine on contemporary Honolulu and Pearl Harbor.

Sometimes a particular point gave special trouble, and a number of participants would be drafted in an effort to solve it. Here too they gave willingly, although the result usually meant that somebody had to be wrong. There was the question, for instance, of what ship Captain Buckmaster was on when the *Yorktown* finally sank. Buckmaster himself thought he watched from the tug *Vireo,* but was not sure. Others recalled seeing him on the destroyer *Balch;* still others on the destroyer *Gwin.*

These conflicting viewpoints just couldn't be reconciled, so finally it was "back to the archives." By piecing together several obscure reports, it gradually became clear that Buckmaster had gone first to the *Vireo* . . . then transferred to the *Balch* later on June 6 . . . and finally transferred again to the *Gwin* at 7:20 A.M. on June 7, shortly after the *Yorktown* sank. So he watched from the *Balch*—just as Admiral Tiemroth had been saying all along.

The Japanese participants were just as patient and helpful. Many vivid pictures still come to mind: Takayoshi Morinaga acting out his escape from the *Kaga's* blazing hangar deck . . . Mitsuharu Noda sipping Johnny Walker as he recalled with relish his extracurricular assignments for Admiral Yamamoto . . . Admiral Kusaka thoughtfully maneuvering a matchstick "fleet" about the polished top of a bamboo table, showing me exactly how Nagumo's force made its famous turn to the northeast on June 4.

Here too several participants were sometimes drafted to help clear up a particular point. From interviews with Admiral Kusaka and Susumu Kawaguchi, for instance, it became clear that not only the torpedo planes but also the dive bombers had to be rearmed when Nagumo made his fateful decision to strike Midway again.

In addition to these personal recollections—both American and Japanese—I've relied on much written material about Midway. The U.S. Navy's Classified Operational Archives offer a treasury of unpublished action reports, war diaries, debriefings, interviews, analyses, interrogations of Japanese prisoners. The material is all there—and so are the people to help. Nothing was too much trouble for Dean Allard and his fine staff. A special vote of thanks must go to Mrs. Mildred Mayeux, who bore the brunt of so many of my problems.

The Marine Archives, too, couldn't have been more helpful. Rowland Gill runs a superb shop. Here, incidentally, are copies of most of the Army Air Force reports, so important in piecing together any account of Midway.

On the Japanese side, Colonel Susumu Nishiura opened wide the doors of his War History Office at the Defense Agency in Tokyo. He even put up with my French. A special word of gratitude is owed to Commander Tsunoda, the office's expert on Midway. Thanks largely to his efforts, new light is shown on the Aleutian phase, which appears to have been more a sop to the Japanese Naval General Staff than an attempt to divert the U.S. fleet.

There's also valuable printed material on Midway. Some of the best comes from government sources. The ONI pamphlet *The Japanese Story of the Battle of Midway* (1947) translates Nagumo's Battle Report. It has its shortcomings (sometimes due to translation difficulties), but it helps pin down the time many incidents happened, and it remains the only source for some of the communications between the Japanese commanders. The USSBS's *Interrogations of Japanese Officials* (1946) includes interviews with 18 participants. *Admiral Raymond A. Spruance* (1966) is a useful biography by E. P. Forrestel. *Marines at Midway* (1948) is a superb account by Robert D. Heinl, Jr., happily free of "officialese." Scot MacDonald's *Evolution of Aircraft Carriers* (1964) is full of useful information on all the carriers involved—both sides. The Pearl Harbor hearings contain nuggets on the organization of the Combat Intelligence Unit and the Japanese code JN-25.

Unofficially, much useful material has also been published. On the battle as a whole, Thaddeus V. Tuleja's *Climax at Midway*

(Norton, 1960) is a stimulating treatment. William Ward Smith's *Midway: Turning Point of the Pacific* (Crowell, 1966) contributes firsthand experience and a fine seaman's eye. In a class by itself is Samuel E. Morison's account in Volume IV of his *History of United States Naval Operations in World War II* (Little, Brown, 1949). On some points my own conclusions stray from Admiral Morison's findings, but there can be no doubt about my indebtedness. His three magnificent chapters on Midway were what fired my desire to do a whole book on the subject.

Other works throw valuable light on particular parts of the story: *The Ragged, Rugged Warriors* by Martin Caidin (Dutton, 1966) covers the B-26s . . . *Torpedo Junction* by Robert J. Casey (Bobbs-Merrill, 1942) conveys the suspense in Task Force 16 . . . *The Flying Guns* by C. E. Dickinson (Scribner, 1942) describes flying with Scouting 6 . . . *Undersea Victory* by W. J. Holmes (Doubleday, 1966) handles the submarines . . . *The Wild Blue* by John F. Loosbrock and Richard M. Skinner (Putnam, 1960) includes Colonel Walter Sweeney's firsthand account of the B-17s . . . *The Sky Is My Witness* by Thomas Moore, Jr. (Putnam, 1943) tells the experiences of a Marine dive bomber pilot . . . *United States Submarine Operations in World War II* by Theodore Roscoe (Naval Institute, 1948) discusses the *Nautilus* and the *Tambor* . . . *The Magnificent Mitscher* by Theodore Taylor (Norton, 1954) views Midway through the eyes of the *Hornet*'s famous skipper.

In addition, there are useful, appropriately loyal ship's histories on all three of the U.S. carriers. For the *Yorktown* there is Pat Frank and Joseph D. Harrington's *Rendezvous at Midway* (John Day, 1967); for the *Hornet* there is Alexander Griffith's *A Ship to Remember* (Howell, Soskin, 1943); and for the *Enterprise* there is Edward P. Stafford's *The Big E* (Random House, 1962).

From time to time interesting magazine articles have also appeared. To name a few of the best: J. Bryan III's beautifully organized "Never a Battle Like Midway" in the March 26, 1949, issue of the *Saturday Evening Post* . . . Joseph M. Worthington's firsthand account of the *Benham*'s role in the January 1965 issue of *Shipmate* . . . Frank D. Morris's description of the PBY torpedo attack in the July 21, 1942, issue of *Collier's* . . . John S. Thach's fine account of Fighting 3 in the December 12, 1942, issue of the same magazine.

Sydney L. James's story of Torpedo 8 in the August 31, 1942, issue of *Life* remains a classic of war reporting. For fuller treatment of Commander Waldron's men, there's the series of nine articles by Lloyd Wendt with George Gay in the *Grafic* Magazine of the Chicago *Tribune,* starting May 30, 1948. Still another important source on Torpedo 8 is H. H. Ferrier's "Torpedo Squadron Eight, the Other Chapter" in the October 1964 issue of the *Naval Institute Proceedings.*

Newspaper coverage was necessarily limited because of censorship and the limited availability of information in wartime. Nevertheless, there are good accounts of the attack on the *Yorktown* (without naming her) by Foster Hailey in the *New York Times* on June 22 and 23, 1942; and another by Wendell Webb in the New York *Herald Tribune* on June 22, 1942. Home-town papers eventually caught up with many of the survivors; for instance, see the interview with William England in the Davenport, Iowa, *Democrat* on September 20, 1942; or that with Hawey Wilder in the Atlanta *Journal* on September 16, 1942.

The B-17 fliers had a field day in the Honolulu *Advertiser* on June 12, 1942. The claims of hits and sinkings are mistaken, but the interviews are no less interesting for the picture they give of these spirited young men flying their first combat missions.

On the Japanese side, the traditional authority has long been Mitsuo Fuchida and Masatake Okumiya's *Midway—the Battle That Doomed Japan* (Naval Institute, 1955). This remains an indispensable work, but other less familiar sources can fill in gaps and contribute a fresh viewpoint. Teiichi Makishima's *The Tragic Battle of Midway* (1956) benefits from the eye of a trained journalist . . . Juzo Mori's *Torpedo Plane Strike* (1956) depicts the battle as seen from the *Soryu* . . . Hiroyuki Agawa's *Isoroku Yamamoto* (1966) throws much new light on the Admiral. The same is true of Kota Hoketsu's article, "Memories of Isoroku Yamamoto" in the April 1, 1966, issue of the magazine *Zaikai*. For the mood in Tokyo at the time of the battle, the back files of the *Japan Times and Advertiser* make fascinating reading—especially the period May 26–June 16, 1942.

There's useful material on this side of the Pacific too. In addition to Fuchida's *Midway,* three books especially come to mind: *The End of the Imperial Japanese Navy* by Masanori Ito (Norton, 1962); *Death of a Navy* by Andrieu D'Albas (Devin-Adair, 1957); and *Zero!* by Masatake Okumiya and Jiro Horikoshi with Martin

Caidin (Dutton, 1956). Also, John Toland's *But Not in Shame* (Random House, 1961) contains a valuable interview with Minoru Genda—generally considered the "brains" of Nagumo's fleet.

Several helpful articles have also appeared in the *Naval Institute Proceedings*. In the October 1949 issue James A. Field, Jr. analyzes Admiral Yamamoto's attitude toward America. In the May 1953 issue Edwin T. Layton offers an intriguing theory on Operation K— and is vigorously rebutted by W. J. Holmes three months later. In the May 1963 issue Commander Yahachi Tanabe (with an assist from Joseph D. Harrington) gives his version of how his submarine sank the *Yorktown*.

In researching this book, scores of helpful people have paved my way. The trail really began in Washington, where Rear Admiral E. M. Eller made available the marvelous resources of his Office of Naval History. Better than that, he gave freely of his wisdom and encouragement. The same can be said of Colonel C. V. Glines, Chief of the Magazine and Book Branch at the Defense Department's Directorate for Information Service. Special thanks go to Lieutenant Commander Dan Dagle in that office, who did so much in helping locate participants.

The Marines were there too. Colonel F. C. Caldwell, head of the Historical Branch, met every request. At National Archives Mrs. J. Coleman turned the place upside down to find the right pictures, and as my deadline neared, the Navy's Lieutenant Commander George P. Bienstadt worked like a Trojan to get them processed.

At the Pearl Harbor Naval Shipyard in Hawaii, Doris Obata made the project her own. She was indefatigable in turning up some of the old hands who won that famous race to get the *Yorktown* ready in time. Getting to Midway itself turned out to be a combined operation, and I'm grateful to all concerned—especially Lieutenant Colonel Jim Sunderman of the Air Force and Lieutenant Commander Bill Stierman of the Navy. On Midway Captain James Savacool proved a perfect host, and Chaplain Robert H. Warren outdid himself to be helpful. Incredibly, he found six people there today who had also been in the battle that fateful June of 1942.

In Japan there were any number of people who took the neophyte in hand and made his visit fruitful. To name a few: Hiroyuki Agawa, Kazushige Hirasawa, Kiyoaki Murata, Walter Nichols, George Saito, Douglas Wada.

Back in Washington again, I descended on Rear Admiral Arthur

ACKNOWLEDGMENTS [307

McCollum along with the year's biggest blizzard. It didn't seem to faze him at all: he gave me the full benefit of his great insight on both the Japanese and the Washington end of things. Vice Admiral George Dyer, one of the few survivors of the early days at COMINCH, helped me pin down numerous dates and times. Adrian Van Wyen, CNO Air Historian, filled me in on many technical details about the planes. A visit to Norfolk found Charles S. Hiles immensely helpful on the intelligence preliminaries.

Throughout my research other Midway writers have been immensely generous. Roger Pineau freely shared his broad knowledge of Japan and the Japanese. Robert D. Heinl, Jr., is a human encyclopedia on the Marines. J. Bryan III, Richard Newcomb, and Thaddeus V. Tuleja lent me valuable papers. Ladislas Farago, Joe Harrington, John and Toshiko Toland were all hard-pressed working on their own new books, but there was always time for a helping hand.

Finally there are those who lived with the project from day to day. Yuzuru Sanematsu was a tower of strength in Tokyo. Maria Look performed wonders on research. Anne Barker valiantly pulled together the index. Evan Thomas contributed his deft editorial touch—plus the free services of his daughter Louisa, who came up with such a fine title. Florence Gallagher rounded out her twentieth year of typing my scribbled foolscap.

But all these individuals—helpful as they were—would not have been enough without the generous assistance of the 388 participants listed on the following pages. In the end, a battle consists of people, and these are the people of Midway. Like everyone else listed in this acknowledgment section, they share no responsibility for my findings—no blame for my failings—but all the credit in the world for any new light this book may throw on what was truly a great moment in our national experience.

List of Contributors

This book represents the combined efforts of both Americans and Japanese, so it seems appropriate that they should be listed together, without regard to nationality. Each name is followed by the participant's vantage point, rather than rank or position at the time of the battle. Where supplied, present rank is also included.

John O. Adams—PBYs, Midway

Capt. Howard P. Ady, Jr., USN (Ret.)—PBYs, Midway

Rear Adm. Frank Akers, USN (Ret.)—*Hornet*

Cdr. Gene L. Alair, USNR—*Astoria*

Rear Adm. Clarence E. Aldrich, USN (Ret.)—*Yorktown*

Maj. Gen. Brooke E. Allen, USAF (Ret.)—B-17s, Midway

Riley Allen—Honolulu

CWO John G. Almand, USN—*Russell*

Takahisa Amagai—*Kaga*

Cdr. Bernard L. Amman, USNR (Ret.)—PBYs, Midway

Brig. Gen. Kirk Armistead, USMC (Ret.)—VMF-221, Midway

Capt. Warren W. Armstrong, USN (Ret.)—*Maury*

Maj. Dorn E. Arnold, USMC (Ret.)—6th Def. Batn., Midway

Rear Adm. Murr E. Arnold, USN (Ret.)—*Yorktown*

Rear Adm. Ralph J. Arnold, USN (Ret.)—*Yorktown*

Rear Adm. William H. Ashford, Jr., USN (Ret.)—*Enterprise*

Lieut. A. M. Bagley, USN—*New Orleans*

Lt. Cdr. George M. K. Baker, Jr., USN (Ret.)—*Astoria*

Lt. Cdr. Thomas W. Baker, USNR (Ret.)—*Astoria*

Lt. J. Clark Barrett, USNR (Ret.) —VB-8, *Hornet*

CWO George E. Bateman, USN— *Yorktown*

Lt. Col. Robert J. Bear, USMC (Ret.)—VMSB-241, Midway

Capt. Walter H. Beckham, SC USNR—*Portland*

Lea Bell, USMC (Ret.)—Carlson's Raiders, Midway

Lt. Col. William M. Bell, USMCR (Ret.)—6th Def. Batn., Midway

Lieut. (j.g.) Floyd H. Bennett, USN (Ret.)—*Yorktown*

Lt. Robert H. Bennett, USN (Ret.)—NAS, Midway

Capt. Vane M. Bennett, USN (Ret.)—*Yorktown*

William Bennett—Shipyard, Pearl Harbor

Rear Adm. Roy Stanley Benson, USN—*Nautilus*

William H. Berlin, Jr., USMC (Ret.)—6th Def. Batn., Midway

Capt. Arthur H. Berndtson, USN—*Enterprise*

Lt. Cdr. Richard H. Best, USN (Ret.)—VB-6, *Enterprise*

Cdr. Daniel T. Birtwell, Jr., USN (Ret.)—*Portland*

Rear Adm. Worthington S. Bitler, USN (Ret.)—*Pensacola*

Cdr. W. P. Blackmore, USN (Ret.)—tug *Keosauqua*, Pearl Harbor

Cdr. Carl M. Blackstock, USNR (Ret.)—PT boats, Midway

Col. George A. Blakey, USAF (Ret.)—B-17s, Midway

Capt. Ben Ward Blee, USN—*Pensacola*

E. E. Blythe, USN (Ret.)—*Phelps*

CWO Jule C. Bode, USN (Ret.)—*Yorktown*

CWO Frank W. Boo, USN (Ret.)—*Yorktown*

Col. Alfred L. Booth, USMC (Ret.)—6th Def. Batn., Midway

Capt. Harold S. Bottomley, Jr., USN—VB-3, *Yorktown*

Cdr. Matthew J. Bouterse, CHC USN (Ret.)—*Astoria*

Cdr. James C. Boyden, USNR—PBYs, Midway

Sgt. Gail B. Brackeen, USMC (Ret.)—6th Def. Batn., Midway

Eugene K. Braun, USN (Ret.)—VB-6, *Enterprise*

Capt. Chester E. Briggs, Jr., USN —*Yorktown*

Capt. Burdick H. Brittin, USN (Ret.)—*Aylwin*

Rear Adm. William H. Brockman, Jr., USN (Ret.)—*Nautilus*

Rear Adm. Charles B. Brooks, Jr., USN (Ret.)—*Yorktown*

Capt. James A. Brown, MC USNR (Ret.)—*Astoria*

Cdr. Robert G. Brown, USN (Ret.)—*Russell*

Vice Adm. Elliott Buckmaster, USN (Ret.)—*Yorktown*

Col. Jean H. Buckner, USMC (Ret.)—6th Def. Batn., Midway

Capt. George S. Bullen, USN (Ret.)—*Pensacola*

Rear Adm. William H. Buracker, USN (Ret.)—*Enterprise*

Rear Adm. William P. Burford, USN (Ret.)—*Monaghan*

Cdr. Arthur T. Burke, USNR (Ret.)—*Enterprise*

S. I. Burke, Jr., USN (Ret.)—*Benham*

Capt. Noel A. Burkey, Jr., USNR—*Astoria*

Rear Adm. Sherman E. Burroughs, USN (Ret.)—*Enterprise*

Lt. Cdr. Nathaniel T. Burwell, USN (Ret.)—*Ballard*

Capt. Norwood A. Campbell, USN (Ret.)—*Yorktown*

Capt. Stanley Caplan, USNR—*Aylwin*

Maj. Eugene T. Card, USMC (Ret.)—VMSB-241, Midway

Col. John F. Carey, USMC (Ret.) —VMF-221, Midway

Cdr. Conrad H. Carlson, USN (Ret.)—*Astoria*

Capt. Charles M. Cassel, Jr., USN —*Anderson*

Lt. Cdr. John K. Chase, USN (Ret.)—*Hughes*

Lt. Cdr. James W. Christie, Jr., USNR (Ret.)—*Hornet*

Ellis Clanton—Shipyard, Pearl Harbor

Philip R. Clark, USMC (Ret.)— 3rd Def. Batn., Midway

Cdr. Philip W. Cobb, USN—VB-3, *Yorktown*

Capt. Oliver D. Compton, USN— *Benham*

Capt. Donald E. Cooksey, DC USN—6th Def. Batn., Midway

Lt. Col. Jack Cosley, USMC (Ret.) —VMSB-241, Midway

Rear Adm. William R. Cox, USN (Ret.)—*Gwin*

Capt. Russell F. Craig, USN—*Pensacola*

Rear Adm. Richard S. Craighill, USN—*Blue*

Carl V. Cramer, USN (Ret.)—*Vincennes*

Rear Adm. Edward P. Creehan, USN (Ret.)—*Hornet*

Edward G. Creighton—*Monaghan*

Capt. Russell S. Crenshaw, Jr., USN—*Maury*

Capt. W. R. Crenshaw, USN— *Yorktown*

Lt. Cdr. Edmund B. Crosby, USN (Ret.)—*Yorktown*

Cdr. Robert B. Crowell, USN (Ret.)—*Benham*

Capt. Arthur A. Cumberledge, USN (Ret.)—*Hornet*

Lt. Col. Daniel L. Cummings USMC (Ret.)—VMSB-241, Midway

Rear Adm. Charles R. Cundiff, USN (Ret.)—*Yorktown*

Vice Adm. John C. Daniel, USN (Ret.)—*Phelps*

Cdr. Douglas C. Davis, USN— PBYs, Midway

Sgt. George F. Davis, USMC (Ret.)—6th Def. Batn., Midway

Capt. Ray Davis, USN (Ret.)— VS-8, *Hornet*

WO Raymond C. Davis, USN (Ret.)—*Yorktown*

Rear Adm. W. Dalton Davis, MC USN (Ret.)—*Yorktown*

Rear Adm. John F. Delaney, Jr., USN (Ret.)—*Yorktown*

Vice Adm. Walter S. Delany, USN (Ret.)—CINCPAC, Pearl Harbor

Lt. Cdr. Stephen Dewey, USN (Ret.)—*Hornet*

Cdr. Cleo J. Dobson, USN (Ret.) —*Enterprise*

Capt. Donald G. Dockum, USN (Ret.)—*Ellet*

Rear Adm. Oscar H. Dodson, USN (Ret.)—*Hornet*

Col. Malcolm O. Donohoo, USMC (Ret.)—*Portland*

Rear Adm. Leonard J. Dow, USN (Ret.)—*Enterprise*

Adm. Laurance T. DuBose, USN (Ret.)—*Portland*

Rear Adm. Claren E. Duke, USN (Ret.)—*Grouper*

Vice Adm. Ralph Earle, Jr., USN (Ret.)—*Ralph Talbot*

Capt. Albert K. Earnest, USN— VT-8 (Det.), Midway

Roger Eaton, USMC (Ret.)—6th Def. Batn., Midway

Cdr. Edwin H. Edgerton, USN (Ret.)—*Astoria*

Rear Adm. John E. Edwards, USN (Ret.)—*Phelps*

Cdr. Roy T. Elder, USN (Ret.)— *Yorktown*

BMC Stanley J. Engels, USN (Ret.)—tug *Tamaha,* Midway

Cdr. Wilhelm G. Esders, USN (Ret.)—VT-3, *Yorktown*

Lt. Cdr. William Evans, USN (Ret.)—*Vincennes*

Jean I. Everest, USN (Ret.)—PT boats, Midway

Capt. Edward T. Farley, USN (Ret.)—*Morris*

Lt. H. H. Ferrier, USN—VT-8 (Det.), Midway

Cdr. Clayton E. Fisher, USN (Ret.)—VB-8, *Hornet*

Cdr. William A. Fisher, Jr., USN (Ret.)—VS-8, *Hornet*

BTC Raymond J. Fitzgibbon, USN —*Hammann*

Cdr. R. E. Flack, USN—VF-6, *Enterprise*

Rear Adm. Allan F. Fleming, USN —*Hornet*

Adm. Frank Jack Fletcher, USN (Ret.)—*Yorktown*

Capt. George H. Flinn, USNR (Ret.)—VT-8, *Hornet*

GMCS Edward T. Forbes, USN— *Anderson*

Rear Adm. John G. Foster, USN (Ret.)—*Hornet*

Vice Adm. Charles W. Fox, SC USN (Ret.)—*Enterprise*

Melvin Frantz, USNR (Ret.)— *Yorktown*

Cdr. George R. Fraser, USN (Ret.)—NAS, Midway

Capt. Lawrence C. French, USN (Ret.)—VF-8, *Hornet*

Capt. Harold E. Fry, USN (Ret.) —*Astoria*

Cdr. Louis Funkenstein, Jr., USN (Ret.)—*Thornton*

Kenneth E. Gaebler, USN (Ret.)— *Enterprise*

CWO William E. Gallagher, USN (Ret.)—VB-3, *Yorktown*

Rear Adm. W. Earl Gallaher, USN (Ret.)—VS-6, *Enterprise*

Rear Adm. Francis H. Gardner, USN (Ret.)—*Ellet*

Gen. Minoru Genda—*Akagi*

Capt. Harry B. Gibbs, USN—VF-3, *Yorktown*

Capt. Robert W. Gillette, USN (Ret.)—*Monaghan*

Cdr. Harold J. Gilpin, USN (Ret.) —*Pensacola*

Cdr. John W. Gilpin, USN (Ret.) —*Monaghan*

Rear Adm. John K. B. Ginder, USN (Ret.)—*Anderson*

Lt. Cdr. Joseph V. Godfrey, USN (Ret.)—VB-3, *Yorktown*

Lt. Cdr. Edgar E. Gold, USN (Ret.)—*Hornet*

Cdr. George H. Goldsmith, USN —VB-6, *Enterprise*

Capt. Leon Grabowsky, USN— NAS, Midway

Daniel Grace, USMC (Ret.)—6th Def. Batn., Midway

Capt. James S. Gray, Jr., USN (Ret.)—VF-6, *Enterprise*

Cdr. Richard Gray, USN (Ret.)— VF-8, *Hornet*

Capt. John E. Greenbacker, USN— *Yorktown*

CG William M. Gross, USN (Ret.) —PBYs, Pearl Harbor

Capt. Troy T. Guillory, USN—VB-8, *Hornet*

Capt. Donald C. Gumz, USN (Ret.)—PBYs, Midway

Rear Adm. Harry A. Guthrie, USN (Ret.)—*Yorktown*

Capt. James W. Haggard, USN (Ret.)—*Enterprise*

Cdr. John E. Halter, Jr., USNR (Ret.)—*Ellet*

Alden W. Hanson, USN (Ret.)—VB-3, *Yorktown*

Capt. Eugene R. Hanson, USN—VT-8 (Det.), Pearl Harbor

WT G. S. Hardon, USN (Ret.)—*Monaghan*

ENCS. W. E. Hare, USN—*Yorktown*

Capt. Charles S. Hart, USN—*Russell*

Rear Adm. Paul E. Hartmann, USN—NAS, Midway

Rear Adm. Glenn R. Hartwig, USN (Ret.)—*Russell*

Col. Toshio Hashimoto—*Hiryu*

Herman Hastrup—shipyard, Pearl Harbor

Rear Adm. John D. Hayes, USN (Ret.)—*Astoria*

Robert M. Haynes, USMC (Ret.)—6th Def. Batn., Midway

Capt. Vincent P. Healey, USN—*Astoria*

Rear Adm. George L. Heath, USN (Ret.)—*Portland*

Capt. John A. Heath, USN (Ret.)—*Mustin*

Capt. Frank M. Hertel, USN (Ret.)—*Vincennes*

Rear Adm. John M. Higgins, USN (Ret.)—*Gwin*

Capt. Thomas W. Hogan, USN (Ret.)—*Nautilus*

Cdr. Don C. Holcomb, USNR (Ret.)—*Ballard*

Robert V. Hollison—shipyard, Pearl Harbor

Rear Adm. Paul A. Holmberg, USN—VB-3, *Yorktown*

Lt. (j.g.) Pressley E. Holmes, USN (Ret.)—*Yorktown*

Capt. W. J. Holmes, USN (Ret.)—14th Naval District, Pearl Harbor

Brig. Gen. Robert E. Hommel, USMC (Ret.)—6th Def. Batn., Midway

Jinjiro Honda—*Kirishima*

Rear Adm. Gilbert C. Hoover, USN (Ret.)—*Morris*

Cdr. Harvey Hop, USN (Ret.)—PBYs, Midway

Capt. Lewis A. Hopkins, USN—VB-6, *Enterprise*

Naoaki Hoshiko—*Tanikaze*

Donat G. Houle, USN (Ret.)—*Hughes*

Cdr. Ralph B. Hovind, USN (Ret.)—VS-8, *Hornet*

J. E. Hoy, USN (Ret.)—*Hornet*

Cdr. Richard Z. Hughes, USN (Ret.)—VF-8, *Hornet*

Col. William C. Humberd, USMC (Ret.)—VMF-221, Midway

Col. Gavin C. Humphrey, USMC (Ret.)—*Vincennes*

Capt. Elgin B. Hurlbert, USN (Ret.)—*Yorktown*

Floyd M. Hurley, USN (Ret.)—*Hammann*

Capt. Roy M. Isaman, USN—VB-3, *Yorktown*

Cdr. Edmond M. Jacoby, USN (Ret.)—NAS, Midway

Capt. Norman D. Johnson, USN (Ret.)—*Minneapolis*

Rear Adm. Robert Ruffin Johnson, USN (Ret.)—VB-8, *Hornet*

E. G. Johnston, USN—*Enterprise*

Takashi Kanoe—*Hiryu*

S1C Peter Karetka, USNR—*Hughes*

Susumu Kawaguchi—*Hiryu*

Virgil E. Keeney, USN (Ret.)—*Yorktown*

Theodore E. Kimmell, USN (Ret.)—PBYs, Midway

Susumu Kimura—*Nagara*

Cdr. Joseph Kisela, USN (Ret.)—
Yorktown
Capt. Norman J. Kleiss, USN
(Ret.)—VS-6, Enterprise
Jay W. Koch, USMC (Ret.)—6th
Def. Batn., Midway
Magotaro Koga—Nowaki
Keizo Komura—Chikuma
Cdr. Rubin H. Konig, USN (Ret.)
—VT-3, Kaneohe
Arthur Kozak, USMC (Ret.)—6th
Def. Batn., Midway
ACCM J. S. Kuhn, USN—PT
boats, Midway
Don J. Kundinger, USAF (Ret.)—
B-17s, Midway
Yoshio Kunisada—Kaga
Stan Kurka, USN—Hornet
Ryunosuke Kusaka—Akagi
EMC Thomas Blair Kuykendall,
USN (Ret.)—Hornet

Cdr. William W. Lancaster, USN
(Ret.)—Yorktown
Lt. Cdr. Charles S. Lane, USN
(Ret.)—VB-3, Yorktown
Capt. Harvey P. Lanham, USN—
VB-6, Enterprise
Rear Adm. Robert E. Laub, USN
(Ret.)—VT-6, Enterprise
Fred H. Laughter, USN—Hornet
Rear Adm. Edwin T. Layton, USN
(Ret.)—CINCPAC, Pearl Harbor
Albert Lee—shipyard, Pearl Harbor
Lt. Col. Steve Lesko, USMC
(Ret.)—Kittyhawk
Rear Adm. Maxwell F. Leslie,
USN (Ret.)—VB-3, Yorktown
Capt. Robin M. Lindsey, USN
(Ret.)—Enterprise
Cdr. Stan Linzey, CHC USN—
Yorktown
Col. John W. Livingston, USAF—
B-17s, Midway

Lt. Cdr. John D. Lorenz, USN
(Ret.)—Yorktown
GY Sgt. Joseph E. Love, USMC
(Ret.)—3rd Def. Batn., Midway
William R. Lucius, USMC (Ret.)
—MAG 22, Midway
CWO Forest E. Lunsford, USN
(Ret.)—Benham
Rear Adm. Richard B. Lynch,
USN—Nautilus
Rear Adm. John B. Lyon, USN
(Ret.)—Enterprise

Capt. John R. McCarthy, USN
(Ret.)—VS-6, Enterprise
Rear Adm. C. Wade McClusky,
USN (Ret.)—EAG, Enterprise
Morris W. McCoy, USMC (Ret.)
—6th Def. Batn., Midway
Capt. William P. McGirr, USN
(Ret.)—Enterprise
Col. Robert C. McGlashan, USMC
(Ret.)—6th Def. Batn., Midway
Capt. Clinton McKellar, Jr., USN
—PT boats, Midway
Lt. Cdr. Boyd M. McKenzie, USN
(Ret.)—Yorktown
Cdr. Philip N. MacDonald, USN
(Ret.)—Yorktown
Hisao Mandai—Hiryu
Teiichi Makishima—Akagi
Col. Ernest R. Manierre, USAF—
B-17s, Midway
CWO Lester L. Marshall, USMC
(Ret.)—VMF-221, Midway
QMCM William C. Martin, USN
—Yorktown
Vice Adm. Charles P. Mason, USN
(Ret.)—Hornet
Lt. Cdr. Stuart J. Mason, USN
—VB-6, Enterprise
Shogo Masuda—Akagi
Rear Adm. Roger W. Mehle, USN
—VF-6, Enterprise
Cdr. Milford A. Merrill, USN
(Ret.)—VB-3, Yorktown

Cdr. Robert S. Merritt, USN (Ret.) —VF-8, *Hornet*

Lt. Col. George E. Metzenthin, USMCR (Ret.)—22nd Prov. Marines, Midway

Capt. Vernon L. Micheel, USN— VS-6, *Enterprise*

Cdr. Edwin B. Miller, MC USN— NAS, Midway

Brig. Gen. Ronald K. Miller, USMC (Ret.)—3rd Def. Batn., Midway

Gishiro Miura—*Akagi*

Maj. Neil W. Mold, USA—Carlson's Raiders, Midway

MG Sgt. Otto M. Moore, USMC (Ret.)—VMSB-241, Midway

Lt. Col. Pete L. Moore, USAF (Ret.)—B-26s, Midway

Cdr. Corwin F. Morgan, USN (Ret.)—VT-8 (Det.), Pearl Harbor

Juzo Mori—*Soryu*

Takayoshi Morinaga—*Kaga*

Cdr. J. S. Morris, USNR (Ret.)— VT-6, *Enterprise*

Cdr. William B. Mosle, USNR (Ret.)— VT-3, *Yorktown*

Capt. Elias B. Mott, USN (Ret.)— *Enterprise*

Rear Adm. Horace D. Moulton, USN (Ret.)—*Enterprise*

Lt. Col. James P. Muri, USAF (Ret.)—B-26s, Midway

WO Meade E. Murphy, USN (Ret.)—*Yorktown*

Cdr. James F. Murray, USN (Ret.)—VB-6, *Enterprise*

Robert K. Nelson, USMC (Ret.)— *Yorktown*

Lt. Cdr. Denny A. Newberry, USN (Ret.)—*Enterprise*

Capt. Robert J. Ney, USN—PBYs, Midway

Rear Adm. Bromfield B. Nichol, USN (Ret.)—*Enterprise*

Paul E. Nichols, USN (Ret.)— *Morris*

Susumu Nishiura—Imperial Headquarters, Tokyo

Mitsuharu Noda—*Yamato*

John Ross Nugent, USAF—Midway

Raita Ogawa—*Akagi*

Hisashi Ohara—*Soryu*

RM1 Lawson Oliphant, USN (Ret.)—*Hughes*

Heijiro Omi—*Yamato*

Tatsuya Otawa—*Soryu*

Capt. Frank A. Patriarca, USN— VS-6, *Enterprise*

Lt. Cdr. James W. Patterson, Jr., USN—VB-6, *Enterprise*

Cdr. Ralph E. Patterson, USN (Ret.)—*Yorktown*

Rear Adm. Oscar Pederson, USN (Ret.)—*Yorktown*

Capt. Joe R. Penland, USN (Ret.) —VB-6, *Enterprise*

Rear Adm. Henry S. Persons, USN —*Enterprise*

Capt. William R. Pittman, USN —VS-6, *Enterprise*

Joe Poffenberger, USN (Ret.)— *Hornet*

Lt. Col. Bruce Prosser, USMC (Ret.)—VMSB-241, Midway

Rear Adm. Donald J. Ramsey, USN (Ret.)—*Hughes*

Capt. Wilmer E. Rawie, USN (Ret.)—VF-6, *Enterprise*

Rear Adm. Clarence C. Ray, USN (Ret.)—*Yorktown*

John A. Reece, USN (Ret.)—PBYs, Midway

ABCM H. J. Reese, USN—VT-3, *Yorktown*

EMC Thomas W. Reese, USN (Ret.)—*Hornet*
CWO George W. Reeves, USNR— YP 349
Cdr. Paul T. Rennell, USN (Ret.) —PT boats, Midway
Lt. Col. Donald E. Ridings, USAF (Ret.)—B-17s, Midway
Rear Adm. Frederick L. Riefkohl, USN (Ret.)—*Vincennes*
Lt. Col. Allan H. Ringblom, USMC—VMSB-241, Midway
Rear Adm. Wilbur E. Roberts, USN (Ret.)—VB-6, *Enterprise*
Capt. Joseph J. Rochefort, USN (Ret.)—14th Naval District, Pearl Harbor
Cdr. Eldor E. Rodenburg, USN (Ret.)—VS-6, *Enterprise*
Fred Rodin—shipyard, Pearl Harbor
BMC E. W. Rollman, USN (Ret.) —*Enterprise*
Maj. J. D. Rollow, Jr., USMCR (Ret.)—VMSB-241, Midway
Cdr. Joseph C. Roper, USN (Ret.) —*Enterprise*
Cdr. Allan Rothenberg, USN (Ret.)—PBYs, Midway
Vice Adm. Richard W. Ruble, USN (Ret.)—*Enterprise*
Capt. Stanley E. Ruehlow, USN (Ret.)—VF-8, *Hornet*
Louis Rulli, USN (Ret.)—*Yorktown*
Cdr. Robert B. Russell, USNR (Ret.)—*Russell*

Goro Sakagami—*Akagi*
Capt. Carl A. Sander, Jr., USN— *Astoria*
Toshisaburo Sasabe—*Akagi*
Rear Adm. Edward P. Sauer, USN (Ret.)—*Balch*
Vice Adm. Walter G. Schindler, USN (Ret.)—*Yorktown*

Cdr. William J. Schleis, USN —NAS, Midway
Capt. Tony F. Schneider, USN— VB-6, *Enterprise*
Clester R. Scotten, Jr., USMC (Ret.)—6th Def. Batn., Midway
Lt. Col. Charles J. Seibert, USMC (Ret.)—3rd Def. Batn., Midway
Benjamin L. Serna, USMC (Ret.) —6th Def. Batn., Midway
Rear Adm. Elliott W. Shanklin, USN (Ret.)—*Portland*
Edward Sheehan—shipyard, Pearl Harbor
Rear Adm. Cyril T. Simard, USN (Ret.)—NAS, Midway
Capt. W. B. Simmons, USMC (Ret.)—*Pensacola*
Capt. Hilliard C. Smathers, USN (Ret.)—PBYs, Midway
Capt. Bert Smith, SC USN (Ret.) —*Hammann*
Lt. Edward B. Smolenski, USN (Ret.)—*Yorktown*
Lt. Cdr. John W. Snowden, USN (Ret.)—VS-6, *Enterprise*
Adm. Raymond A. Spruance, USN (Ret.)—*Enterprise*
Col. Edward A. Steedman, USAF (Ret.)—B-17s, Midway
James Stevens, SC USN (Ret.)— *Hornet*
Maj. James E. Stone, USMC (Ret.)—MAG 22, Midway
Rear Adm. Hubert E. Strange, USN (Ret.)—*Yorktown*
J. F. Sutherland, USN (Ret.)—VF-8, *Hornet*
Lt. Marvin Sutliff, USMC (Ret.)— 6th Def. Batn., Midway

Yahachi Tanabe—*I-168*
Adm. John S. Thach, USN—VF-3, *Yorktown*
ADC Allen J. Thompson, USN (Ret.)—PBYs, Midway

Lt. Oliver C. Thore, USN (Ret.)—*Yorktown*

Rear Adm. Alexander C. Thorington, USN (Ret.)—*Yorktown*

Capt. Theodore S. Thueson, USN (Ret.)—PBYs, Midway

Rear Adm. Harold H. Tiemroth, USN (Ret.)—*Balch*

Col. Charles T. Tingle, USMCR (Ret.)—6th Def. Batn., Midway

Lt. Cdr. Kengo Tominaga—Navy Department, Tokyo

BTC Norman R. Touve, USNFR (Ret.)—*Astoria*

Yasumi Toyama—*Jintsu*

Shunichi Toyoshima—*Isokaze*

Capt. Ignatius N. Tripi, SC USN (Ret.)—*Portland*

Rear Adm. Arnold E. True, USN (Ret.)—*Hammann*

Brig. Gen. Marshall A. Tyler, USMC (Ret.)—VMSB-241, Midway

Kazuomi Uchida—*Yamato*

CWO George Vavrek, USN (Ret.)—*Yorktown*

Gunner Jefferson M. Vick, USN (Ret.)—*Yorktown*

Lt. Col. Harold R. Warner, Jr., USMC (Ret.)—6th Def. Batn., Midway

Col. Jo Kyle Warner, USAF—7th A.F. liaison, Midway

Yasuji Watanabe—*Yamato*

Capt. William G. Weber, USN—*Balch*

Sgt. Maj. Edwin Wehinger, USMC—Carlson's Raiders, Midway

George K. Weise, USN (Ret.)—*Yorktown*

Capt. D. E. Weissenborn, USN (Ret.)—*Yorktown*

CWO Joseph O. Weist, USMC—6th Def. Batn., Midway

Col. E. C. Wessman, USAF (Ret)—B-17s, Midway

Col. Narce Whitaker, USAF—B-17s, Midway

Cyril D. Williams—shipyard, Pearl Harbor

Lt. James E. Wilson, MC USN (Ret.)—*Yorktown*

Newton Harry Wilson, USN (Ret.)—NAS, Midway

James M. Winants, USMC (Ret.)—VMSB-241, Midway

Cdr. Leonard A. Wingo, USN (Ret.).—*Yorktown*

Master Sgt. Edward D. Winslow, USMC (Ret.)—NAS, Midway

Rear Adm. Theodore R. Wirth, USN (Ret.)—*Portland*

Joseph Y. Wisener, USMC (Ret.)—*Yorktown*

Cdr. Maurice E. Witting, USN (Ret.)—*Yorktown*

Cdr. Thomas J. Wood, USN—VB-8, *Hornet*

Col. Willard G. Woodbury, USAF (Ret.)—B-17s, Midway

Rear Adm. Joseph M. Worthington, USN (Ret.)—*Benham*

Alfred Wright, Jr., USNR (Ret.)—*Saratoga*

Maj. Carl E. Wuertele, USAF (Ret.)—B-17s, Midway

Masaki Yamauchi—*Mogami*

Shiro Yonai—*Argentina Maru*

Chuichi Yoshioka—*Akagi*

Frank E. Zelnis, USMC (Ret.)—VMSB-241, Midway

Index

Navy War College (Newport, R.I.), 28

Navy Yard, Pearl Harbor, 37, 88, 254, 287. *See also* Yorktown, repairs on

"Negat," Station, 18

New Caledonia, 4

New Orleans, 58

Nichol, Lt. Cdr. Bromfield, 189

Nimitz, Adm. Chester W., 4, 19–34, 36, 39, 41, 45–47, 49–50, 54, 61, 67, 79, 82, 256, 286–287

Nira Luckenbach, 54

Nishibayashi, Cdr., 184

Noda, Yeoman Mitsuharu, 187, 284, 286

Norfolk, 55, 85

Norris, Maj. Benjamin, 97, 120, 128–129, 254

Northampton, 30–31

Northern Force (Japanese), 7, 12, 76, 243

Norton, Seaman Bill, 62

Nowaki, 43, 131, 183–184, 209, 246–247

Nuuanu Valley, 37

Occupation Force (Japanese), *see* Invasion Force

Ogawa, Lt. (Assistant Air Officer on the *Kaga*), 182

Ogawa, Lt. Raita, 43, 116–118, 159–160, 208, 247

O'Halloran, Maj. James S., 98

Ohara, Cdr. Hirashi, 173, 179, 209, 286, 296

Oishi, Capt., 57, 252, 284

Okada, Capt. Jisaku, 150, 171

Oliver, Lt. Robert J., 31

Olivier, Boatswain, 98

Ominato, 12, 13

Omi, Petty Officer Heijiro, 1, 6, 14, 284

Ono, Cdr., 124

Operation "K," *see* "K" Operation

Operation Plan No. 29–42, 35–36

Osterloh, Cdr. Erwin H. (Sam), 58

Ota, Capt. Minoru, 9

Otawa, CPO Tatsuya, 133, 174, 180, 247

Oto, Capt. Masanao, 76

Parks, Maj. Floyd B. (Red), 80–81, 97, 101

Patrol Squadron 23, *see* PBYs

Patrol Squadron 24, *see* PBYs

Patrol Squadron 44, *see* PBYs

Patrol Squadron 51, *see* PBYs

Patterson, ARM3c James W., Jr., 166, 224, 226

Payne, Capt. Paul, 70, 126–127

PBYs, 26, 40, 280, 289; May 30–June 2, search operations, 29, 45, 46, 52–53, 56; June 3, Invasion Force located, 65–66, 68, 69; June 3–4, night torpedo attack, 71–75, 78, 86; June 4, Striking Force located, 78–79, 94–95, 97, 112, 116, 136, 153, 185, 193, 211; June 5, search operations, 253, 261–262; June 5–21, rescue work, 281–282

Pearl Harbor, 2, 3, 4, 9, 10, 12, 14, 16–18, 20, 21, 23–28, 30–32, 35–36, 39–41, 42, 44, 52, 54, 55, 57, 61, 63, 71, 88–89, 136, 188–190, 200, 254–255, 273, 286–287

Pederson, Cdr. Oscar, 154, 194

Penland, Lt. Joe, 165, 176

Pensacola, 235

Pensacola, 200, 216, 220–221, 287

Pfingstag, Lt. Cdr. H. J., 33–34

Pichette, Seaman Norman, 266

Pittman, Ens. William R., 151–152, 162, 164–165, 176

Planning, Japanese, 4 ff, 185–186

Planning, U.S., 23, 25–26, 28–29, 31, 34, 35–36

Plyburn, Boatswain's Mate, 203

"Point Luck," 39, 61–62, 82

"Point Option," 93, 138, 190

Portland, 62, 193, 220–221, 241

Port Moresby, 19

Prideau, Fireman, 229

Prince of Wales, 2

Princeton University, 131

Propst, Ens. Gaylord D., 72–74

Wilson, Chief Pharmacist's Mate James, 273
Winslow, Pfc Edward D., 99
Wiseman, Lt. (j.g.) Osborne B., 170, 235
Wood, Ens. Thomas J., 84, 150, 177, 253–254
Woodbury, Capt. Willard G., 70
Worthington, Lt. Cdr. Joseph M., 286
Wright, Lt. Cdr. W. A. (Ham), 24
Wright, CEM William E., 276
Wuertele, Capt. Carl, 126–127, 238

Yamaguchi, Rear Adm. Tamon, 131–133, 135, 187–188, 202–203, 214–215, 232–233, 243, 249–251, 285
Yamamoto, Adm. Isoroku, 1–8, 10, 12–15, 22, 39, 41, 43, 44, 60, 75, 76, 131, 134, 150, 185–187, 241–246, 251, 256–260, 264, 270, 278, 282, 284–285
Yamasaki, Cdr., 171
Yamato, 1, 6, 8, 10–11, 13–14, 43–44, 75, 185–186, 242–243, 278, 284, 286
Yamauchi, Lt. Cdr. Masaki, 259
Yanagimoto, Capt. Ryusaku, 2, 133, 179–180, 208, 245
Yankee Doodle, 70, 126
Yokochi, Petty Officer, 171
Yokosuka Naval Base, 12
Yonai, Cdr. Shiro, 10, 75
Yorktown, at Coral Sea, 11, 23; May 15–27, recalled to Pearl Harbor, 23, 26, 33; May 27–29, repairs on, 33–

35, 36–39; May 30-June 4, en route, 60–62, 82–84, 87, 93–95, 141, 153–155; June 4, attack on Nagumo, 155–159, 168–170, 175, 179, 190, 192–193, 196–197, 205–208, 214, 230, 231, 234–236, 241–242, 290–295; attacked by dive bombers, 193–205, 216–217; attacked by torpedo planes, 217–223; ordered abandoned, 223–229, 240–241; June 5-6, attempt to salvage, 241, 255, 265–268, 273–274; June 6, attacked by submarine, 265, 274–278; June 7, sinking of, 279–280, 288
Yoshida, Chief Radioman Katsuichi, 282
Yoshida, Cdr., 248
Yoshimatsu, Lt. Cdr. Tamori, 62
Yoshino, Lt. Cdr., 130
Yoshioka, Lt. Cdr. Chuichi, 184, 244
Yugumo, 248
Yunoki, Lt. S., 69

Zelnis, Sgt. Frank, 130
Zero (fighter plane), 102, 165, 293; attacking Midway, 90, 100 ff; defending own force, 113–114, 117, 121–123, 146–147, 149, 159, 163, 169, 175, 179, 191, 192, 211, 230, 232, 254, 271; escorting strikes against U.S. fleet, 135, 161, 188, 194–195, 214, 218
Zuiho, 14, 243, 278
Zuikaku, 11, 27, 154